Twirling Jennies

Twirling Jennies:

A History of Social Dance
(and other mischief)
in the City of Spindles
1820–1920

Ruth Evans

**Co-researched with
Charles Worsley**

Misenchanted Press

Twirling Jennies: A History of
Social Dance (and other mischief)
in the City of Spindles 1820–1920

Revised edition

Copyright 2015, 2016 by Ruth C.
Evans. All rights reserved.

Published by Misenchanted Press,
Takoma Park, MD

ISBN 978-1-61991-018-8

Library of Congress Control
Number: 2015912496

Printed in the United States of
America

Cover art, layout, and book design
by Ruth C. Evans

Website: www.twirlingjennies.com

This book is dedicated to Lawrence, Diana, Rick, and Barbara for their help in getting me off the path I started dancing down at fifteen, and onto one I expect to follow happily for the rest of my days.

And to Evan, Gayle, and James, for growing up to be good people in spite of it all.

—R. C. E., 2015

About the Author and her Co-Researcher:

Long before they were husband and wife, Ruth Evans and Charles Worsley were dancers. Ms. Evans began English and American Country Dancing in the 1970s, Middle-Eastern and Historic Ballroom in the 1980s, and Modern Ballroom in the 1990s. Mr. Worsley has been participating in various forms of Country Dance and Ballroom Dance since the 1980s. He has been researching and performing Period Ballroom for over thirty years.

While Ms. Evans has previously sold fiction under a pen name, this is her first non-fiction work. But her ability to put together a story is tried and true, and her empathy with the mill girls—on and off the dance floor—is indisputable. She began sewing as a child, worked fourteen-hour days as a costume apprentice in her teens, spent two decades as a dressmaker and another decade with a textile company, has served as a volunteer for Lowell's Industrial History Center, and now works for a local manufacturer helping to guide projects from development to the factory floor. She attended her first contra dance at the age of fifteen and still clearly remembers the sights, sounds, smells, and emotions that greeted her then.

The couple was married in 1999 and moved to Lowell ten years later. They recently welcomed their second grandchild.

Ms. Evans' fantasy novel, *The Raven Coronet,* is published by Misenchanted Press under the penname, Christina Briley.

About this book:

This book is the result of a project that didn't happen. After Ruth Evans and her husband, Charles Worsley, moved into one of Lowell's converted mills, they thought it would be fun to tailor their performances of nineteenth and early twentieth century dancing to their new environs. Having spent a decade performing then-and-now foxtrots, waltzes, and more for the ballroom community, focusing on re-enacting the story on their doorstep made perfect sense. So they started investigating dancing in early Lowell.

They quickly discovered two things: dancing was a hugely popular pastime during Lowell's first hundred years, and no single source contained more than a few lines about it. They also discovered that Lowell's numerous historic organizations had no idea what to do with a lone pair of renegade vintage dancers. Busy with their jobs and family, and lacking the nerve to start busking on street corners without a sponsor, the project was set aside.

In the summer of 2013, after four years of on-and-off research, Ms. Evans decided to take the bull by the horns and try writing a book on the history of dance in Lowell herself. Apparently she succeeded. This revised edition corrects a few fine points of dance history that historian Susan de Guardiola (kickery.com) was kind enough to bring to the author's attention. It also includes a handful of other minor tweaks and clarifications.

About the images:

Writing a book about dance is daunting; the ability of words to capture the essence of such an activity is limited. Images are particularly important, but as photography was in its infancy during the era, pictures of dancers in action are not possible. Other documents are often faded, yellowed, and damaged. Because this book is intended to bring a vibrant history to life, the author has used her skills to clean, crop, and enhance the illustrations. But in no instance has she changed the *substance* of what is being portrayed.

The modern photographs from outside sources have not been altered or significantly cropped by the author. She would like to thank Doug Plummer, Meyer Billmers, and Corey Sciuto for their generosity in allowing her to use their work. Ms. Evans would also like to thank Ella Carlson—who photographed the author and her husband in 2011—for giving her free rein to use those photos as she saw fit (which *did* include some cropping).

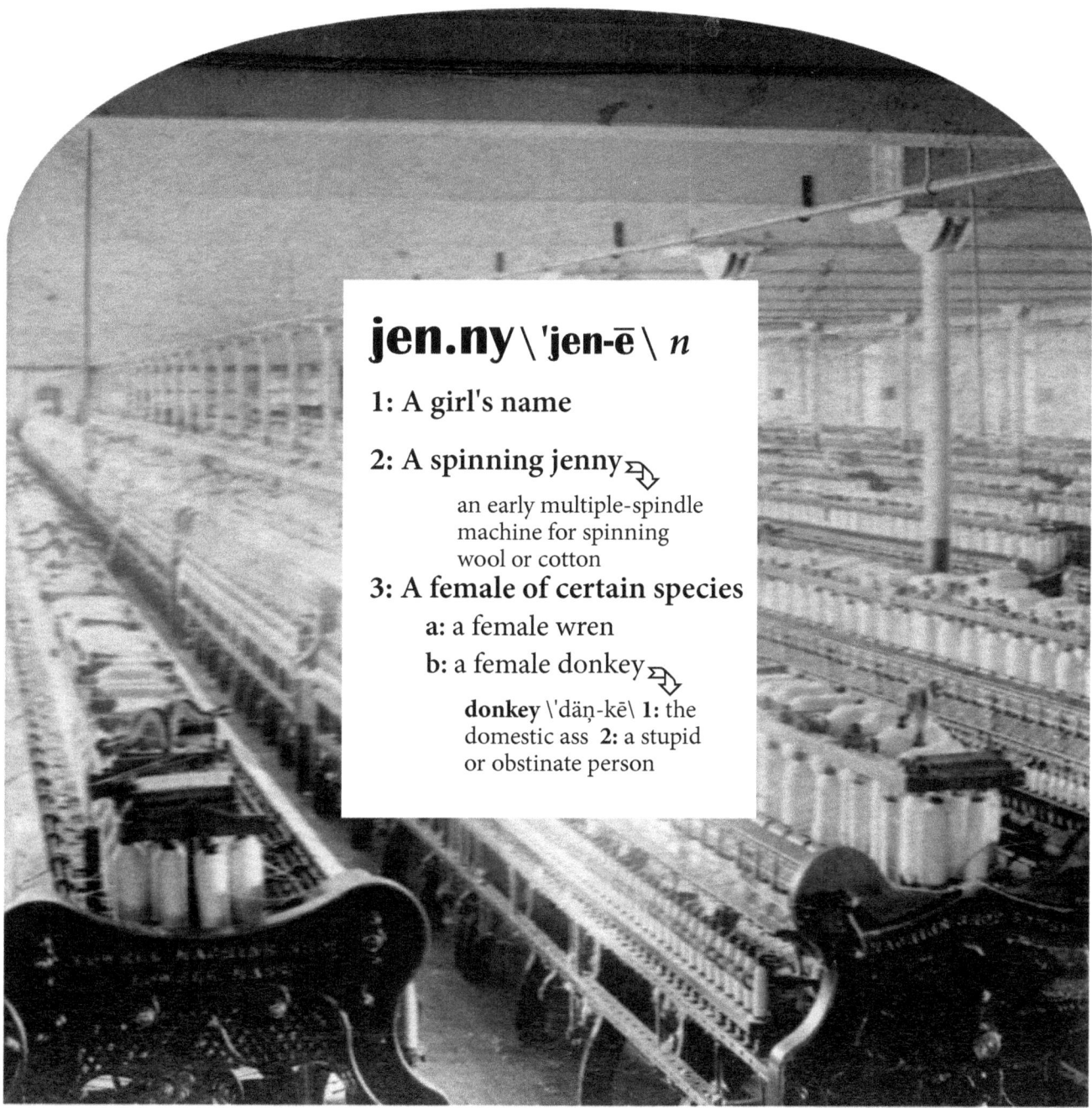

jen.ny \ˈjen-ē\ *n*

1: A girl's name

2: A spinning jenny ⇨
 an early multiple-spindle machine for spinning wool or cotton

3: A female of certain species
 a: a female wren
 b: a female donkey ⇨
  donkey \ˈdäŋ-kē\ 1: the domestic ass 2: a stupid or obstinate person

A selective definition as it pertains to the book's title, the last line being a common nineteenth century view of dancers. Drawn from Webster's Seventh New Collegiate Dictionary, *1976.*

Above and opposite page: The Spinning Room of Lawrence Mill, Lowell, Massachusetts, from a vintage stereoscope card.

Contents:

Introduction   1

A Word on Context   2

1. At the Bend in the River: Dancing before Lowell   4

2. The Early Days: Lowell's Beginnings   12

3. Mixt Dance: Kissing, Courtship, and Damnation   24

4. Country Dance: Contras and Quadrilles, Past and Present   36

5. 'Round the Room: Galop and Polka and Waltz, Oh My!   54

6. The Middle Years: Dancing 'Round Every Corner   64

7. The Ballroom: Its Decorum, Dimensions, and Delights   80

8. A Short Tour: The Victorian Dance Halls of Downtown Lowell   96

9. Out of the City: The Trolley Parks   126

10. The 1900s Arrive: Ragtime Dances Come to Town   138

11. Germans, Grizzlies, and More: Novelties and Fads   164

12. The Last Waltz: From Flappers to Folk Festivals   176

Illustrations   182
Appendix I   192
Appendix II   194
Endnotes   196
Bibliography   204
Index   209

Introduction: Why Lowell? Why Dancing?

Throughout much of the nineteenth century, Lowell, Massachusetts was at the cutting edge of technology, the very center of America's Industrial Revolution. It was there, on the banks of the Merrimack River, that automation and water-power combined to manufacture textiles on a scale previously unimaginable. The "Lowell Experiment," as it was originally known, was the work of a group of investors, and the land that became the city of Lowell was carved out of the surrounding towns of Chelmsford, Dracut, and Tewksbury.

Building a planned city in the middle of farms and open fields not only required finding the labor to build it, but the labor to staff it, as well. Many of the bricklayers and ditchdiggers who constructed Lowell's mills and canals were Irish immigrants brought up from Boston. But for the workforce to run the looms, the investors turned to a segment of society they considered more reputable and easier to control. Farm girls were recruited from across New England to populate this modern utopia. In the company boarding houses, the girls' morals would be protected; in the mills, their purses would be enriched; and in the churches and schools, their minds would be educated.

Although Lowell was a business venture, it also became a major tourist attraction, a sort of futuristic theme park: *See the animatronic looms move as if by magic! Watch the beautiful young women tend to them! Hear the thundering noise of hundreds of machines running in concert! Wonder at the towering brick factories that spring up virtually overnight! Touch the miles of fabric churned out! Experience modern man's ingenuity at its finest!*

When the author's own great-grandfather traveled from his home in western Pennsylvania to Boston in November of 1866 for a railroad convention (The Third Annual Convention of the Grand International Brotherhood of Locomotive Engineers), the delegates were treated to a tour of Lowell.

But Lowell wasn't a make-believe world; it was a manufacturing city where capitalism ruled and sexism was the order of the day.

Dancing was both scorned and embraced by the residents of the city. Looking at the history of dancing in Lowell offers insights into pastimes, social mores, courting, sex, sexual harassment, prostitution, etiquette, social status, and religion. It dusts off the mill girls of history books and breathes a bit more life into their world.

There have been many books written about Lowell, but dance has been relegated to a line here or a mention there. Trying to write a book on the subject reminds one of the archaeologist who must put together mere shards of artifacts scattered throughout a dig site to tell a story. But the pieces *are* there and, combined with material from period dance manuals and etiquette books, plus personal experience with the dances of the time and the promises and pitfalls of the dance hall, it is possible to offer an in-depth look at a lively— and scandalous—piece of Lowell history.

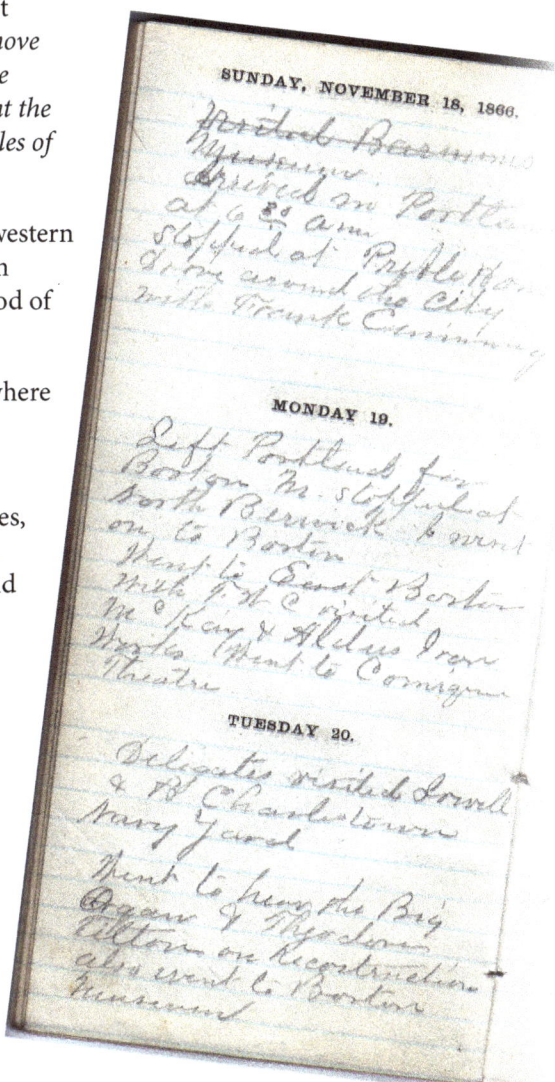

A Word on Context: Sex, Sin, and Scare Stories

Making outrageous claims to scare young people into behaving is a time-honored tradition. These days, when some judicious web searching will easily debunk the lies, such threats have fallen into disuse. But fifty, or one hundred, or two hundred years ago, it was a different story. When it came to sex, misinformation was not only common, it was often deliberately promoted. And since mixed-gender dancing might later lead to sex, it, too, was credited with a number of ills so as to discourage young people from indulging. A single tale of woe loosely linked to dancing might be turned into a prediction of universal doom. Perhaps sometime, somewhere, a woman happened to fall ill and die shortly after attending a dance, but it was surely from germs or a pre-existing condition—not from her dancing or her décolleté—and it was hardly inevitable!

All of which begs the question, *why* was sex outside of marriage—for women, anyway—considered so dreadfully shameful? Pregnancy and disease could certainly derail a young woman's life given the era's lack of antibiotics and reliable birth control. But the historical taboo against sex goes beyond that. If one of the driving instincts of all living things is to reproduce, then women hold the upper hand. Recent scientific advances notwithstanding, a woman knows that the child she bears is her own; a man only knows what the woman tells him. So controlling women and their wombs has long been of utmost importance in a patriarchal society. In Victorian Lowell, rules and customs furthering that aim were rigidly enforced through shame, myth, and punishment.

It may surprise modern readers to know that the idea of "free love" did not originate with the hippies of the 1960s and 1970s; it likely goes back almost as far as does the taboo against sex. In the mid-1800s, the concept was embraced by some followers of a movement called "Individual Sovereignty."

"The advocates of 'Individual Sovereignty' hold that where certain affinities are found in two persons of opposite sexes, no human law or civil institution should keep them asunder. [One adherent's treatise] denounces the restraints imposed on the intercourse of the sexes by the present institutions of society. He observes that all our social gatherings, our balls, parties, and public amusements of every kind are instinctive efforts to escape, for short intervals, from the prison of the social institution, into the freedom of human society—efforts miserable and abortive, like prisoners dancing in their chains, and holding them the more tightly to prevent them from clanking." —*Lowell Daily Journal & Courier,* June 14, 1854.

The above article also included the reporter's take on the subject: "We must be permitted to say, that such a dogma as this is calculated to unsettle and undermine the whole fabric of human society—to restore chaos once more."

Opposite: "Husking the Corn in New England" and "The Dance After the Husking" both from Harper's Weekly, *fall of 1858. Romanticized depictions of country life were popular in the nineteenth century, and here the artist takes on a traditional New England corn-husking festival.*

While dancing was often blamed for leading young people astray, it's interesting to note how much more mischief is shown in the wholesome, folksy, corn-husking scene than at the dance; people at the dance are, well, just dancing. According to Harper's, corn-husking *tradition entitled a young man finding a red ear of corn to kiss the girl of his choice—whether she liked it or not!*

At the Bend in the River: Dancing Before Lowell

On the banks of the Merrimack river, long before there was a city of Lowell, there was dancing.

For the Native Americans of the lower Merrimack Valley, the Pennacooks, dance was an important part of their ceremonies and celebrations. It was a means to curry favor with their gods, and a means to ask the gods' forgiveness or to thank them for their largesse. European settlers believed that the Pennacooks' boisterous and colorful dancing was akin to devil worship, but they wrote wondering

accounts of it nevertheless. In books of the late nineteenth and early twentieth centuries, local historians would describe how tribe members "threaded the fantastic mazes of the dance"[1] and declared that the natives "were fond of extravagant dancing and reveling."[2]

Dance was also part of life for many of the encroaching settlers. Squire John Varnum, born in Dracut of European stock, made the following entries in his diary:[3]

Jan. 15, 1778. "About 2 of ye Clock the company viz: Hezekiah Coburn and wife, Parker Varnum and wife, Roger Ray and Hannah Brown, Henry Coburn and Samuel Richardson, Samuel Coburn and Rhoda, Jonas Varnum and Polly Parker, John Parkhurst, Isaac Parker, Abijah Hall and Bradstreet Coburn set off in three double shays to go to Billerica, went as far as Capt. Miniers. Took a drink of Flip and toddy and returned through the town. Got here about Sun setting. The Company set off for Joseph Varnum's to sup there with fife and fiddle and returned home at about 2 A.M."

Above: Old-time sleighing scene from vintage postcard.

Left: Joseph Varnum (1751-1821) and his house (shown late 1800s), at which a group of friends enjoyed "fife and fiddle" one evening until the wee hours.

Opposite page: A map of what would eventually become the center of Lowell (Norman B. Leventhal Map Center, Boston Public Library).

March 4, 1779. "Parker had a great entertainment. Mr. Brown & his wife Rhoda, Elijah Fletcher & wife, Michael Hildreth & wife, Philip Parker & wife, Bradley Varnum & wife, Capt. Peter Coburn & wife, Doctor Little & wife, Nathan Parker & wife, Jonas Varnum & Polly Parker, Isaac Parker & Abijah Hill and myself & wife, all dined & supped here. Jonas & Polly went to a Dance the same evening at Abijah Fox's. Henry Coburn, Thomas Varnum, Bradstreet Coburn & a large number of young people went to the [said] Fox's to the Dance there that evening."

10 Dec. 1779. "Thos. Varnum had a Dance at his house in the Evg. As same fell by lot there."

There is no way to know for certain what was being danced at these events, but it's safe to assume that it was primarily contra dancing. There is some disagreement over the origins of the name "contra." Is it a mispronunciation of "country"? Or does it come from the Latin phrase "contra saltare"—to dance opposite—and refer to the formation of the dancers? Either way, it was a style of dancing that pre-dated Squire Varnum's diary entries by well over a century, and continued to be popular for the century that followed Varnum's words.

Thomas Wilson's 1825 *Analysis of the London Ball-room* states that "The general character of this style of dancing is simplicity, ease, freedom, and liveliness," and then goes on to say that contra (or "country") dancing is more mirthful than graceful, more cheerful than elegant.[4] In other words, it is a style of dance well suited to an evening with friends, though perhaps a bit cramped in the average parlor!

Contra dance formation consists of a line of men facing a line of women, and the most familiar contra dance to the average non-dancer today is the Virginia Reel. Centuries old, with a number of variations, many readers will remember being taught this reel in gym class. By the time of Lowell's founding, the moves in contra dances had begun to echo those seen in square dances—ladies chain, do-si-do, right and left through, heys, turns, stars, and so forth.

> For my sixteenth birthday, my parents allowed me to hold a contra dance at home. We had a large room that ran the length of the house and, with the rug rolled up, the couches pushed against the walls, and the tables stashed elsewhere, there was enough space for three musicians at one end and a longways set of five or six couples down the center. The big concern was keeping one's elbows tucked in when dancing by the mantel, or else risk cracking them painfully on the marble!
>
> Many years later, I had a contra dance in my own home in a much narrower room. This meant dragging all the furniture to other parts of the house. The one thing we left in place was a child's toy kitchen, for it took up barely any space. Yet even that should have gone. Halfway through each dance, without fail, there would be a loud "thunk" as the oven door was jarred open by the springing of the floor under our feet.   —Author

Frontispiece from The Dancing Master, *written by H. Playford and published in 1698, showing contra dance formation.*

But the contra dances of the eighteenth and nineteenth century should not be confused with movie images of rowdy barn dances. There was proper etiquette, and proper footwork, and countless guides were written for both.

In his 1917 *History of Chelmsford,* Reverend Wilson Waters writes that "there always was a genuine, hearty, social life in Chelmsford." He speaks of corn huskings, and house raisings, sleighing parties, and sewing bees. And dancing—"which the minister winked at, because he knew he could not stop it."[5]

Waters also tells of a fondness for practical jokes among the locals. A tipsy tavern patron might clamber awkwardly into his wagon in the dark and cluck to his horse, only to find himself moving backwards, someone having quietly unhitched the horse and re-hitched the animal tail forward. The reverend mentions the time that the parson, who regularly crossed a plank over the brook on his way to court a certain widow, got dunked because some pranksters had earlier sawed the board practically in two.

But, Reverend Waters insists, "Dancing schools and parties were conducted in a polite and genteel manner."[6]

And, despite the misgivings of numerous ministers and other guardians of morals, there were plenty of people who viewed dancing as a pleasurable and important social skill.

In January of 1816 the opening of a new dancing school was announced in Chelmsford, complete with the names of the anticipated pupils. This would seem a clear sign that while dancing might be shameful in some quarters, it was a point of pride in others.

"A school will be opened at the Hall of Ezra Blodgets this evening at 6 o'Clock by Mr. Robbins to Instruct in the polite accomplishment of Dancing. Terms: three dollars fifty cents per quarter, last six weeks half price.

"Ladies – Clarisa Howard, Lucretia Varnum, Hannah Adams, Sally Colburn, Sally Sherborm, Irena Bowers, Louisa Butterfield, Edna Varnum, Sarah Wood, Abagail Spalding."

Above and above right: Mock-ups of invitations as described by Rev. Waters in The History of Chelmsford.

At right: An early nineteenth century dance lesson in France, as depicted on a vintage postcard. Mr. Robbins' dance students would be practicing in a much less opulent setting, but would still be striving to master proper deportment and the ballet-like footwork dictated by French dancing-masters.

"Gentlemen – Charles Howard, John Spalding, Parker Varnum, Jr., Saml. Penst [prob. Priest], John F Adams, John Hunt, Henry Adams, Benjamin Adams, James Coburn, Ebn. Adams, Capt Adams, Capt J Bowers, Samuel Wook, John Butterfield, Major N. Howard, Parker Varnum, Jeremiah Varnum, [G.] Blodgett, George Hunting, Varnum Spalding, James Varnum, Charles Melvin, Esra Blodgett, Benja Pierce, Alex Wright, _____ Chase, William Adams, Lewis Sticklemire, Otis Howard, William Spaulding, Charles Blood, Aron P. Richerson."[7]

In 1822, just a year before the incorporation of Lowell, a Thanksgiving Ball was held in a hall at Middlesex Village (a section of Chelmsford that would become part of Lowell). The unusual invitations were handwritten on common playing cards—one wonders if fifty-two invitations were sent out!

"The company of Mr. S. Parker and lady is requested at Mr. S. Spalding's Hall, at the head of the Middlesex Canal, Chelmsford, On Thursday evening, December 5, 1822. Managers: G. L. Sticklemire, Z. F. Fletcher, J. T. Sheppard, E. Proctor, Jr."

And on the other side: "Dancing to commence at 6 o'clock."

Mr. S. Spalding's Hall would have been at S. Spalding's Hotel, which seems to have been the structure later known as Middlesex Tavern. Middlesex Tavern was also called Clark's Tavern for a time after innkeeper Col. Jonas Clark and nearby Clark's Ferry.[8]

Unlike the eighteenth century house parties mentioned by Squire Varnum, a detailed description of dancing at Middlesex Tavern

Above: Front and back of 1822 invitation to a Thanksgiving Ball to be held at Middlesex Tavern (Lowell Historical Society).

Right: Photo of Middlesex Tavern from vintage postcard.

Far right: A cotillion, or quadrille of the era.

has survived the years. Several decades after the Thanksgiving Ball, the Honorable Samuel P. Hadley recorded his childhood memories of the tavern during the 1830s:

"In the winter, balls were given in the hall of the old Village Tavern. They were attended by the very best people of both sexes, and were admirably conducted. The hall was gaily decorated, and the ladies and gentlemen appeared in the full fashion of the day. The music consisted of a half dozen pieces [instruments] and was inspiring. Dancing began at about 7 and continued until 12, when the whole company sat down to a hot turkey supper with all the other dishes. After supper the dancing was resumed, and often continued until daybreak."

"There were no round dances in those days. Fisher's Hornpipe, Money Musk, Chorus Jig, Portland Fancy, Lady Washington's Reel, Speed the Plough, and other old contra dances, which called for real dancing, and the cotillion, were in order."

"When I was a small boy I was permitted to go down to the hall, dressed in my very best, and sit on a seat near the entrance to observe the gay dancers. I had to be in my bed at nine o'clock however."[9]

A "round" dance would have referred to a couple dance that traveled in a circle around the room. The waltz would have been one such dance, but it had not yet caught on in rural New England when Mr. Hadley was a child. The waltz was considered quite scandalous for many years, the difference between a contra dance and a waltz being similar to the difference between the family dinner table and an intimate table for two.

The word "cotillion" has had various meanings; in this instance it would have been a quadrille, or what we call a square dance today.

Although these dances took place in tavern halls, they would not have been public; hence the invitations. Even among those people who defended mixed-sex dancing, many frowned on public balls.

Well south of Massachusetts, around the same time that the city of Lowell was springing up, a young man was navigating the social world of Philadelphia and, in 1836, this anonymous gentleman shared what he had learned in *The Laws of Etiquette; or Short Rules and Reflections for Conduct in Society*. He conceded that the elaborate manners of his time were "abundantly absurd," but insisted that "still they must be attended to,"[10] for society would judge a person's value by his (or her) manners. Despite the formal nature of his topic, this fellow set forth his instructions with a certain wry humor, and occasionally used terms more appropriate to battlefields than ballrooms. His advice regarding dances appears below. Note the especially short and direct admonition that he saved for last.

"BALLS
▸Invitations to a ball should be issued at least ten days in advance, in order to give an opportunity to the men to clear away engagements; and to women, time to prepare the artillery of their toilet [*"toilet" refers to dress or garb; the phrasing would seem to indicate the importance of dress as a way to show up one's peers*]. Cards of invitation should be sent—not notes.
▸Upon the entrance of ladies, or persons entitled to deference, the master of the house precedes them across the room: he addresses compliments to them, and will lose his life to procure them seats.
▸While dancing with a lady whom you have never seen before, you should not talk to her much.

▸The master of the ceremonies must take care that every lady dances, and press into service for that purpose those young gentlemen who are hanging round the room like fossils. If desired by him to dance with a particular lady you should refuse on no account.
▸If you have no ear, that is, a false one, never dance.
▸To usurp the seat of a person who is dancing is the height of incivility.
▸Never go to a public ball."[11]

There were others who condemned "mixt" dancing entirely; to them it didn't matter whether a ball was public or private. The Ministers of Christ at Boston had published *An Arrow Against Profane and Promiscuous Dancing Drawn Out of the Quiver of the Scriptures* a full century and a half before the founding of Lowell but it still resonated with many. Written by Increase Mather, this 1684 pamphlet admonished: "The miserable Dancer knoweth not, that as many Paces as he makes in Dancing, so many steps he makes to Hell."[12] *An Arrow* declared further: "The unchaste Touches and Gesticulations used by Dancers have a palpable tendency to that which is evil."[13]

More specifically, Mather stated: "From the Seventh Commandment [thou shall not commit adultery]. It is an Eternal Truth to be observed in expounding the Commandments, that whenever any sin is forbidden, not only the highest acts of that sin, but all degrees thereof, and all occasions leading thereto are prohibited."[14]

Of course, Mather was absolutely right. If the act of lusting is a form of adultery—as those versed in the bible, from the Puritans to Jimmy Carter, have long said—then there's no question that adultery goes on virtually anywhere that there's dancing. In what other nineteenth-century situation could men and women hold hands, put their arms about each other, and move together in rhythm in front of friends, neighbors, and family?

Away from the dance floor, there were other explorations of intimacy among the younger set in the form of "kissing games." The description below comes again from Mr. Hadley and refers to Middlesex Village in the early 1800s.

> **What is the difference between a *Dancer* and a *Mad-man*?**
> **Replied:** *There was no other difference, but only this; that the person who is really Phrentick, is mad all the day long; when as the Dancer is only mad an hour in a day perhaps.*
>
> —Attributed to Prince Alphonsus by Increase Mather

"Pleasant gatherings, particularly in winter months, were held in various homes, and if these occasions were not characterized by so many artificials and by so much of what is now termed good form, they were none the less hospitable and enjoyable. Whist parties, singing parties, and among the younger portion, kissing parties, were common enough; while the elders met once a week...for prayer and meditation, or the study of the Scriptures."[15]

But, unlike dancing, the kissing games were widely considered an innocent introduction to courtship and do not seem to have provoked the wrath of the righteous to any significant degree. Kissing games did not involve the sweaty, breathless, body contact that was found between couples exerting themselves on the dance floor. Dancing was, in fact, illegal in the early days of Massachusetts. The following comes again from Rev. Waters' *History of Chelmsford*:

"A few items from the printed volume of Laws & Liberties; revised, 1672, may be interesting. Gaming and dancing and the observance of Christmas were punished by fine. The law forbidding the celebration of Christmas was repealed in 1681."[16]

The reverend does not mention when the prohibition against dancing was repealed. Other sources tell us that Massachusetts banned "dancing and revelling" in taverns from 1646 until 1832 when the law was quietly dropped because it was so widely ignored.[17]

In 1842, some years after the city of Lowell had sprouted along its northern edge, the town of Chelmsford built the basement of a new meeting house. This basement was above ground, made of brick, and was heated by a large wood stove. It served—rather inadequately—as town hall while the structure above housed religious services. This arrangement continued until an entirely new Town Hall building was erected in 1879.[18]

Said basement also served as the site of various social events and dances.

A hot stove in the center of a dance floor would create a significant hazard, and so the stove was removed before each ball. But not in advance by anonymous workmen; no, a tongue-in-cheek ceremony grew up around the removal. The fire would be allowed to die down, two sizeable sticks of cordwood would be slid under the stove, and then four men would serve as pallbearers for the "deceased" while the orchestra played one particular funeral anthem—Handel's *Dead March* from the oratorio, *Saul*.[19]

Just picture such a scene: four men in evening wear, solemnly pacing out of the hall with their burden while the rest of the guests stand by in feigned mourning. Until, much like a New Orleans jazz funeral, the somber part of the ceremony ends and the party begins.

Or, as Lord Byron once wrote, and a great many dance cards of the day quoted: *"On with the dance! Let joy be unconfined!"*

> I've danced in a lot of different town halls over the years and many of them had their little quirks. South Acworth still had an attached outhouse back when I danced there, and Nelson was known for the slope of its floor—one particular corner of the hall tended to get very crowded as dancers literally gravitated toward it. Fitzwilliam initiated a dress code for their dances after a magazine article had photos of young women showing more skin than the town fathers thought proper. And I remember one town hall that we drove right by because there was no town in sight, just a lone building in a clearing at the side of the road—Easton I think that was. As I recall, some of the dancers went skinny-dipping in the isolated brook out back after the dance. But for all the halls I've seen, I can't say as I've ever encountered one with a stove that had to be moved! —Author

Above left: Increase Mather.

Far left: Excerpt from An Arrow Against Profane and Promiscuous Dancing.

Immediate left: Waltz image from Howe's Complete Ball-Room Hand Book.

Above: Clip art by author.

Junction of the Concord and Merrimack Rivers

The Early Days: Lowell's Beginnings

Francis Cabot Lowell, for whom Lowell is named (and who happens to be the author's fifth cousin four times removed), was born the 7th of April, 1775 in Newburyport, Massachusetts. He was the son of John Lowell II—a judge and member of the Continental Congress—and Susanna Cabot. His upbringing was a privileged one and included attendance at Phillips Academy and graduation from Harvard College.

Lowell became a successful merchant engaging in overseas trade. Much of his business was with the Orient, and many of his imports were textiles. He also invested in real estate, excelled at mathematics, and held a fascination with improving on existing technology.

In June of 1810, Francis Lowell, his wife Hannah, and their four children embarked on a two year tour of the British Isles. During that time, they enjoyed the high life, and their letters talked of balls and dance lessons:

"I was at two private balls last week, besides another evening in company, and have to struggle hard not to have company all this week," Hannah confided to a friend.[1]

"We get two lessons dancing every day that take up a great deal of time that we used to have for other lessons," five-year-old Edward noted.[2]

But Francis Lowell also had business reasons for being in Europe. He believed that for the United States to be truly independent of her former English masters, the young country needed to develop a healthy manufacturing base and cease to rely on the fabric mills of Great Britain. With that goal in mind, he was determined to learn all he could about their spinning and weaving technology. Because English law forbade the export of any written materials describing these processes, anything Francis could learn needed to be consigned to memory.

So Lowell's personal itinerary included visits to the mills of Lancashire and Shropshire, where he spent hours contemplating the power looms, water wheels, and spinning machines that were the heart of textile production.

At left: 1856 image of the river junction at Lowell, Massachusetts.

Above: Stereoscope card, "Their First Dancing Lesson." While this card is from 1900, it shows a well-to-do family spending time encouraging their children's dance skills, much in the same way the Lowell family did.

There has been speculation that Lowell also visited Robert Owen's mills at New Lanark, Scotland, despite a lack of evidence. Much of the musing has centered on similarities between Owen's efforts to improve working conditions for his employees and the efforts that Lowell eventually made in his own mills. Such efforts were noticeably lacking in England's sordid factories. But Owen's motive was a "spirit of universal charity—not for a sect or a party, or for a country or a colour, but for the human race, and with a real and ardent desire to do them good."[3]

That is a very different view than that of Lowell and his peers. For the men who brought the city of Lowell into existence, their aversion to a degraded workforce was rooted in their pocketbooks rather than their ideals. Granted, they considered themselves moral men and good Christians (Owen, on the other hand, rejected established religion), but they were trying to solve a labor shortage by offering decent working conditions. Raising up the downtrodden was not part of their agenda.

Right: A vintage postcard showing an idealized view of England's Lancashire Cotton Mills.

Below: This 1892 image of Lancashire mill workers includes a barefoot child. English factories drew their workers from slums and poorhouses and frequently employed entire families struggling to survive.

> Workers in the Lancashire mills often wore wood-soled shoes; they were inexpensive and stood up to hard use well. Clog dancing is said to have come, in part, from this. The workers would break the monotony of their day with songs and a bit of fancy stepping as they tapped out the rhythm of the looms.
> –Author

Above: *An early engraving of New Lanark showing schools as well as factories—and even a village band!*

Below: *Dance lessons at New Lanark. Visitors often watched these well-behaved, working-class children learn their steps.*

When it came to the subject of dancing as recreation for the workers, the two camps held outright opposing views. Compare Owen's beliefs, as described by a visitor to New Lanark in 1819, with the Yankee mentality as described by a visitor to Lowell fifteen years later:

"Human nature, [Owen] says, is not understood by any class of society, and he has discovered that dancing is one of the means of reforming vicious habits. This he thinks it effects by promoting cheerfulness and contentment, and thus diverting the attention from things that are vile and degrading."[4] —John Griscom, 1819.

"The rigid spirit of Puritanism has been carried to its utmost in Lowell, owing to the great number of young girls collected together in the factories. In 1836, a man was fined by the municipal authorities for exercising the trade of common fiddler; he was treated as if he had outraged the public morals, the magistrates fearing that the pleasures of the dance might tend to corruption of manners."[5] —Michael Chevalier, 1839.

Regardless of whether Francis Lowell ever saw Owen's enlightened treatment of the laborers at New Lanark, he most certainly came away from the mills of Great Britain with both a head full of new technology and a distaste for the squalor of the typical English textile factory.

When the Lowell family set sail for Boston at the end of their European visit in June of 1812, the United States had just declared war on Britain. Their ship, the American *Minerva*, was diverted to Halifax and their luggage searched, the British being certain that Francis was smuggling designs for England's advanced textile machinery. But with the only evidence in Francis' head, nothing was found and the family returned safely to Boston.[6]

Lowell soon assembled a team capable of implementing his plans. Early in 1813, at the behest of Lowell and his associates, the Massachusetts legislature passed an act to incorporate the Boston Manufacturing Company "for the purpose of manufacturing Cotton, Woolen & Linen goods, at Boston, in the County of Suffolk, or within fifteen miles thereof."[7]

Directly above: Owen believed that the crass behavior of the poor resulted from their dire straights, while most of his peers saw behavior as the cause rather than the result. The woodcuts above are from Owen's Essays on the formation of the Human Character, *illustrating the effect of bad and good circumstances respectively.*

Above right: Detail from "The Power of Music" showing a visiting fiddler.

Right: Waltham, Massachusetts' Main Street in 1856, two decades after the Boston Manufacturing Company established their first mill within Waltham's borders.

16

A list of Lowell's associates reads like a street directory of modern Lowell, with names like Appleton, Jackson, Gorham, Moody, and Thorndike. This group built their first factory in Waltham and began producing cloth late in 1814. There were other textile mills already operating in the United States, but Boston Manufacturing was the first to take raw fiber all the way to finished fabric under one roof.

This unified approach to textile production quickly began turning a profit. The company built a second mill in 1818 and a third in 1819.

Francis Cabot Lowell didn't live to see the extent of his plans' success. He died of pneumonia August 10th, 1817. The Boston Manufacturing Company thrived anyway. When it became obvious that the power of the Charles River at Waltham was inadequate to support further expansion, Lowell's surviving partners went looking for a new site. They eventually came to name it for him.

As the search progressed, someone suggested: "Why don't they buy up the Pawtucket Canal? They can put up as many mills as they please there, and never want for water."[8]

Top: Photograph of The Boston Manufacturing Company's Cotton Mill in Waltham from a vintage postcard.

Above left: Wash Room at Boston Manufacturing's Bleachery.

Above right: Boiling Room at Boston Manufacturing's Bleachery.

Left: Image of Pawtucket Falls and the adjoining dam from a vintage postcard. This section of the Merrimack drops 32 feet over a short distance—a nightmare for navigation but a superb source of water power.

The canal in question had been built late in the eighteenth century to bypass the rapids on the Merrimack River known as Pawtucket Falls. Its creation made river shipping from New Hampshire to points south possible. By the time the Boston Associates came along, the Pawtucket Canal was underutilized, having been supplanted by the later, more convenient, Middlesex Canal. Yet it was well suited to the needs of this group of visionaries.

In 1821 the investors acquired four hundred acres at the junction of the Merrimack and Concord Rivers by purchasing controlling interest in the corporation that owned the Pawtucket Canal, *The Proprietors of Locks and Canals on Merrimack River*. Early in 1822 the Merrimack Manufacturing Company was incorporated. The company quickly set about building a dam at the falls and enlarging the Pawtucket Canal into an ample power canal.

In those early years Lowell did not yet exist. The new mill buildings springing up were within the borders of East Chelmsford, a simple farming village. Investors, engineers, designers, mechanics, and other experts needed for the great industrial adventure that was to be a "City of Spindles" descended on the area to patronize taverns and inns that had once catered primarily to river travelers.

Historian Coburn writes: "Much social gayety centered at the Old Stone House on Pawtucket Street, which was built in 1824 by Phineas Whiting, Sr., the material being slaty stone taken from the river bed."[9]

And Cowley says in his *History of Lowell*: "In the first years of the Merrimack Company, the annual meetings of the stock holders were held in Lowell. The dinners eaten on those occasions, at the Mansion House, and at the Stone House, were interesting incidents in the lives of those who had the great pleasure to be present."[10]

The Old Stone House became the Ayer home and is now a convent. The long-gone Mansion House was a house near today's Kearney Square that the Merrimack Company bought and turned to an inn.[11]

Above: The Old Stone House (or Ayer home) as seen on a vintage postcard.

Left: The Marshall Tavern on Parker Street.

Top opposite page: Washington Tavern on Central Street as shown on a vintage postcard.

Middle opposite: Upstairs hall at the former Davis Inn. A panel that could be swung down to split the hall into two smaller rooms can be seen latched to the ceiling.

Bottom opposite: "Barroom Dancing," an American painting showing tavern festivities from around 1820.

Other hostelries came and went. Davis Inn, also on Pawtucket Street, had become a private home by the time of Lowell's founding; the historic structure is today known as the Spaulding House. Washington Tavern on Central Street was built in Lowell's first decade and remained standing until 1960. Marshall Tavern on Parker Street, built in 1794, was another spot that oft "resounded with laughter and hearty greetings" prior to becoming a private home, now gone.[12]

And any place there were taverns or inns, there was likely dancing— some of it proper and organized, some of it much less so. It was not unusual for traveling dance teachers to rent a tavern's assembly rooms to give dance lessons. This in turn brought renewed interest in dancing and more income to the innkeeper in the form of food, drink, and ballroom rentals.[13]

As East Chelmsford became first the town of Lowell in 1826, then the city of Lowell in 1836, many of the country taverns were gradually replaced by large, downtown hotels such as Merrimack House or Lowell House. Of the earliest inns, the Old Stone House is the one best known for its dances as town grew to city:

"Here, in the town period of Lowell history, were held the famous seasonal balls, known as the "lighting up" and "blow out" balls, occurring respectively on September 21 and March 21. These were the most distinctly democratic social festivities of the year, at which employers and corporation officers danced with factory operatives. Much more select was a series of twelve socials given at the house each winter. In 1836 took place a celebrated ball at which a price of six dollars was asked and secured."[14]

The "Lighting Up" balls marked the beginning of the shorter days of winter when whale-oil lamps were brought in to allow the mills to operate past sunset. The "Blow Out" or "Blowing Out" parties marked the putting away of the lamps and a reprieve from their fumes for another six months.

Staffing the mills were a group of women that became known as the Lowell Mill Girls. Here, as in Waltham, the investors sought to avoid the dismal state of England's mills while satisfying their labor needs in what had been, until then, a rural area. Since the surrounding towns were mostly farmland, the companies turned to farm families to provide their workers.

Word went out that paying work was available for industrious women of good moral character. And the wages being offered were high, high enough to overcome the stigma attached to mill work by conditions in Europe, where a factory girl was "but a brute, a slave, to be beaten, pinched, and pushed about."[15]

On a New England farm, "a woman had always been a money-*saving*, rather than a money-earning member of the community, and her labor could command but small return."[16] Now, in this "Yankee El Dorado" springing up on the banks of the Merrimack, a farm girl was being promised real earning power. Her virtue would be carefully guarded in company boarding houses and she could enjoy activities and opportunities impossible in an isolated village. She could work in the mills for a few years before returning home richer and wiser to marry and fulfill a woman's "proper" destiny.

The founders of Lowell believed that this use of temporary workers would prevent the degradations seen in Europe's mills; no permanent factory population meant no slums. Equally important was that these farmer's daughters would work for less than men and would—being properly raised nineteenth-century women—do as they were told. Profits would be assured.

The prejudice against factory work faded quickly as the young women who entered Lowell's mills brought home tales of "new fashions, new books, and new ideas."[17] Some of these girls also brought home new dance steps.

> *I work, these days, for an athletic shoe company located in a refurbished textile mill. The room where I spend my days making prototypes is adjacent to the factory floor. On my first few visits to the factory, I was overwhelmed by the heat and noise generated by hundreds of machines, and by the rush of the workers to get each operation done in the allotted time. I was very relieved when I got back to the safety of my own department. Over time, the factory became much less intimidating, and I began to be aware of the rapport between the operators and the friendly joshing that went on.*
>
> *But this is in the days of air conditioning and OSHA, and at a company that takes its commitment to its employees seriously. It's hard to imagine just how horrifying those first days in the factory were in the mill girls' time.*
>
> *—Author*

Right: The weave room of one of Lowell's cotton mills as shown on a vintage postcard.

Top opposite: Front and inside of an 1857 invitation to a Thanksgiving Ball in Maine.

Bottom opposite: Two clippings from the Lowell Courier, *October 10, 1837, with dance-related advertisements.*

Not every young woman danced. Some didn't have the inclination, or the time, or the money, or the energy. And some held either religious or personal beliefs that forbade such intimate contact with the opposite sex. Yet for many, it was a popular pastime.

Plenty of girls had enjoyed dancing back home, long before they arrived in Lowell. Across New England, young and old would have been dancing what are today considered classic contra dances: Fisher's Hornpipe, Hull's Victory, Money Musk, Chorus Jig, Portland Fancy, and the Virginia Reel.

In Lowell, these dance enthusiasts could take real lessons and learn the steps of dances too new or too scandalous—such as the dizzying waltz—to have gained popularity in less urban areas. They could also shop for the latest in dance wear.

The 1837 notice below offers lessons at either Mechanics Hall or a student's home. Private lessons would have been for the well-to-do, for the families of the corporations' agents and investors or those of other successful businessmen. The mill girls and their peers would have attended the group classes.

In 1892, Parker Lindall Converse of nearby Woburn described dance lessons of the early 1800s in her book, *Legends of Woburn*. She also bemoaned the sorry skills of later, more-coddled students.

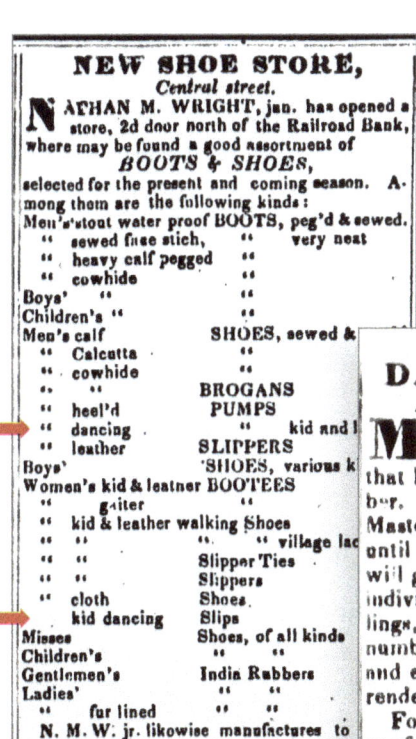

"Then, the dancing master meant business. The question was not so much how soon the pupils could dance, as how well they could do it when they finally got at it. The scholars were not only required to behave as orderly as those of our High schools, but each was drilled most thoroughly in the steps and position of the feet, ...as many as ten evenings being sometimes necessary to devote to drill before any dancing at all was permitted. Even then, frequent stops occurred to bring up the poorer ones to the proper standard."

"The final public balls, at the end of each term, exhibited almost perfectly the 'poetry of motion;' for the 'manual exercise of heels' was brought down to a strict science... Each dancer had his or her feet in position; each started on time; each took the steps gracefully; and all arrived at their proper places exactly together. The *tout ensemble* of the ball room was perfect."[18]

Others were less impressed with the idea of dance lessons. In 1853, a boy working at the Lowell Machine Shop wrote home: "My boarding place proves as good as I could wish. There [are] only two things I dislike, one is the children think themselves pretty important in the family and no wonder the way they are bringing them up. They must have their own way about everything and if they do not there is a noise I tell you. They have three children, one boy and two girls, the oldest not above the age of twelve years and they are going to the dancing school. Their mother thinks that a great accomplishment. I think [their mother] would rather dance anytime than eat."[19]

Harriet Martineau, an English sociologist, toured the Waltham and Lowell mills in the mid-1830s. She commented in her writings: "I saw a bill fixed up in the Waltham mill which bore a warning that no young lady who attended dancing-school that winter should be employed: and that the corporation had given directions to the overseer to dismiss any one who should be found to dance at the school."[20]

When Ms. Martineau asked the overseer why, she was told: "They are very young, many of them; and they forget the time, and everything but the amusement, and dance away till two or three in the morning. Then they are unfit for their work the next day; or, if they get properly through their work, it is at the expense of their health."[21]

Of course, if dancing when you were supposed to be resting was bad, dancing at work was worse. One researcher tells us that in 1837 two women were dismissed from the Hamilton Mill for dancing in the spinning room—not so much for any loss of production, but because "this incident flew in the face of the puritanical moral code advocated by the management and, as such, was defined as detrimental to the order and discipline of the mill." Levity of any type (a balm that might lighten the drudgery of the mill) could result in dismissal.[22]

Lowell's churches were split on the morality of dancing. Harriet Robinson, a mill girl in the 1830s and 40s, was raised a Congregationalist. She writes in *Loom and Spindle*: "We were well taught in the literal devil, in a lake of brimstone and fire, and in the 'wrath of a just God.'"

"I used often to wish that I could go to the Episcopal Sunday-school, because their little girls were not afraid of the devil, were allowed to dance, and had so much nicer books in their Sunday-school library."[23]

The Episcopalians might allow dancing, but Reverend Theodore Edson, first pastor of Saint Anne's Episcopal Church, was concerned about dancing among the working classes for multiple reasons. In an 1839 diary entry, Edson muses: "Last night was the annual Ball at the Mechanics Hall. It has been for several years last past got up with an extensive interest and I have felt sorry and grieved to see so many of our own people concerned in the matter; the plan is intended to embrace all classes of people and they are to mingle together in the dance once a year."

"There are several objections in my mind. One, that dancing here publicly is a step to licentiousness and I am sorry that influential people should give countenance to a practice which in other forms is doing much harm. But further, the laboring man and woman who go there and dance make themselves ridiculous in the eyes of those who have nothing to prevent their dancing. Well, it is not to be expected that a hard working person once a year should be able to leave his hammer, anvil or saw and dance as elegantly as a child who has been taught and practiced; the awkwardness of the mechanic and his hardworking wife is a matter of sport and such dancing is indeed most thoroughly and truly ridiculous. It is a pity they should put themselves in a way to be laughed at."[24]

When it came to the different social classes of Lowell, Harriet Robinson divided the factory population of the early 1830s into four groups: the agents of the corporations and their families, the mill overseers (and their families), the factory operators, and "the lords of the spade and the shovel"—the predominantly Irish workers who built the factories and the canals.[25]

The introduction to 1836's *The Laws of Etiquette; or, Short Rules and Reflections for Conduct in Society* explains that people frequently confuse America's social system with its political system. In the European countries with a monarchy, the author states, they are indeed the same. "But in America the two systems are totally unconnected; there is perfect freedom of political privilege...but this equality does not extend to the drawing-room or the parlors. The distinction of classes...is actually more clearly defined, and more rigidly observed in America, than in any country in Europe."[26]

Attempts to muddy those distinctions, particularly on the dance floor, often resulted in the type of embarrassment noted by Reverend Edson. But there could be much more dire results for a mill girl than just ridicule. The threat to a young woman's virtue from a man of her own station was bad enough, but an upper-class dandy whirling her about the ballroom had an even better chance of sweeping her off her feet. And no amount of PR from the corporations of Lowell about the virtue of their workers or the respect they were afforded could totally erase the truth of the matter.

Left: Image from vintage postcard.

Above: St. Anne's Episcopal Church on Merrimack Street as shown on a vintage postcard.

There is a certain anti-dance screed that turns up periodically as a novelty item. People come across reprints of 1892's *From the Ball-Room to Hell* and chuckle at the melodramatic and oh-so-yesterday title. Thumbing through the book, most people are even more amused to find that the dance the author condemns most strongly is the waltz!

But if the modern reader can look past the writing style and a few misguided claims, there's a lot of truth to the text. And, as a former dancing teacher and championship dancer, T. A. Faulkner knew what he was talking about:

"Some one has said that few people know better than the dancing master and saloon keeper; how many souls are sent through the port holes of hell between the ages of fourteen and twenty by these two agencies of the devil."[1]

Books, treatise, and sermons warning of the evils of dancing were many; ones written by repentant dancing masters with an inside knowledge of the predators of the ballroom were much rarer. Faulkner claims that "two-thirds of the girls who are ruined fall through the influence of dancing."[2]

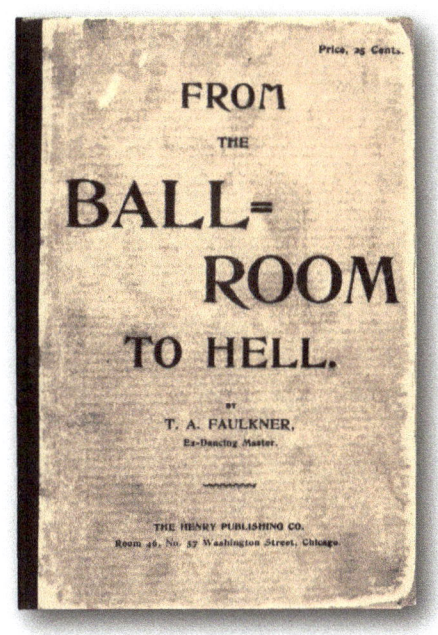

Mixt Dance:
Kissing, Courtship, and Damnation

He offers two reasons for this. First is the intimate hold of the waltz, and the "emotions which must come to every woman who has a particle of warmth in her nature when in such close connection with the opposite sex."[3] Even if a young woman successfully guards her chastity, she still soils her reputation: "It is a noticeable fact that a man who knows the ways of a ball room rarely seeks a wife there. When he wishes to marry he chooses for a wife a woman who has not been fondled and embraced by every dancing man in town."[4]

Opposite page: Three postcard images from the early 1900s. The text is shown exactly as it appears on the cards. Just what the "right direction" meant was left to the imagination. And how it was imagined undoubtedly varied between individuals, as well as genders.

Above: Cover of T. A. Faulkner's From the Ball-Room to Hell.

Below: 1856 waltz illustration.

"The second reason why so many dancing girls are ruined is obvious, when one considers how many fiends there are hanging about the dancing schools and ballrooms, for this purpose alone, some of them for their own gratification, and others for the living there is to be made from it. I am personally acquainted with men who are professional seducers, and who are to-day making a living in just this way. They are fine looking, good conversationalists and elegant dancers. They buy their admittance to the select dancing school by paying an extra fee, and know just what snares to lay and what arts to practice upon the innocent girls they meet there to induce them to yield to their diabolical solicitations, and after having satisfied their own desires and ruined the girls they entice them to the brothel where they receive a certain sum of money from the landlady, rated according to their beauty and form."[5]

Faulkner wrote in California near the turn of the century. But many years earlier, very similar stories had appeared in the *Boston Daily Times* as part of a series of articles about Lowell's manufacturing population.

A SOLEMN WARNING TO DANCERS.

Wo unto them who chant to the sound of the viol, and invent to themselves instruments of music, like David, Amos vi, 5.

Seventy years before T. A. Faulkner wrote From the Ball-Room to Hell, *the Methodist Episcopal Church published a tract titled* A Solemn Warning to Dancers. *The first of the pamphlet's four pages includes the illustration above. Gambling paraphernalia sits on the table and a serpent lurks underneath as the couple dances off the precipice to their doom.*

The themes of the two publications are frequently so similar that one suspects that Faulkner was familiar with the earlier work. From A Solemn Warning to Dancers: *"Stop! And think a little. Would you be willing to go from the ball chamber to the judgment seat of Christ? But you are commanded to be* always ready.*"[6] And from* The Ball-Room to Hell: *"The Son of man cometh at an hour when ye know not. If he should come and find you at the dance, locked in the embrace of another woman's husband, do you feel that he would consider you ready? Do you not feel the slightest fear that He would say, 'Depart from me, I never knew you'?"[7]*

Also from A Solemn Warning: *"Dancing is not only a notorious conformity to the world, but is directly calculated to divert the mind from every thing of a serious nature, and, by the manner in which it is conducted, tends to awaken in the breast of youth every unhallowed passion, and to set on fire of hell the whole course of nature."[8] And from* The Ball-Room to Hell: *"The more profitable things upon which she has been accustomed to spend her time and thought, lose all attraction for her, she feeds her romantic passion on novels, unfit for any person to read, and which would have been without special interest to her before she entered the dancing school. She spends much thought upon those things which tend to develop her lower nature, for 'as a man thinketh, so is he.'"[9]*

"We know, from good testimony, that many men employed in the mills take every opportunity to seduce such girls as fall in their way. It has been done by overseers as well as laborers, and many have fallen victims to those who should have been their guardians and protectors. There used to be in Lowell an association of young men, called 'the old line,' who had an understanding with a great many girls in the factories, and who used to introduce young men of their acquaintance, who were visiting the place, to these girls, for improper purposes. Balls used to be given at various places, attended mostly by these young men and factory girls, with some others who did not know the object, and after the dancing was over the girls were carried to infamous places of resort in Lowell or in the immediate vicinity; and were not returned to their homes till day-light."[10]

Another article from the same series also disputed the rosy and pure Mill Girl image. Not only did the *Times* claim that girls were being "ruined" by various lechers, it said that there were professional prostitutes working in the mills and lowering the morals of those around them.

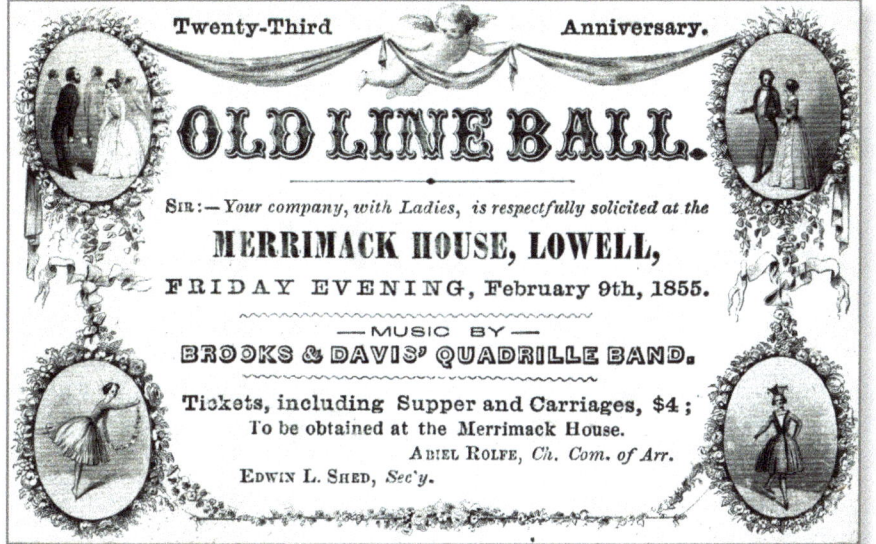

Left: 1855 Invitation to an Old Line Ball (Lowell Historical Society).

Above: An undated dance card shows three young gentleman mulling over who shall be their "catch" for the evening.

"We shall first state some facts which go to show that the amount of prostitution is greater among the girls than is generally supposed; and greater than is probably supposed by the immediate agents and overseers of the mills. A medical practitioner—[one]by no means having the largest business in that way—once assured us, in reply to inquiries we made for information, that, within one week, more than seventy different persons applied to him for remedies against the loathesome disease contracted in the promiscuous intercourse of the sexes. The most of them were females. The thought is dreadfully revolting; but it is true, and ought to be known."[11]

Dancing was clearly only one of a number of threats to a Mill Girl's purity and future. A doctor's letter to the *Times* in response to the paper's series of Lowell articles offers another situation that might lead women to the brothel.

"I have practiced here now about 4 years, and have had, God knows, too often occasion to see the general decay of health produced on the bodies, and consequently, minds of the 'Factory Girls,' under the present system. This is so evident, that it is common for them to calculate 'how long they can work before they are down sick.' You have already stated very truly their unhealthy condition, together with the causes. The immorality you mention, as existing among some of them, I think may be fairly attributed (in spite of the strict rules by which they are governed) to the same cause. For instance, a girl arrives in Lowell; (many sometimes 100 or 200 miles from home,) she goes to work in the mill for awhile; she is taken sick, and perhaps has no one to attend her as a nurse except the boarding-house keeper; and although they are generally exceedingly kind and attentive, yet, with their various and many duties, they cannot pay that strict attention required. The girl's money (what little she may have earned) goes for board. She has then the worst of all bills—a doctor's—to pay out of her future earnings, provided she recovers. Her visions of laying up money are gone, and she reflects only on her present destitute condition. When she is raised from her sick bed she may be weeks, or months, perhaps, before she can return to her former laborious occupation in the mill. In the meantime she seeks out some easier one, or saunters about the streets; the consequence of which is, that she runs the risk of forming bad connections with others, who may entice her from the path of duty. We all know that a feeling of destitution begets a feeling of desperation, urging on to profligacy and destruction."[12]

Needless to say, these revelations did not sit well with many of the people of Lowell, and a sniping war between the *Boston Times* and the corporation-controlled *Lowell Courier* ensued. The *Times* was disparagingly referred to as a "penny paper" and the *Courier* was accused of "low blackguardism" and called "destitute of decency."[13] The factory girls themselves were furious at having their reputation tarnished; the *Times'* assurance that "By far the larger portion of the girls are pure, high-minded, and virtuous"[14] did little to appease them. A flurry of articles appeared in Lowell tallying up churches built and pennies saved and insisting the girls were well protected.

Despite the *Boston Times*' 1839 exposé, nothing changed. The Lowell factories continued to ruthlessly pursue profits at the expense of their workers; a certain number of unscrupulous men from all walks of life continued to seek ways to use and abuse the city's large population of young women; and the 'Old Liners' continued their famous parties for decades.

From the *Lowell Sun*, January 24th, 1893: "Another of the delightful assemblies of the 'Old Liners' was held last evening at the Highland club house, and like all preceding ones was full of fun and social enjoyment. At 7:30 the dancing began with an 'old line' march…Then until intermission it was kept up without a hitch, and some of the most enjoyable features of the evening were the revivals of the old time dances."

When I first discovered that some stories cast the Old Line dances as dens of sin while others waxed nostalgic about these "delightful assemblies," I was puzzled. The two views seemed incompatible.

Then I realized an obvious parallel. When I was a young contra dancer in the 1970s, there was various mischief going on; one musician in particular used the dance floor as his personal hunting ground. This man seemed to have a special fondness for girls a fraction of his age, ones too young to know how to say "no" to an adult. They were no more likely to resist this charismatic grown-up than they were to stand up in the middle of a schoolroom and tell their teacher to shut up.

Some of these teens—having been denied the power to say "no," while simultaneously given a sense that they held power as seductresses—would take years to find their own voices and reclaim their lives.

There were dancers at the time who knew what was going on and winked; others looked away or made only feeble attempts to intervene. The majority of people heard merely whispered rumors or nothing at all. Mention of the misbehavior to a bystander years later was answered with: "Yes, but didn't we have fun?"

The fellow is today a respected and much-lauded member of the dance community. But some of us still cringe every time we hear him praised.

—Author

Regardless of the presence or absence of cads at their parties, the term "Old Line" actually refers to a town's local aristocracy, to well-established and respected families in a given area. An 1869 report on the "Old Liners" of Swanzey, NH, went further: "The 'Old Line' is one of the peculiar institutions that nobody wishes to abolish, founded on the old-fashioned custom of sociality between families and neighborhoods, and the rendering of assistance to one another in cases of sickness."[15]

Securing an invitation to one of Lowell's Old Line parties would have seemed like a coup to many a young woman, perhaps even her ticket to a rich husband and freedom from the mills. Working class couples would most likely have been excluded, but the Factory Girls were both novel and vulnerable: starry-eyed maids to enjoy and discard. As such, they would have been welcomed—by some, at least—at many events normally closed to their social group.

One historian—a twentieth-century *Lowell Sun* columnist named Charles Sampas—liked to pepper his writing with juicy bits gleaned from old newspapers and elsewhere. The presence of factory girls at society dances came up more than once.

"A very prominent early-Lowell-days industrialist got resoundingly slapped by his wife when he was caught holding hands with a blonde mill girl at the Old Stone House on Pawtucket St. in one of the soirees there…[His wife} made him take a trip with her to Europe for a year or so to get over 'the scandal.'"[16]

"In the 1830s and 1840s, Lowell was quite socially-conscious and Pawtucket Street was definitely the Lowelltown's Number One 'Social Street'…One of the most-talked-of occasions was the appearance at one of these parties of a very pretty Lowell millovely. She was the 'secret' sweetheart of a big mill agent here—and was 'sort of' an unofficial 'queen' of the Lowell social life. (Also a few other things). At any rate, the agent had the first dance with her; other mill biggies followed suit. It was the story of the Era of the Common Man—and the millmen tried to keep up with the times in their own special way—this time dancing with a girl who 'worked' in the mills."[17]

Far left: 1913 postcard image of the Highland Club where some of the later "Old Line" dances were held.

Above: A romanticized depiction of the waltz calls the dance "One little minute of love."

Left: Titled "After the Ball," this painting (image from a vintage postcard) certainly suggests that the dancing was followed by something more.

The fact is that the Lowell System was ripe for abuse.

"Look, then, at the unnatural composition of such a society. On one hand a large mass of females, a large portion of whom do not expect to get married; and on the other, a considerable number of single men, engaged in the factories, or dwelling in the surrounding village, too often without principle, and eager to gratify their baser appetites."[18] —*Boston Daily Times,* 1839.

The mill directors insisted such gratification wasn't happening, and if it was, the men involved were doing the honorable thing.

"There have never been more than three cases of illicit relations in our establishment, and, in the three cases, the parties were immediately married, many months before the birth of the infant; thus we do not count any births which are positively illegitimate."[19] —Quoted in 1834.

This, of course, omits all the girls who left before they were found out, or who avoided pregnancy, or who chose abortion or death over disgrace.

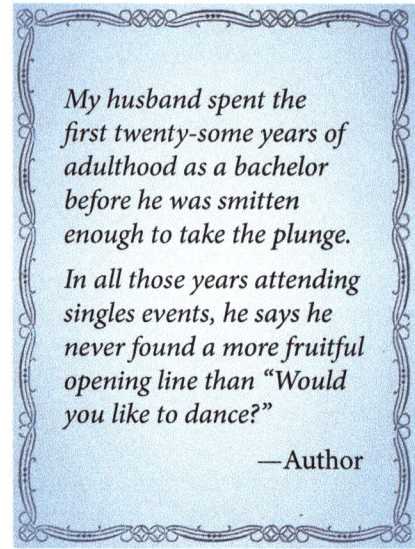

My husband spent the first twenty-some years of adulthood as a bachelor before he was smitten enough to take the plunge.

In all those years attending singles events, he says he never found a more fruitful opening line than "Would you like to dance?"

—Author

Lowell's famous canals did more than just power the mills; they also hosted a number of suicides.

While there were certainly many factors that might bring a mill girl to ruin, the dance world had a uniquely tempting blend of men, women, movement, and music. Yet, it still had plenty of defenders. Allen Dodworth, a New York City dancing master, best summed up the "pro" side of the argument late in the century:

"Dancing in well-ventilated rooms, under proper regulation, is an excellent and healthful physical exercise, from which the most feeble may receive benefit. Physiologists inform us that exercise is doubly beneficial when accompanied by exhilaration of mind. This being true, where can the two be so happily united as in dancing to good music amid pleasant associations?"[20]

In a western Massachusetts textile town, out near the state line, a pair of poems was written in 1861 protesting society's hypocritical demonization of dancing.[21] It is easy to hear the voices of exasperated young women from all across Massachusetts in the words. One of these poems appears at right in its entirety. The page following *Moral* offers a guide to its many nineteenth-century social references—along with some supporting excerpts from the second poem, *The Donation* (see the Appendix I for a complete recitation of *The Donation*).

Left: 1910 postcard image.

Moral

Oh, Fathers! Oh Mothers!
Why quake at mere names,
While you take to your bosoms
These "hug-and-kiss *games!*"

You hate the word "Dance"—
Say "dancing's a sin:"
What dancing hath such "scence,"
As Cop'nhagan "ropes in?"

You the violin scorn—
Yet what "vial of wrath,"
E'er poured out such woe"
As *one* "kissing play" hath?

If to *chassez* is "wrong"—
Then what of that chase
Wherein—will-he, nill-he—
A kiss ends the race!

If to glide through "the Lancers,"
Or walk through quadrilles;
If that's under ban, sirs,
Then stop your "Grab" Mills!

Why must Polka or Waltz
Hurry me to Old Lamiel
While your "Needle's Eye"
Swallows such a huge camel!

Of course, those old "Balls"
Where you danced till day-light;
While the Bar-Room ran *liquor,*
Could never be right.

But in your own home,—
Or 'mid friends you invite,—
If such dancing's wrong,
Then there's no play that's right.

But the eye of True Faith,
Looks not to mere forms,
So the feelings are right,
Human Love true and warm.

True Faith will not quarrel,
With Schottisch and Reels;
But looks more to the *heart,*
And less to the *heels.*

And may find no great odds
In the Good "Kingdom Come,"
Twixt my "tweedle d——,"
And your "tweedle—um!"

And here's a Commandment,
For Kith and Kin:
*"Accurs'd be that man
Who CREATETH A SIN!"*

That is: who of things,
In themselves no way wrong,
Makes a Bug-a-boo Monster,
To frighten the young.

Selected excerpts and their explanations:

While you take to your bosoms, These "hug-and-kiss games!"

What dancing hath such "scence," As Cop'nhagan "ropes in?"

*You the violin scorn—Yet what "vial of wrath,"
E'er poured out such woe, As one "kissing play" hath?*

*If to chassez is "wrong," Then what of that chase
Wherein—will-he, nill-he—A kiss ends the race!*

*If to glide through "the Lancers," Or walk through quadrilles;
If that's under ban, sirs, Then stop your "Grab" Mills!*

*Why must Polka or Waltz, Hurry me to Old Lamiel
While your "Needle's Eye," Swallows such a huge camel!*

Of course, those old "Balls," Where you danced till day-light;

True Faith will not quarrel, With Schottisch and Reels;

*And may find no great odds, In the Good "Kingdom Come,"
Twixt my "tweedle d——" And your "tweedle—um!"*

- Hug-and-kiss games and kissing plays were a regular part of life for young people in the eighteenth and nineteenth centuries: "Social parties among the young were called 'kissing parties' because in all the plays, either as a penalty or as part of the play, all the girls who joined in the amusement had to be kissed by some of the boys" wrote William James McKnight in *A Pioneer History of Jefferson County.*[22]

- Copenhagen was a popular form of tobacco; the odd spelling of scence is a play on scents/sense. Copenhagen was also a game. *Hood's Sarsaparilla Book of Parlor Games* describes it as a raucous game where a player known as "the Dane" was encircled with a piece of rope held by all the other players.[23] *The Donation* singsongs: *"And plays with the girls, Where you pull 'em and haul 'em, Now chase 'em, now miss 'em; Now catch 'em, now kiss 'em, 'Roped in' by that Drag-on, They call Copenhagen:"*

- Vial of wrath has religious roots: "The fire of hell is such as multitudes of tears will not quench it,—length of time will not finish it,—the vial of God's wrath will be always dropping upon a sinner."[24]

- Chassez refers to a sliding dance step (side-together-side). It is also the French word for "pursue."[25]

- Will-he, nill-he, or willy-nilly means "randomly" nowadays but the older meaning is "with or without consent"—whether "wills he or not wills he."[26]

- The Lancers was a popular nineteenth-century quadrille (see the Country Dance chapter).

- Grab Mills may have been a reference to widespread sexual harassment in the textile mills. But a "mill" is also a classic, turning dance move for four people, a move now called a star (and no relation to today's breakdance/hip-hop mill). Lines from *The Donation* suggest there was a kissing game incorporating a dance mill: *"But 'round goes the Mill again, Music you trill again; Hands clasp hot hands, till they tingle and thrill again; Your cheek in a blaze—Your blood in a bound—You romp and you race, While the Mill goes round. Sly glances, half-hidden, Bold kisses unbidden, But not any 'dancing' For that is forbidden!"*

- Lamiel is presumably a typo—or perhaps an alternate spelling—for "Ramiel." Ramiel was a fallen angel, one of the Watchers cast out of heaven for taking human wives and sharing forbidden knowledge.[27] To be "hurried to Ramiel" suggests becoming betrothed to a servant of Satan.

- **While your needle's eye swallows such a huge camel** is a biblical reference: *"It is easier for a camel to pass through the eye of a needle than for a rich man to enter the kingdom of God."* (Matthew 19:24).

- **"Ball"** is in quotes as a sign of disdain; there would not be a Bar-room running liquor at a *proper* Ball.

- **Schottisch and Reels** are both types of dances popular in the 1860s.

- **Tweedle dee and tweedle dum** refers to two things that are virtually the same. It dates to a rivalry between Handel and his fellow musician, Buononcini; some listeners felt that their styles of "tweedling" were all but identical.[28] Here, the reader is invited to fill in the blanks in the phrase—"my tweedle-dance and your tweedle-games," perhaps? Regardless, the line clearly questions whether God will judge dancing to be any more sinful than all the other mischief going on in society.

With so many double entendres crammed into just over a dozen stanzas, there can be little doubt that the poem's author was literate, intelligent and enjoyed wordplay. It also seems clear that *Moral* was written by a woman.

One of the things the author defends is dancing at home amid friends. Yet the dance nay-sayers considered even that to be a gateway vice.

"Dancing is too fascinating, and they who were at first content with parlor dancing soon want something else, and will for the sake of dancing, go to almost any place"[29]

Not only that, but the desire to dance would cause young people to further sin by lying to their parents and deceiving them about where they were going.

Yet, the kissing games mentioned earlier were hardly innocent. The author of *Moral* was not alone in pointing out this hypocrisy. In 1872, journalist T. W. Higginson coined a particularly memorable phrase when he described even the clumsiest of dancing as better than "coarse string games"—although what he meant by "string games" is unclear: were they rope games like Copenhagen or did Cat's Cradle somehow involve lips? Either way, dancing was:

"...not so objectionable as the coarse 'string games' which even now prevail in those regions of New England where dancing is still prohibited, and *a maiden's lips are held less sacred than her feet.*"[30] (emphasis added).

The smooching part of the games listed in *Hood's Parlor Games*—published in Lowell in the latter half of the 1800s—is not immediately obvious. Kissing doesn't appear until the "Forfeits" section, a list of "punishments" for failing to achieve the goals set forth in all the earlier-described games.

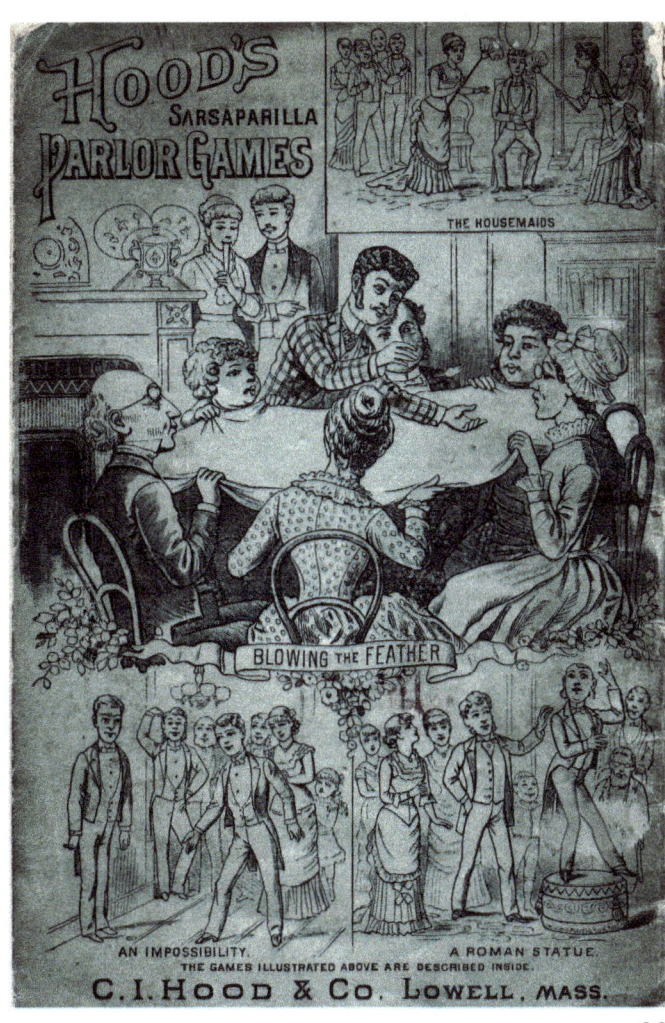

Far left, below and above: Front and back covers (respectively) and inside image from Hood's Sarsaparilla Parlor Games, *c.1885.*

"*Forfeits.* Perhaps the most enjoyable portion of the whole evening's pleasure is 'crying the forfeits,' which usually takes place at the conclusion of the games. A record or score of the forfeits should be kept, and one or more persons should be chosen as judges to assign the tasks to be performed in redeeming the forfeits. Sometimes the forfeits are written upon pieces of paper beforehand, are folded and placed in a hat, and are assigned by drawing from the hat, each person who draws to perform the forfeit named on the paper. Either way ought to be satisfactory, as every one should remember that the pleasure of the evening will be seriously marred by losing temper or by obstinacy."[31]

Many of the forfeits are pleasantly silly with no kissing involved: singing "quack, quack" to a given tune; using a feather duster to dust the "parlor ornaments" (any gentlemen in the room); pretending to be a statue which the other players may pose as they see fit; etc. But several of the forfeits are a tad more titillating:

"Run the Gauntlet.—In this, the gentlemen stand in two rows, facing each other, while the lady who is to pay the forfeit, is to pass between them. Each gentleman who can, is to get a kiss, but he must stop her with hands only, while she can resort to any means to escape, except leaving the row."[32]

"To become a sofa, a gentleman must get down on his hands and knees while a lady and gentleman leisurely sit down on his back and kiss."[33]

CRESCENT MOON—AT THE DANCE

"Kiss Nun-fashion. (A lady and gentleman kiss through the back of a chair.)"[34]

"Kiss each other back to back. This is done over the shoulder."[35]

"Bow to the wittiest, kneel to the prettiest, and kiss the one you love best."[36]

"Kiss yourself in the looking-glass."[37]

"Say 'Quizzle, Quizzle, kiss me quick,' ten times in one breath."[38]

Mid-nineteenth century sources from Maine and Pennsylvania talk about musical games where kissing was an integral part of the play rather than simply a postlude. Boys "lived and played [these games] in the 'pleasures of hope,'" while an older chaperone would sit nearby watching and basking in the "pleasures of memory."[39]

The games usually had a group of young people holding hands in a circle with one or two players in the center. One common game began by players circling a boy and singing that he must choose the one that he liked best. Things progressed from there.

"The gentleman in the centre then chose a lady from the circle, and she stepped into the ring with him. Then the circling was resumed, and all sang to the parties inside,—'Down on this carpet you must kneel, just as the grass grows in the field; Salute your bride with kisses sweet, And then rise up upon your feet.'"

"The play went on in this manner until all the girls present were kissed."[40]

There were dozens of these "play songs" where children acted out various stories, and romance was often a part of them. In fact, the notion of dancing and singing in a ring was viewed with such fond nostalgia that it was a regular part of advertising in Lowell.

It's hard to imagine older teenagers today doing anything but scoff at such play songs, even if they did involve a little lip-to-lip action. Yet, when John M. Todd wrote of growing up in the mid-1800s, he mentioned participating in these games at the age of seventeen.[41]

It was once said by a French visitor to Lowell that American manners completely prohibited "a full and free expression of the stronger feelings of the soul." Compared to the French, the English were cold, and the "double-distilled English" of *New* England were doubly so.[42]

But people are people. And the youth of nineteenth-century Lowell were like the hormone-steeped youth of every other place and time. As such, any chance to dabble in the forbidden world of sex was welcome right up until one entered into marriage where, at last, one could indulge one's passions with the blessing of society.

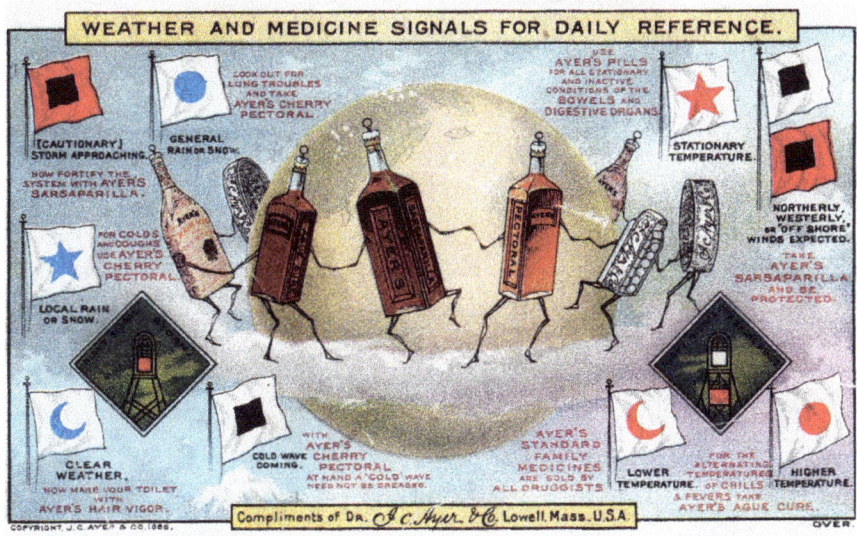

Far left: Another vintage postcard image (1915) linking dancing to seduction.

Above: E. W. Hoyt & Company's 1892 image of children dancing in a circle was designed to inspire feelings of youth, health, and good times. The J. C. Ayer & Company's 1886 advertisement has a similar goal, even if its imagery is a bit more bizarre.

Above: 1907 print of "Sir Roger De Coverly," better known now as "The Virginia Reel."

Immediate right: Illustration of the five positions from an 1811 dance manual.

Far right: The five positions from an 1882 ballroom dance manual.

Social dancing does not exist in a vacuum. It as much about "social" as it is about "dancing" and, as such, reflects the manners and mores of its era. Dance evolves, absorbing or rejecting the influence of other dances and of world events, both big and small. And virtually every new style is based on the ones that came before.

The contras and quadrilles of nineteenth century Lowell shared their roots with ballet; both originated in the courts of Europe. Contras and squares have come a very long way since then. But when Lowell was young, learning to dance properly meant learning the five basic positions that are still used in ballet. Terms such as *Jété, Assemblée, Pas de Bourré, Battement, Chassé, Entrechat, and Glissade* appear as moves in dance manuals of the 1830s and will all be familiar to the modern ballet dancer.

Even so, by the time Lowell sprang up, the steps were less important than in prior days. The preface to 1841's *Ball-Room Instructor* says: "There are many unacquainted with dancing, who labor under an erroneous impression, that 'the steps' are all that are necessary to be learned to fit a person for the ball-room. In our modern assemblies, scarcely one person in ten is acquainted with them; and if they are, they make use of steps to please their own fancy..."

Country Dance:

Contras and Quadrilles, Past and Present

He further states that it is far more important that one knows the *figures* than any fancy footwork: "A person well skilled in graceful and classic steps, [but] unacquainted with figures, would certainly make a ridiculous appearance."[1]

Not to mention being a hazard on the dance floor!

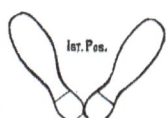

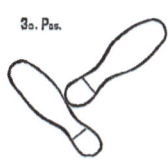
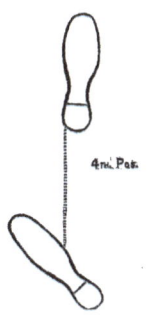
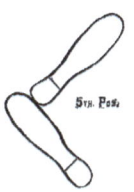

By the 1860s, the elaborate, ballet-like footwork was rarely seen. In dances for two, such as waltz or polka, there was new footwork to learn and flaunt. In the contras and quadrilles, "the change of manners and customs, the fickleness of fashion, and, above all, the exigency of the modern laiser aller" had contributed to the abandonment of the more formal dance steps.[2]

Nonetheless, the posture, positions, and elegant movements of the earlier dances remained essential all through the nineteenth century, even if the footwork itself had fallen out of favor: "It would be an error to suppose that the new dances, despite their apparent facility of acquirement, can in the least dispense with those preliminary exercises which give ease to the body, are the necessary preparation for the steps and attitudes, and which have in all times formed the foundation of every description of dance."[3]

It is hard to imagine how the mill girls would have had the time and energy to learn to dance up to these standards, although some of them clearly made the effort. Back home, in New England villages where the only dance

Above: Frontispiece from A Complete Practical Guide to the Art of Dancing *by Thomas Hillgrove, 1863.*

Left: Photograph by Doug Plummer, 2013.

Right and Far Right: Pages explaining the proper bow and curtesy with which to "honor your partner." From Hillgrove's Guide, 1863.

teachers were itinerate ones merely passing through, one suspects that posture and footwork were considerably laxer.

It thus comes as no surprise that St. Anne's Reverend Edson felt working class men and women "put themselves in a position to be laughed at"[4] on those occasions when they joined the upper classes on the dance floor.

But as the nineteenth century drew to a close, "the neighbourly community dances were gradually ousted by the less sociable couple dances from Europe, the waltz and polka, and the later [American] dances, the Boston, the one-step, fox-trot and tango."[5] Contra dances survived in rural New England, but in cities such as Lowell, only one or two favorites were still done in formal ballrooms except at "old-timers" events. The excruciatingly correct steps and attitudes fell by the wayside.

A 1918 book of American contra dances, "Largely from the New England States," describes the walking step that had by that time become the norm.

> *In the forty-some years I've been attending contra dances, I've never known of one held in Lowell. But in nearby Concord, two or three are held every week in a beautiful hall that was once a barn.*
>
> *If one wants to see footwork suggestive of the type danced in early Lowell, his or her best bet would be to look into Scottish country dance, where pointed toes and graceful leaps live on.* —Author

"The Usual Country-Dance Step"

"The invariable step used throughout these dances is an easy, natural, springy walking step. This is executed, especially by the men, with a certain slight emphasis and complacency of manner, which almost suggest a swagger. There is a slight raising of the elbows at each step, and a slight scuffling of the feet."[6]

This is the step that is seen today in dance halls across New England. The amount of scuffle, the level of bounce in the knees and elbows, the force with which feet strike the floor, and the degree of (or total lack of) proper posture all vary from one decade to the next and one area to another. Still, the picture drawn by the 1918 description is as familiar to contra and square dancers now as it was to dancers a century ago.

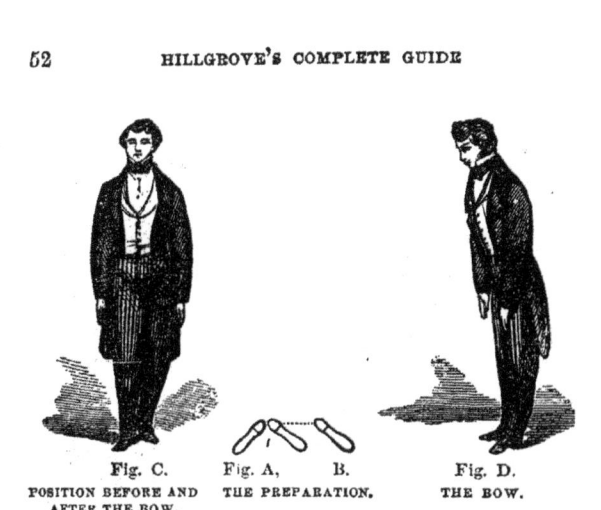

Although any resemblance to ballet is gone, the figures themselves have stayed much the same. Reviewing several gives more of a sense of continuity than of change.

Honor your partner is rare now in contra formation. But in a quadrille—that is to say, a square dance—it remains the opening move. The bows may lack the precision of bygone days, yet they are there nonetheless.

Lawrence De Garmo Brookes asserted in 1887 that the "honor" existed because "at the beginning of all our Acts, we should do due Honour to God, which is the Root of Prudence, which Honour is compact of these three things, Fear, Love and Reverence."[7]

That claim is, perhaps, overstated. For most New England dancers in recent centuries, the "honor" is simply a polite greeting to their partner. It is invariably followed by nods to other nearby dancers.

A *Star* has had several names over time; *Hands Across* appears most often. The French word, *Moulinet* is common in the older manuals while its English equivalent, *Mill*, is used in Burchenal's 1918 *American Country-Dances.*

But for all that, the move is essentially unchanged, excepting the modern use of an interlocked, hand-to-wrist hold among many contra and square dancers.

Above: 1863 illustration of a Star *or* Moulinet.

Left: Photo by Doug Plummer showing a traditional Star *hold.*

Immediately below: Modern wrist hold for a Star.

Bottom of page: 1822 illustration of the figure Right and Left.

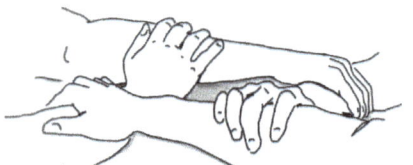

The *Right and Left* of the 1820s varied; Wilson's *Complete System of English Country Dancing* stated that it was one move in a quadrille and another in a longways set.[8] Usually it was a type of weaving figure, or "hey." Men traveled clockwise, and women counterclockwise, taking right and left hands alternately.

The vagaries of the manuals and the passage of time took their toll. The handclasps became optional. The figure became two dancers passing through two dancers, exchanging places, and returning the same way.

That exchanging of places has evolved a fair bit over the years. In nineteenth-century Lowell, the man might grasp the woman's left hand in his own to lead her gracefully to place before doing a smart about-face himself.

Today, the man may spin the lady to place under his arm, or use a chummy, arms-about-the-waist turn, or perhaps the more proper courtesy turn. When the dancers are the same gender, the exchange is sometimes a contact-free, shoulder-to-shoulder, wheeling motion.

Ladies Chain (2.d Part) Diagram 8. LE PANTALON.

Above right: 1822 illustration of a Ladies' Chain.

Immediately below: Waist hold for a Courtesy Turn.

Below left: 1841 Balance definition.

Below right: 1918 instructions for a Balance.

In another classic figure, *Ladies Chain,* two women take right hands, pass by, and offer their left to the opposite man who turns the lady around and sends her back the way she came.

As in the Right and Left, that left hand turn to exchange places has become something else. The most frequent choices now are a courtesy turn—women's left hand in man's left and man's right hand atop woman's right at her right hip—or a spin or two under the man's arm.

The *Balance* is ripe for interpretation, as much then as now. The 1841 description below is decidedly vague; here is where dancers would be likely to "make use of steps to please their own fancy." In early Lowell, gentle leaps and stylishly pointed toes would have been the order of the day.

A 1918 source offers more detail and covers several variations, all still in use in twenty-first century New England. Improvisation remains common—if less refined than in days past!

Balance—Performed by both couples at the same time. Gentleman and partner face each other, dancing one or two steps to the right, then to the left, or in one place (see cut No. 4)

[No. 4.]

Balance Step
The following are five different ways in which the balance step is done:
- **(A)** (Meas. 1-2.) Take two walking steps forward and two backward.
- **(B)** (Meas. 1.) Step forward on the right foot (one); then swing the left slightly forward and at the same time raise and lower the right heel (two).
(Meas. 2.) Step forward on the left foot; then swing the right foot forward.
- **(C)** Same as **B**, but continuing forward during the second measure.
- **(D)** (Meas. 1.) Step to the right with the right foot (one), and close the left foot to the right (two).
(Meas. 2.) Repeat the same to the left.
- **(E)** Same as **D**, but taking it forward and back, instead of to right and left.

One style of balance that has only appeared in the last half-century or so is sometimes called the Boston Stamp Balance. Based on description "B," it turns the first step (count 1) into a stomp and incorporates hall-shaking heel strikes into the kick (1-*and*) and on the heel drop (2). This style is particularly popular in a dance titled *Hull's Victory*, written to celebrate the 1812 capture of the HMS Guerriere by the USS Constitution. While the turns and balances of the dance may have quietly mimicked the maneuvering of the ships and the firing of their guns for over two centuries, there is lately a fondness for also reproducing the *sound* of the cannon as well.

The *Swing* is the move that has changed the most over the years, though its name has stayed the same. While Thomas Wilson, dancing master, describes a right hand turn as simply "turn your partner" in an 1808 manual, by 1815 he states that "turn your partner" is a two hand turn; the right hand turn has become "swing your partner." He also specifies the ballet-style steps that go with this early swing:

"The only difference between this Figure and [turn your partner] is that in lieu of taking both hands, you give the right hand only, and move in the directions as above; if you give the left hand, you move contrary-wise; this is performed *by three Chasses Jetté and Assemblé—four bars.*"[9]

A right hand turn using three slipping steps, a graceful leap, and an elegant return to position actually sounds like a lovely move—but absolutely nothing like a modern swing. It also sounds like a move difficult to execute well and another reason that the laboring class of early Lowell would have had a hard time fitting in on the dance floor with their "betters."

Though the slips and leaps soon fell out of fashion, the swing as a one-hand turn lasted through the nineteenth century. Manual after manual includes such instructions as "join right hands and swing half round." It wasn't until the early twentieth century—when Ragtime was breaking all the rules and couple dances were driving the last of the old contras from the ballroom—that the swing became what it is today.

> When the dance is going full blast and the music lively, I'm partial to using a stamp balance myself; I even like to add heel strikes to every half-count. At least, I did until I realized that a clogging-style balance had become passé and the extra end "thump" stood out like a sore thumb.
>
> I only remember two injuries during the years I danced heavily, and both involved balances. I often danced barefoot and in one instance I did a stamp balance onto an unseen shard of glass.
>
> But no pair of mere dance shoes would have saved me from a later, more painful injury that took place during *Hull's Victory.* My usually-skillful partner forgot the turn that preceded one of the balances; I did not. As I attempted to make the turn, I swung around behind him and my foot slipped under his heel—just in time to take the brunt of the "cannon fire."
> —Author

Left: Dancers take hands for a two-hand turn. Photo by Doug Plummer.

Top Right: A modern swing as done at the New England Folk Festival. Photo by Doug Plummer.

Middle Near Right: Diagram of footwork for a buzz step from a 1918 book.

Middle Far Right: 1815 diagram of Swing Corners, a move now known as Contra (or Country, or Contrary, or Contr'y) Corners.

The "new" swing used a closed ballroom hold and introduced something called a buzz step:

"Buzz Step—This is a sort of pivoting step, used when swinging partners in place. The man holds his partner in ordinary dance position, but well out to his right, so that they are practically side by side, with right shoulder to right shoulder. (Diagram 6)."

"In fitting the step to the music, each measure should be counted ('one, and, two, and'). On 'one,' put down the right foot in place; on 'and' step forward on the ball of the left foot; on 'two,' put down the right foot on the same spot as before; on 'and,' step forward on the ball of the left foot, and so on."[10]

To put it more simply than in the 1918 description given above, the right foot becomes the pivot point and pushing with the ball of the left foot is what powers the spin.

Diagram 6

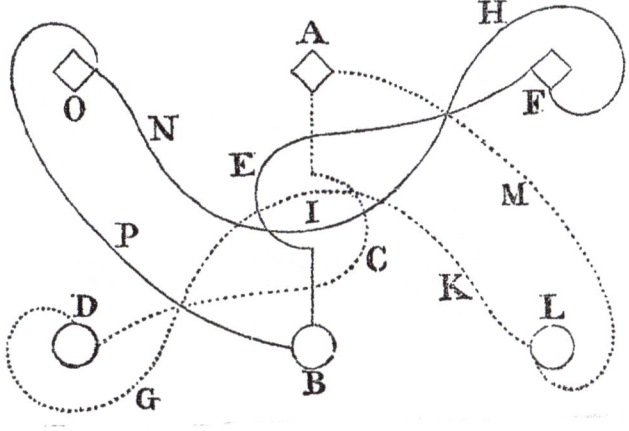

Swing corners.
The whole of the Figures as performed by the Lady and Gentleman.
FIG. VII.

A more advanced figure among the dancers of early Lowell would have been *Swing Corners*. Today that move is called *Contra Corners*. Although the 1815 diagram above makes the move look terribly confusing, once learned, it's not that hard. The dancers doing the move turn their partner part way with the right hand, then the person to the right of their partner's place with the left hand; the partner again in the center with the right hand, then the person to the left of their partner's place with the left hand. Finally, they turn their partner back to place with the right hand. These days, a balance and (buzz step) swing are usually substituted for the final turn to place.

By now, the average reader has had quite enough of these step descriptions (and the average dancer would rather be dancing). But for all the specifics available, it is impossible to say *exactly* how the figures were executed in nineteenth-century Lowell, and not just because so much time has passed. Dance manuals of the period differ. Different events drew different classes—and different mixes of classes—especially in a growing city like Lowell. Different dance teachers would have stressed different aspects of dancing.

> *There is a contra dance group that has been performing the old dances for audiences since the 1920s. For all their efforts to stay true to the nineteenth-century version of each dance, I came away from their performance with the feeling that they had shown only a single person's style from a single time and a single place with none of the variety or improvisation among the dancers that brings a dance hall to life.* —Author

Even more importantly, dancers of any time period have their own personal style. The better dancers add their own flourishes "to please their fancy" and to show off their skill; the less accomplished dancers may corrupt the moves into something a bit different and a tad simpler.

That remains the case today. New England contra dancing is a vibrant, living tradition, readily accessible for study. Yet it is almost as difficult to try to nail down the exact way a move is executed now as it is to nail down how a move was performed 200 years ago!

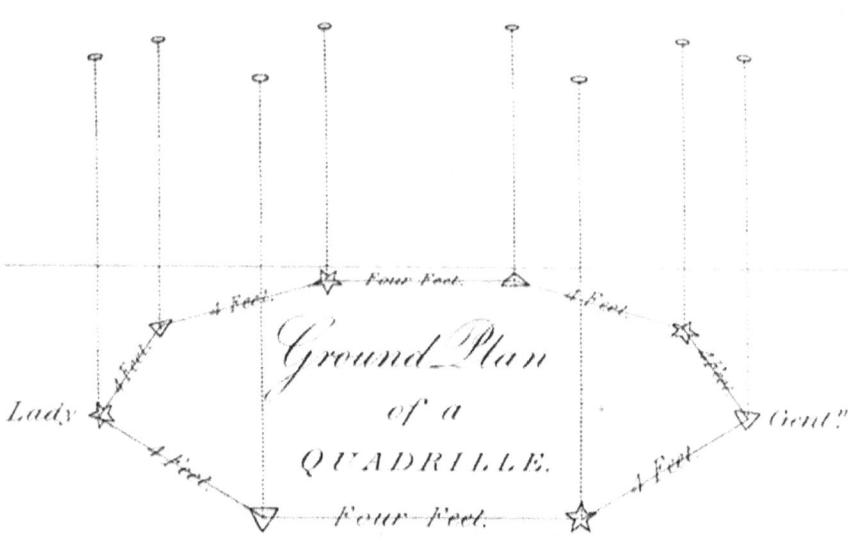

In any case, all of these dance figures (plus a great many others) were done within a specific framework or formation. The more common of these remain, for the most part, unchanged.

The *Longways Set*, or *Contra Set*, is a line of couples, partner facing partner. Many older dances call for a specific number of couples, usually three, and all the figures take place between those couples. But as Lowell was growing, so were the number of dances for "as many as will," where the lines are as long as space allows. In most of these sets, every other couple, or sometimes every third couple, is designated "active." The active couples lead the majority of the figures and gradually move down the set with each run-through of the sequence. When they reach the bottom, they start their way up again as a so-called "inactive" couple. For the inactive couples reaching the top, it is their turn to become active and strut their stuff.

The *Quadrille*, or *Square*, is a set of four couples arranged as shown at left. These couples have numbers, although the numbering has changed since Lowell was young.

In the course of the dance, moves may involve anywhere from one to all of these couples. There is often an exchange of places and/or partners during the dance, but in the end everyone is returned "home"—if they don't foul things up, that is! Unlike contras, which may repeat indefinitely, a quadrille usually ends once its figures have been done four times and each couple has danced each position.

In the early-to-mid nineteenth century, quadrilles were also called *cotillons*, as the ladies' turns were likely to show a flash of petticoat or, in French, *cotillon*. Technically, a cotillon was an earlier and simpler form of quadrille but the terms were frequently used interchangeably.

Then, there are the circular dances. The image at right comes from an 1858 dance manual by Elias Howe, a musician from Framingham, Massachusetts who authored and published numerous music instruction books.[11] The diagram shows a formation usually described as "couple facing couple around the room." This arrangement still turns up occasionally for the waltz-based "Spanish Dance" and a few other numbers. Other circular formations include two couples facing two couples around the room or a single circle where each man has his partner on his right. The single circle dances done today are invariably "mixers," where every run-through of the dance brings a new partner.

There are other country dance formations that are rare or have totally vanished into obscurity, and at least one newer one that was unknown until the late twentieth century. But for the most part, these are the ways couples array—and would have arrayed—themselves on New England dance floors.

And once so arranged, what dances would they have been doing? Judge Hadley's recollections of Lowell's early years mention Chorus Jig, Fisher's Hornpipe, Money Musk, Portland Fancy, Lady Washington's Reel, and Speed the Plough.[12] These are all contra dances, at least two of which—Money Musk and Fisher's Hornpipe—appear by name in dance manuals as far back as the 1700s. But the manuals are inconsistent. A bit of dance history shows why.

When the nineteenth century began, dance figures were primarily mixed and matched to suit any given music. It was during the 1800s that specific sequences of figures began to be regularly paired with a specific piece of music and came to be known by that tune's name. This was a somewhat haphazard process. Two entirely different dances might routinely be done to—and take their name from—the same tune. Or a single sequence of figures would use different tunes in different locales and end up with multiple names. By mid-to-late century the dances listed above (with the possible exception of Speed the Plough) seem to have been fairly standardized.

CIRCULAR
Form of the *Spanish, and also of several Country dances.

> No. LIV. *Money Musk.*
> Six hands half way round and back, first and second gentlemen balance together and turn round, the 1st and 2nd ladies do the same, down the middle, up again, cast off, right and left.

Left: Money Musk is one dance where instructions varied significantly. These directions are taken from 1798's The Gentleman & Lady's Companion.

Below: In 1858, Elias Howe described Money Musk quite differently. Howe's version is what is danced today and still uses a one-hand turn in place of a modern swing.

MONEY MUSK.
First couple join right hands and swing once and a half round, go below 2d couple, (the 1st lady goes below 2d gent. on the outside, 1st. gent. at the same time goes below and between 2d and 3d ladies), forward and back six, 1st couple swing three quarters round, 1st gent. goes between 2d couple (on the inside), first lady goes between 3d couple inside, forward and back six, 1st couple swing three quarters round to place (below one couple), right and left four.

Opposite page top: 1864 diagram of contra dance formation.

Opposite page left: 1822 diagram of quadrille, or square, formation.

Top of page: 1858 diagram of one common, circular, dance formation.

A number of Lowell dance cards have survived to the present. Of the fourteen pre-1920 ones that the author was able to access, all but two included Portland Fancy on the program—sometimes more than once. Between 1853 and 1908, it appeared on every single one.

Sets for Portland Fancy can be arranged in multiple ways. Most often it's done as two couples facing two couples around the room like spokes on a wheel, or as two couples facing two couples in parallel sets. These formations both have couples progressing from one set on to the next.

Fifty miles from Lowell, in Prescott (a town submerged by the Quabbin Reservoir in 1938), Portland Fancy was also popular. In *The History of Prescott, Massachusetts,* Lillie Pierce Coolidge described the local version:

"Join hands and swing eight, head couple (gentleman, opposite lady) down the middle, foot couple up the outside (at the same time), back to places; head couple down the outside and the foot couple up the middle, back to places; ladies' chain at the head, right and left at the foot, right and left at the head and ladies chain at the foot, all forward [and back], forward and cross by opposite couple and face the next four and repeat."[13]

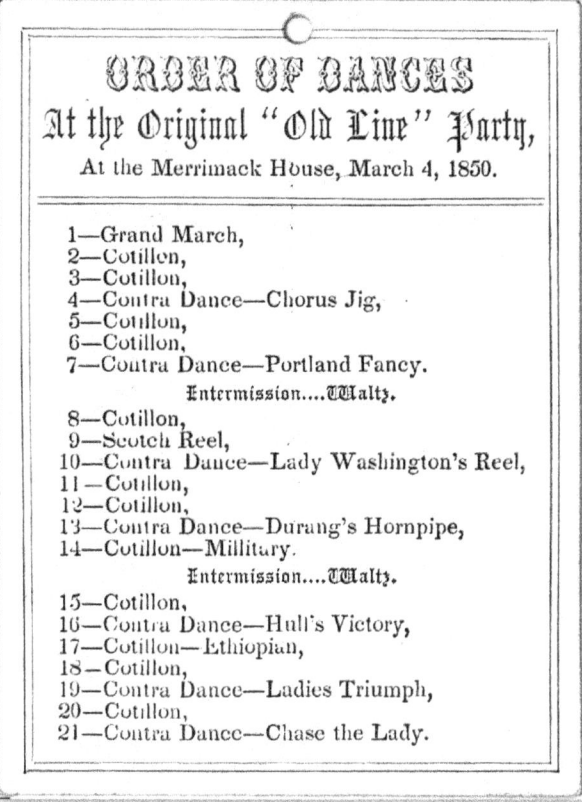

That "swing eight" would be now called "circle eight" or, perhaps, "eight hands 'round."

Lady Washington's Reel appeared on the old dance cards almost as often as Portland Fancy but is a bit harder to find in manuals of the period. With a little digging, it becomes clear that this reel is one of those dances that picked up more than one name. Ralph Page, a well-known twentieth-century caller and dance historian, confirms as much:

"Without a doubt the most popular contra dance of the late nineteenth and early twentieth centuries was 'Lady Walpole's Reel.' When I first began attending public dances it frequently was danced three times during an evening. Twenty miles away from my home town of Nelson, New Hampshire, in the towns of Antrim and Bennington, the identical dance was known as 'Lady Washington's Reel.' Why the difference in that short distance? Who knows?"[14]

The sequence of figures in question is still done in New England today, most often as Lady Walpole's Reel. Dance lore has it that Lady Walpole must not have cared much for her husband; more of the dance's figures are done with one's neighbor than with one's partner!

Happenings in Lowell were also of interest elsewhere. Newspapers across the country delighted in printing reports of unusual social events in the City of Spindles. In February of 1856, *The Weekly Wisconsin* had the following item.

"*The Lowell News* says that the Leap Year Ball of the carpet factory girls…was a very pleasant affair. 'The ladies, to the number of about seventy-five healthy, robust, cheery and lovely, took their carriages, called for their beaux, were driven to the hall, where ladies managed, selected their own partners, ordered the supper, and gloriously paid all their bills!'"

"*The News* says: 'We were amused, however, on observing bright eyed lasses, with roguish eyes trip up to demure young gentlemen, and solicit the honor of their hand for the 'next cotillion!' Who could refuse?

BALANCE FOUR IN A LINE.

One enraptured soul engaged himself to eight different ladies for Money Musk and to six others for Hull's Victory!'"[15]

Ah—Money Musk and Hull's Victory again. Hull's Victory was another regular in the ballrooms of Lowell. It's signature move is balancing four in a line as (partially) shown in the illustration above from Howe's *American Dancing Master and Ballroom Prompter*.

Other contra dances listed on Lowell's dance programs included Durang's Hornpipe, Ladies Triumph, Chase the Lady, Scotch Reel, College Hornpipe, Maid in the Pump Room, Highland Reel, The Tempest, Twin Sisters, Roger De Coverly, and the Virginia Reel.

It is interesting to note that the two most popular dances, Portland Fancy and Lady Walpole's Reel, are the ones where there is minimal distinction between "active" and "inactive" couples; everybody is moving most of the time. The next most popular, the Virginia Reel and its twin, Roger De Coverly, are the exact opposite; they are the ones where much of the set is stationary while a single couple is active. The Virginia Reel would be something of a breather in an evening's program, a dance that even beginners could do and that offers ample time to flirt and exchange pleasantries with those nearby. But Portland Fancy and Lady Walpole's Reel are dances that bubble with enthusiasm—everyone's feet moving gaily to the music. And there is too much actual *dancing* with one's neighbors to leave room for chatting!

Top left: Dance card from an 1850 party (Lowell Historical Society).

Left: Music for Lady Walpole's Reel. Its 32 measures and its AABB repeat are common in contra tunes, but exceptions abound. Portland Fancy uses an AABBCC pattern to total 48 bars.

Above: An 1862 illustration of Balance Four in Line.

Right: An 1889 card from a Knights of Pythias Concert and Ball at Huntington Hall (Lowell Historical Society).

Following pages: A montage and poem depicting an evening of sleighing and dancing in New England from 1874.

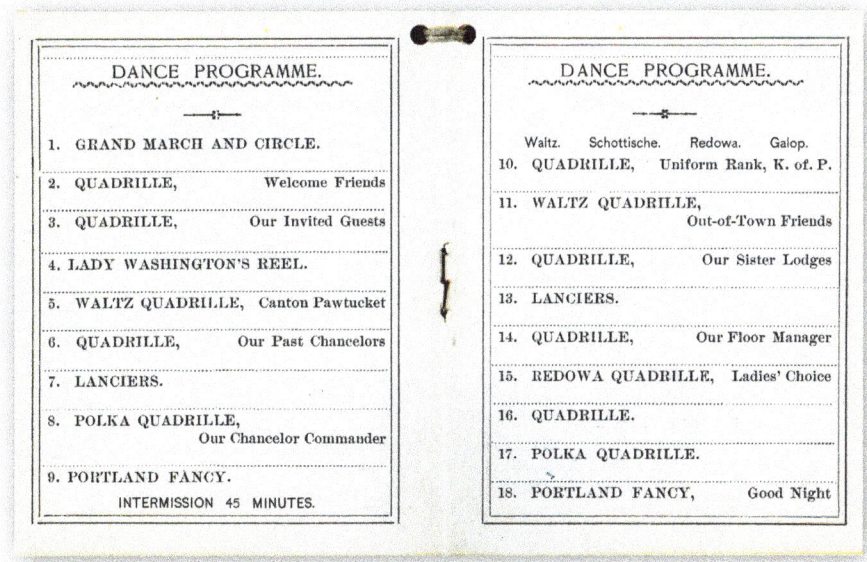

47

COUNTRY SLEIGHING, NEW ENGLAND: 1. "PRINKING."—2. READY FOR THE ROAD.—

ON THE ROAD.—4. THE SINGLE CUTTER AND UPSET.—5. THE VIRGINIA REEL.—6. GETTING SUPPER.

Country Sleighing in New England[16]

Tune: "Come, Lasses & Lads"

In January when down the dairy
    The cream and clubber freeze,
When snow-drifts cover the fences over,
    We farmers take our ease.
At night we rig the team,
    And bring the cutter out;
Then fill it, fill it, fill it,
    And heap the furs about.

Here friends and cousins dash up by dozens,
    And sleighs at least a score;
There John and Molly, behind, are jolly,
    Nell rides with me, before.
All down the village street
    We range us in a row:
Now jingle, jingle, jingle, jingle,
    And over the crispy snow!

The windows glisten, the old folks listen
    To hear the sleigh-bells pass;
The fields grow whiter, the stars are brighter,
    The road is smooth as glass.
Our muffled faces burn,
    The clear north wind blows cold,
The girls all nestle, nestle, nestle,
    Each in her lover's hold.

Through bridge and gateway we're shooting straightway,
    Their tollman was too slow!
He'll listen after our song and laughter,
    As over the hill we go.
The girls cry "Fie! for shame!"
    Their cheeks and lips are red,
And so, with kisses, kisses, kisses,
    They take the toll instead.

Still follow, follow! across the hollow,
    The tavern fronts the road.
Whoa, now! all steady! the host is ready,—
    He knows the country mode!

The irons are in the fire,
        The hissing flip is got;
So pour and sip it, sip it, sip it,
        And sip it while 'tis hot.

Push back the tables, and from the stables
        Bring Tom, the fiddler, in;
All take your places, and make your graces,
        And let the dance begin.
The girls are beating time
        To hear the music sound;
Now foot it, foot it, foot it, foot it,
        And swing your partners round.

Last couple toward the left! All forward!
        Cotillons through, let's wheel:
First tune the fiddle, then down the middle,
        In Old Virginia Reel.
Play Money Musk to close,
        Then take the "long chassé,"
While in to supper, supper, supper,
        The landlord leads the way.

The bells are ringing, the ostlers bringing
        The cutters up anew;
The beasts are neighing; too long we're staying,
        The night is half-way through.
Wrap close the buffalo robes,
        We're all aboard once more;
Now jingle, jingle, jingle, jingle,
        Away from the tavern door.

So follow, follow, by hill and hollow,
        And swiftly homeward glide.
What midnight splendor! how warm and tender
        The maiden by your side!
The sleighs drop far apart,
        Her words are soft and low;
Now if you love her, love her, love her,
        'Tis safe to tell her so.
        —Edmund Clarence Stedman

As a matter of fact, one of the major changes that has come over the New England contra dance scene in the past forty years is the triumph of what some have termed "aerobic" contra dances. In the majority of the dances done now, an "inactive" couple is anything but. The days when one filled up time on the sidelines clogging or flirting or sneaking a swing with another "inactive" are a thing of the past.

New Englanders have generally had a fondness for contra dances over quadrilles, especially in the long, narrow kitchens of the farms and villages from which the mill girls originally came. But the ballrooms of Lowell played host to plenty of quadrilles, and the nineteenth century dance manuals list page after page of them with names like The Caledonian, The Imperial, The Hibernian, or even simply The Plain Quadrille and The Social Quadrille. Some of the other names were indications of the tempo and footwork involved: Polka, Schottische, Waltz, or Mazurka Quadrilles were common, particularly in the Civil War era.

An 1841 book, *The Ballroom Instructor,* comments that "Quadrilles differ materially [from each other] in figures, but generally are set to particular pieces of music, or the music arranged to suit them in which case they are always danced the same; and different sets are known by different titles...but when a person becomes acquainted with the different figures, he need pay no attention to the set named as the one to be danced, only observing what figures are called by the leader of the orchestra.[17]

THE LANCERS' QUADRILLES,

AS THEY ARE NOW DANCED IN NEW YORK.

And, in truth, while programs named each contra dance, they were much vaguer about quadrilles. A Sleigh Bells Quadrille appears on a few of the old, Lowell cards and is probably similar to a Sleigh Ride Quadrille listed in Howe's *Ballroom Prompter*. The Continental Quadrille done at Urban Hall in 1874 can be found in Hillgrove's *Complete Guide*. But in many instances, the dance cards failed to designate a name for each quadrille, preferring to leave the line blank or to offer a dedication rather than a name (see the Knights of Pythias card on page 47). Some of the dance names that do appear may have been the creations of local dance masters and never made it into any manuals. As a result of all this, exactly which figures Lowell's square dancers danced in what sequence at which event are lost to time.

Yet there is one set of quadrilles whose name appears repeatedly in both books and on local dance programs: Lanciers—or The Lancers'— Quadrilles. This dance was wildly popular and variations abounded. Guests at an 1893 reception in Huntington Hall danced not only Lanciers itself, but Tuxedo Lanciers (twice) and Double Lanciers, as well.

THIRD FIGURE.

Music—Two Parts.

Head Couples Forward and back, four steps each way. (Fig. 51—4 bars.)

Forward and Salute—The head couples forward again four steps, and stop in the centre to salute the opposite couple—here the musicians must pause while the dancers bow and courtesy—and then they retire back into places. (4 bars.)

Four Ladies Cross Right Hands—Half Round in the Centre—Thus: the four ladies advance, each one giving her right hand to the opposite lady, and then the four ladies, turning to the left, go half round in the centre (Fig. 52).

While the four gentlemen at the same time go half round, passing to the right on the outside of the ladies in a contrary direction to them. (4 bars.)

All face about and return back again in the same manner—Thus: the four ladies cross left hands, turning half round to the right, while the gentlemen march round to the left. Here they meet partners—each one giving the right hand to the right hand of their own partners (Fig. 53),

and at the same time, without stopping, the four ladies release hands in the centre, and turn their partners half round to places. (Fig. 54—4 bars.)

☞ Repeated four times—twice by the head couples and twice by the sides.

A lancer is defined as "a member of a military unit formerly composed of light cavalry armed with lances."[18] *Lancier* is the French term. Both the military man and the military term are today obsolete; it took a 1903 French dictionary to find the word *Lancier*. Associating dance figures with cavalry exercises was not new. A "quad-drill" was originally a four-sided military maneuver done on horses; only later did a quadrille come to be something humans danced.

The Lancers' Quadrilles first appeared in the early decades of the nineteenth century. While the manuals generally call the dance by its English title, most of the Lowell dance cards use the French term instead—probably to advertise the cosmopolitan nature of their fair city. Lancers is usually referred to in the plural—The Lancers' Quad*rilles*—although the distinction between singular and plural in quadrille titles of the time appears random. Lancers and its brethren all had five sections, each consisting of a particular sequence of figures. Directions for Lancers' third "figure" (sequence) from Hillgrove's *Complete Practical Guide to the Art of Dancing* are shown at left.

Lancers was done regularly at Lowell events right through the late 1890s. But at the dawn of the twentieth century, it vanished from the programs while other quadrilles yet remained—it seems the craze had faded out. By the nineteen-teens, quadrilles were rarely seen in the chic ballrooms of the city at all; they were deemed unfashionable and unsophisticated. Because of Lancers overwhelming popularity during the 1800s, it is today a favorite among historic dance re-enactors; beyond that, it is almost never done in the United States anymore.

Even as first contras and then quadrilles fell from grace in cities like Lowell, the country folk of New England went right on enjoying these sociable set dances. One theory holds that settlers heading west were inclined to take only the more fashionable dances of the latter 1800s—those done in quadrille formation—along with them to their new homes. Thus, contra dancing was relegated to rural northeastern town halls and granges while square dancing grew to be seen as the signature dance of America's cowboys and pioneers.

In the past half-century, New England contra dancing has experienced a revival and has spread across the country. The traditional dances of the mill girl era have been joined by hundreds of newly written longways dances for "as many as will." Today, legions of new dancers, musicians, and callers are embracing this once nearly forgotten pleasure.

Opposite page: Instructions for one section of The Lancers' Quadrilles from an 1864 manual.

Left: Photo by Doug Plummer. From a 2013 dance event in Clarkdale, AZ.

WALTZ NOTES

Round dances, as they were called in the day, are those dances where each couple travels *around* the room on their own—usually in a counterclockwise direction. Among contra dancers today, they're called "couple dances," as opposed to "set dances." In modern ballroom competition, they would be the "standard" dances: waltz, tango, Viennese waltz, foxtrot, and quickstep.

Of those modern dances, waltz has been around the longest. And, since the very beginning of its time in the ballroom, there has been a basic, common, turning waltz that has changed very little. But if one considers any dance using waltz's distinctive three-quarter time signature to be a waltz, then each era has had its own unique style of this two-hundred-year-old stalwart.

'Round the Room:
Galop and Polka and Waltz, Oh My!

Above: Painted around 1900, this image harks back almost a century earlier with its dated clothing and dainty dance slippers. The foot position and hand-hold appear correct for the opening of a French Waltz in 1816: "Four steps, 'a-la mode de marcher' precede the falling into of the waltz movements."[1] Not that the move looks like "march style" to the modern eye!

Left: Front page of The Daily Graphic, February 1878 (page heading, or "banner," appears below). Shown at two-thirds of its original size, this illustration offers a bit of waltz history as well as poking fun at the dangers of fashion. A close look shows falling waiters and jostled dancers! The center caption reads "One of our many manners of waltzing at the present date." Other captions are—clockwise from top left—"How they waltzed in Poland where waltzing first started" [which is debatable]; "How they waltzed in 1800;" "How they waltzed in 1875: The Boston Dip;" and "How they waltzed in 1840."

THE DAILY GRAPHIC
AN ILLUSTRATED EVENING NEWSPAPER
39 & 41 PARK PLACE

VOL. XV.   All the News. Four Editions Daily. | NEW YORK, SATURDAY, FEBRUARY 23, 1878. | $12 Per Year in Advance. Single Copies, Five Cents. | NO. 1538.

Waltz was fairly new to the world when Lowell was founded. The earliest of the English dance manuals on the subject had only appeared a few years earlier and the waltz was still widely considered shocking and sinful, especially in Puritan-based New England.

The origins of waltz are murky but its name is clearly from the German word, Wälzen (see box below). It is believed that the dance is based on earlier European folk dances, such as the Austrian Ländler.

One theory holds that the French Revolution triggered the appearance of waltz in Europe's ballrooms. When the monarchy fell, being too close to the aristocracy might mean the guillotine. As a result, French dancing masters combined the ballet-like court dances that they had long taught with the twirling, closed-hold dancing of the peasants. This left both their jobs and their heads intact.

The Correct Method of Waltzing by Thomas Wilson is among the first—if not *the* first—of the English language waltz manuals. Published in 1816, its full title is absurdly long; Sylvanus Urban wryly called it "ample" in his 1817 review before expressing his opinion of the book itself.

"The volume is splendidly printed; and will be a curious morsel for some Bibliomaniac of the next Century. Disapproving in toto of the art of Waltzing, we cannot say more of the mode of teaching it."[2]

Disparaging descriptions of the vigorous and unseemly waltz were quoted in New England newspapers.

"The rude grasp during such dances, do they become the modest nature...?" "...the attitudes, now violent, and now languishing, of a dance better suited for a Bacchanal..."[3]

Above: When court dances like the minuet, a couple dance in 3/4 time, fell from grace, European trend-setters turned to the dances of the common people for inspiration (below).

Opposite page: Frontispiece and title page (recreated for legibility) from Wilson's waltz manual. Figures 1 & 2 show the opening March Steps of the Slow French Waltz; 3 & 4 are the French Waltz itself. Figures 5–7 are of the Sauteuse Waltz; 8 is of the Jetté Waltz; and 9 is the German Waltz. Frontispiece image courtesy of John Drury Rare Books.

A little digging through my 1906 German dictionary not only finds "Wälzen" defined as to roll or revolve; it also finds a number of industrial references: "Wälzen-apparat is a rolling frame; Wältzen-brechmachine is a flax-dressing machine.

And, on another note, "Wälzen sich vor Lachen" would probably be expressed nowadays as ROFL.

—Author

A
DESCRIPTION
OF THE
CORRECT METHOD
OF
WALTZING,
THE
TRULY FASHIONABLE SPECIES
OF
DANCING,
That, from the graceful and pleasing Beauty of its Movements, has obtained an accendancy over every other Department of that Polite Branch of Education.

PART I.
Containing a Correct Explanatory Description of the several Movements and Attitudes
In German and French Waltzing.
BY
THOMAS WILSON,
Dancing-Master,
(FROM THE KING'S THEATRE, OPERA HOUSE)
Author of "The Analysis of country Dancing," "The Treasures of Terpsichore," and a Variety of other Works on Music and Dancing.

Illustrated by Engravings, from Original Designs and Drawings,
By J. R. A. RANDALL.
LONDON,
PRINTED FOR THE AUTHOR,
2, Greville Street, Hatton Garden;
Published by SHERWOOD, NEELY, and JONES, Paternoster Row and sold by MANNERS and MILLER, Edinburgh; and J. CUMMING, Dublin
1816.

The Waltz, 1816 style: Some years ago, armed with scans we'd made of microfilm from the Library of Congress, my husband and I set about learning Mr. Wilson's waltzes. Like most turning waltzes, they have a "he goes, she goes" action; one person turns in place as the other goes around and then that person goes around while the other rotates.

In the most basic of the waltzes described by Wilson, The Slow French Waltz, the "goes" part is essentially three steps forward, right-left-right. The "in place" part involves crossing the right foot behind the left, rising on the toes, and pivoting until the back foot becomes front.

Of course, it's not that simple, given that we're speaking of a dance that was more ballet than ballroom. The "goes" part is called a Pas de Bourée and the "in place" part is a slow pirouette. The toes are turned out and pointed, the knees straight, and the posture, foot position, and timing precise. The other Wilson waltzes—The Sauteuse, the Jetté, and the German Waltz—look more and more like ballet as increasingly elaborate footwork is added.

At one point in our efforts, we took a few private lessons with a ballet teacher. She knew nothing at all about ballroom, but every time we showed her a step from Wilson, she'd exclaim excitedly: "Oh, that's a [something-or-other-in-French]," and then elegantly interpret the move in question. —Author

Curious young women on both sides of the Atlantic experimented with the new steps and practiced waltzing with their friends—but only the bravest of the Yankee girls could see themselves dancing it with a man.

"I am passionately fond of this exercise—but could I for a moment suppose that my partiality for it would ever induce me to attempt it in public, or with a gentleman, I should never try it again—Most religious people so decidedly disapprove of dancing that I often have doubts as to its being an innocent amusement—One thing I am sure is that in cities, waltz parties lead to much evil," wrote Sophie Dupont in 1831.[4]

Waltz had several features that made it scandalous: its close hold, its intimacy as a dance for two rather than for a set of couples, and a dizzying rotation that left one's partner in focus while the rest of the world was reduced to a blur. In addition, the quicker waltzes could be very high energy, a feature which might make a woman—gasp—sweat!

"And she bore on her alabaster and shining cheek the deep round flush of consumption, which parched her throat, and dried up her lips, and made her fly at the termination of each performance to the refreshment-room with her partner there to quench…the inward fever."[5]—Bangor, ME newspaper, 1837.

BYRON ILLUSTRATED—THE WALTZ.

Hail, nimble nymph! to whom the young hussar,
The whisker'd votary of waltz and war
His night devotes, despite of spurs and boots,
A sight unmatch'd since Orpheus and his brutes,
Hail, spirit stirring waltz!—

Judge Hadley may have said that "there were no round dances in those days"[6] when describing the winter balls of the Lowell area in his youth, but there were dance teachers offering waltz lessons at Mechanics Hall by 1837—segregated by gender, of course. Surviving Lowell dance cards, dating back to 1850, consistently have a waltz or two amidst the contras and cotillons of the evening, often during the intermission.

These waltzes would have been "plain" or "common" waltzes, similar to Wilson's Slow French Waltz. His Sauteuse waltz also danced on through much of the 1800s as a "Hop Waltz." But the tempo of Wilson's Jetté waltz—also called a Quick Sauteuse—was so fast that the dancers only took one step per measure; a pivoting action filled beats two and three. And the footwork for Wilson's German waltz was too elaborate for casual dancers. No, only the framework set forth by the slow waltz and its kissing cousin, the sauteuse, survived; their basic footwork still fits in well on a dance floor today.

Another couple dance of the era was the Galopade, or Galop. Perhaps the simplest—and most exhausting—of all ballroom dances, the participants moved sideways with a sliding step, rotating 180 degrees periodically so as to lead with the other foot yet continue in the same direction. The galop appears on vintage Lowell dance cards—again, during the intermission.

The galop gave rise to two other popular Victorian dances. The first of these was the Valse à Deux Temps. This Valse, or waltz, followed the pattern of the galop instead of the rotary movement of the plain waltz, traveling sideways along the line of dance for beats one and two before making a 180 degree turn on beat three to continue onwards. The Valse à Deux Temps was apparently much more taxing than other waltzes.

"The Deux Temps should not be danced for a long time without resting, as it soon becomes laborious, and where effort is apparent, grace is wanting."[7]

The second dance whose arrival was foreshadowed by the galop was the Polka. The polka is, at heart, a turning galop, albeit with much fancier footwork when done nineteenth-century style. Similar dances under different names are reported to have existed for years but the polka shot to fame as a ballroom dance in 1843 when the best known of the French dance masters embraced it. In 1884, a *Lowell Sun* article about the introduction of the polka forty years prior included the following paragraph:

> I learned a basic waltz step in Mrs. Magavero's ballet class when I was six. Beat one was a flat step and beats two and three were done on tip-toe. The group of us would parade around the room in a circle: "down, up, up, down, up, up..."
>
> That waltz has served me well for decades, far better than the box step learned in junior high. And the rise and fall still apply, even in modern, competitive waltz. —Author

Far left: One of a series of popular postcards in the late 1800s, this painting illustrates a verse of Lord Byron's poem "The Waltz." Byron had no love for the waltz—which may have been, in part, due to a deformed foot that prevented him from dancing—and the verse presented speaks of coarse soldiers consorting with "nimble nymphs" as if bewitched by the music.

Above left: This 1901 postcard bears a French caption which translates to: "Waltzers, They turn, turn, like great flowers in gossamer gowns, Intoxicated with wind, with whirl, and with dizzying music." Below that has been hand-written: "In truth, I have neither their charm nor their grace nor their beauty but like them, I love to waltz."

Below: "The Polka Fashions," from Godey's Lady's Book, *1845. At center is a common, semi-closed, mid-1800s, dance hold.*

THE POLKA FASHIONS

"It must have put money into the pockets of dancing masters; for when the polka was suddenly introduced, every one had to learn it. It seemed novel both in rhythm and in step, though, as a matter of fact, the rhythm was precisely that of the Polish national dance, known as the Krakoviax, or in French Cracovienne, the traditional dance of the peasants about the neighborhood of Cracow."[8]

Polka mania spread across Europe and the United States. Merchants attached the word "polka" to almost anything as a marketing gimmick; an 1848 *Lowell Courier* advertisement for Ladies' Polka Gaiters appears at right (a gaiter is a shoe covering similar to a spat.) The single, well-known, polka prefix that remains today is "polka dot."

The *Lowell Courier* wrote that not everyone was enamoured of the new dance: "A gentleman describing the absurdity of a man dancing the Polka, said 'that it appeared as if the individual had a hole in his pocket, and was futilely endeavoring to shake a shilling down the leg of his trowsers.'"[9]

This is, perhaps, not so far from the truth. The nineteenth-century polka was not the shuffling two-step of recent days, nor the bounding frolic preferred by the author and her husband. Master Hillgrove wrote that "All the violent gestures that characterized it on its first appearance in France and England—which are very suitable perhaps for a national dance, or to express the rude mirth of the peasantry—have been replaced by a movement more in accordance with the rules of good taste, and more congenial to the quiet refinement of a ball room."[10]

The Polka—and several other mid-century favorites—can be broken down into four moves:

Hop – A hop in place on one foot, usually done with the other foot tucked against the ankle with toe pointed. (A hop might be a good opportunity for getting that annoying shilling out.)

Slide – The free foot glides along the floor, toe pointed and top of foot angled out, before transferring weight onto it.

Top right: An advertisement for Ladies' Polka Gaiters. "Polka" gaiters most likely had nothing to do with the dance and everything to do with selling spats to the Lowell public by latching onto the polka craze.

Above: Illustration of a polka step from an 1858 manual by Elias Howe.

Opposite page: Vintage postcard depictions of two Polish dances that became nineteenth-century ballroom favorites. At top is shown the boisterous Mazourka; at bottom, the more refined Varsovienne is represented.

Cut – The free foot replaces the standing foot by "cutting" underneath it from behind as the standing foot kicks out, toe pointed. (Another chance to fling that darned shilling across the room with a good, crisp kick.)

Leap – A graceful leap from one foot to the other, usually taken across the line of dance to get past one's partner in a turn.

Thus, the ballroom polka becomes *hop, slide, cut, leap, hop, slide, cut, leap*—with a 180 degree turn on the leaps. Repeat ad infinitum.

> My friends and I were quite horse-crazy as kids. We spent our recesses in equine games galloping about the schoolyard. We were show ponies and barrel racers and practiced switching from one lead to the other with a small hop. We became adept at changing with every stride: "gallop, skip, gallop, skip."
>
> It wasn't until years later that I learned that this was a simple polka. —Author

With the polka's arrival, the common waltz seemed rather a bore; a dusty, old relic that belonged to the elder generation. Dancing masters looked to Europe's folk dances for ideas, and polka-rized just about anything they found. Suddenly there were any number of closed-hold, ballroom dances in three-quarter time, all of them full of slides, cuts, hops, and leaps.

Polka Mazourka—derived from the Mazourka (originally a Polish dance)—*slide (beat 1), cut (2), hop (3), slide (1), cut (2), leap (3); repeat.* The first measure is done along the line of dance with no rotation, the second has a half turn on the leap.

Polka Redowa (from the Czech, rejdovák; its roots mean "whirl" and "cavort")—*slide, cut, leap, slide, cut, leap,* turning on each leap. One version crams a *hop/slide* into the first beat.

Varsovienne (French for "from Warsaw")—*slide, cut, leap, point free foot forward and hold for two beats, repeat three times; follow with three measures of Polka Redowa, point and hold; three measures Polka Redowa, point and hold; Repeat all.*

La Carlowitzka (Polish)—a.k.a. the Gitana—*slide, hop, hop (turning on hops with free foot out behind), slide, hop, hop, two measures of Polka Mazurka and repeat from beginning.* The *slide, hop, hop* has a skating feel, leading with one shoulder and then the other, the free foot pointed to side and behind.

The list goes on; the dances above are just a few examples.

The Redowa and Mazourka were also waltz-time dances in their own right—without the word "polka" attached—but their footwork was too involved for this brief overview.

Waltz-time was but one rhythm among many. The polka and the galop were both in two-four time and spawned numerous variations, including a well-loved combination, the Esmerelda. There was a Five-Step Waltz, done in five-four time, that was described as "very similar to the Polka Mazourka and [at one time] a great favorite."[11] The German Schottisch was brought into ballrooms mid-century; it was done in four-four time.

The schottisch is still—or perhaps, again—popular in New England even though its contemporaries have been forgotten.

As Hillgrove's *Art of Dancing* noted: "It requires less practice than many of the other dances, and when properly danced is very elegant and pleasing. Its combination of two movements, a polka and a circular hop, make a most agreeable variety."[12]

Hillgrove also cautioned in his 1864 manual that the "double movement" makes it "difficult for the gentleman to guide his partner through the Schottisch without encountering many awkward mishaps, such as treading upon toes and dresses, to which unskillful dancers are constantly subject."[13]

In the early days of round dances, a number of different holds were used (see the waltz illustration on page 57) but by the mid-1800s most of the more exotic ones had been abandoned. The great majority of the polka era dances were done in a slightly looser hold than is favored nowadays, one halfway between a closed hold and a promenade position (see illustration on page 59, center couple). This allowed both halves of a couple to angle themselves in the direction of all those hops, cuts, and slides as they traveled around the room. Even the schottisch—half of which is done in a wide open, side-by-side position today—was usually done entirely in this semi-closed hold.

"The gentleman should pass his right arm round the lady's waist, holding her with sufficient firmness to be able to take her through the mazes of the dance with perfect safety. Her right hand should be held in his left hand, which he should raise to about the height of the waist. The lady rests her left hand on the gentleman's right shoulder, her head slightly inclined towards the left."[14] —Hillgrove, 1864.

> *Trying to track down a dance's country of origin isn't as simple as it seems. "Schottische" is German for "Scottish Dance;" does that make it German or Scottish? (probably a German imitation of Scottish) And did the Varsovienne really come from Warsaw? (maybe) When I took Flamenco lessons, I was told that that quintessentially Spanish dance actually came to Europe from India via travelling Romani!* —Author

There is one very important difference between Victorian couple dances and those of the present day: the man did not *lead* the woman; he *guided* her. Today's ballroom crowd refers to proper guiding as "floorcraft." Actual *leading* is less about navigation and more about using subtle—or sometimes not so subtle—movements to signal the next step or move to one's partner.

Nineteenth-century round dances were not led; the footwork was far too elaborate. Everyone was expected to know the sequence and follow it. Only a fool would try to improvise on the fly; on a crowded floor it could spell disaster. It was hard enough to dance and steer without also choosing steps!

"To waltz or perform any of the round dances well, requires considerable practice, especially on the part of the gentleman, who is expected to guide the lady gently through the confusion usually attending these dances, and also to preserve the step and time, and perform the various evolutions in a graceful and easy manner, and to avoid all collisions with other couples in whirling by them."[15]—Hillgrove, 1864.

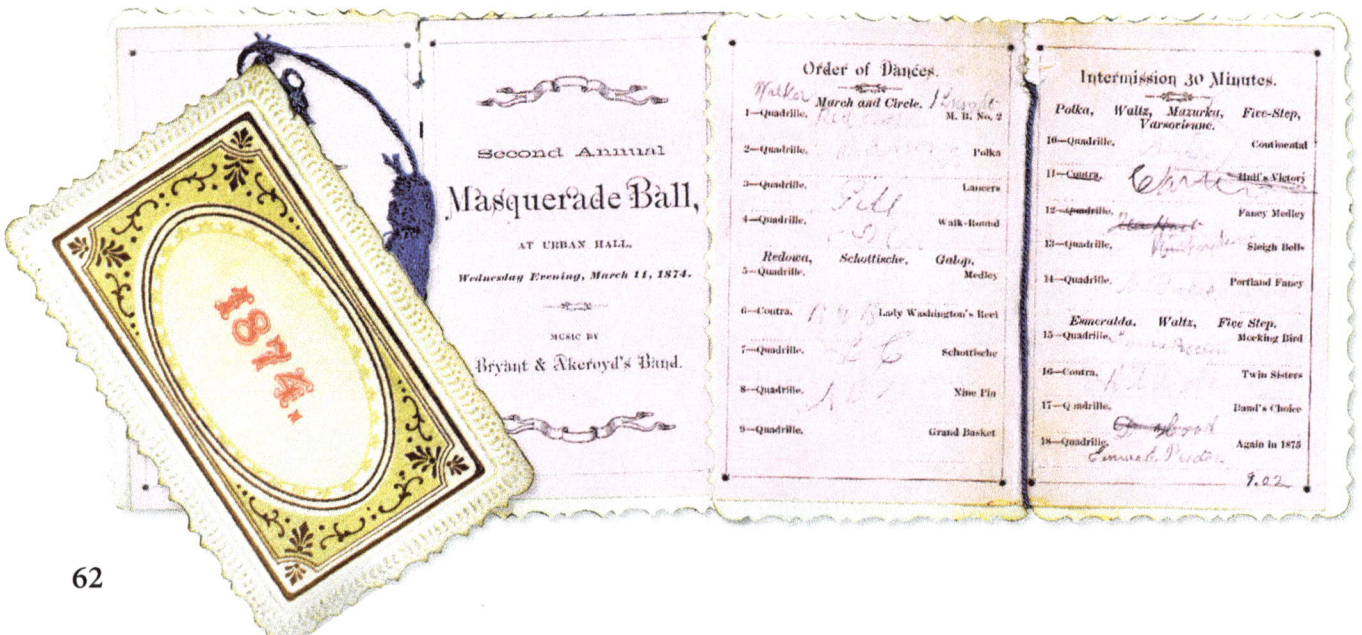

THE POLKA
Glide Polka
Coquette Polka
Rush Polka
Three Slide Polka
Cross Step Polka
La Esmeralda
Bohemian Polka
Heel and Toe Polka
Combination Polka
The Berlin
The Wave
The Ruchter
Babies on our Block
Little Sallie Waters
The Portland
Polka Militaire
The Duchess
New Side Step Polka
The Alsacian
Berlin Polka
German Polka
American Gavotte
Hornpipe Polka
The Metropolitan
The Carlton
The Antlers
The Ashland
Polka Russe
Baby Polka
PAS DE BASQUE
The Waltz
Glide Waltz
The Original Waltz
La Valse à Trois Temps
La Valse à Deux Temps
Hop Waltz
Redowa-Waltz
Racket Waltz
Fascination
La Madrilaine
La Metropole
The Society
Valse Les Patineurs
Waltz Minuet
The Rosita
Military Times
Military Waltz
THE GALOP
Three Step Galop
Four Step Galop
The Racket
One Slide Racket
Two Slide Racket
Three Slide Racket
Waltz-Galop
The Jersey
Ripple Galop
Ripple Combination
Le Galop à Pas Sauté
The Puritan Waltz
Polish Galop
The Gaity
L'Eclair
Wave Galop
Narraga sett Pier
Hecla Galop
The Jubilee
The Fairy
Le Beau
Military Galop
THE SCHOTTISCHE
Military Schottische
Dancing in the Barn
Kentucky Jubilee
Gavotte Schottische
Glide Schottische (#1)
Five Step Schottische
Star Schottische
The Caprice
Imperial Gavotte
Bon Ton Gavotte

The Harvard
Polka Schottische
Schottische à Pas Sauté
Redowa-Schottische
New Schottische
Schottische Gavotte
Stephanie Gavotte
Loomis' New Gavotte
The Knickerbocker—
(Masters)
Glide Schottische (#2)
Edinburgh Schottische
The Gavotte
Caprice Schottische
The Vienna
The Columbia
The Mettlesome
The Skaters
The Knickerbocker—
(Dodworth)
The Celtic
Highland Schottische
Highland Gavotte
Highland Glide
Redowa and Mazurka
The Redowa
POLKA-REDOWA
The Mazurka
Polka-Mazurka
The York
The New York (Cartier)
The Newport
The Ripple
La Mode
The Ocean
Ma Belle
The Russia
La Russe
La Cosca
Loomis' Glide Mazurka
Glide Mazurka
The Rye
Harriet Mazurka
The Rye
Harriet Mazurka
Loomis' Yale U. York
Spanish Mazurka
Two Slide Racket
Le Galop à Trois Pas
Gitana Waltz
La Zingarella
The America
The Latest York
The New York (Brenneke)
Five Step York
The Musette
Independent York
Redowa L'Eclair
The Maniton
MISCELLANEOUS DANCES
La Réve
The Detroit
La Marjolaine
Imperial Polka
Waltz Gavotte
The Sicillienne
The Glissade
The Rockaway
Cadet Waltz
The Bronco
The Victoria
The Varsouvianna (#1)
The Varsouvianna (#2)
The Varsouvianna (#3)
Advance Varsouvianna
The Maryland (Varsouv.)
Danish Dance (#1)
Danish Dance (#2)
Five Step Waltz (#1)
Five Step Waltz (#2)
Shall I have the Pleasure?

Having a specific sequence of steps was all well and good, but it could make the novelty of a given dance wear off fairly quickly. The trendsetters of the dance world responded by inventing variation after variation, each with its own slightly different series of steps. The content list at left comes from a manual titled *Round Dancing*, published in Maine in 1890; it has the names of over 150 dances. At right are diagrams from the same book of two dozen foot positions that a student was expected to learn in order to dance properly.

How in the world was anyone to remember all those step patterns? Or which name went with which one? And even if one kept the names and patterns straight, could one master each well enough to enjoy dancing it? Or find a partner equally capable? By the end of the 1800s, the entire system was beginning to come apart. Clearly, a fresh approach was needed.

A new century was coming, and just over the horizon lay a new way of dancing—and the dawn of Ragtime!

Far left, top: The round dances chosen for the Butcher's Dress Ball in 1873 at Goddard's Hall included Waltz, Polka, Schottische, Varsovienne, Five-Step, Esmeralda, Redowa, and Galop (Lowell Historical Society).

Far left, bottom: A similar group was danced at a costume ball at Urban Hall in 1874—along with an added Mazurka (Lowell Historical Society).

Left & Right: Dance index and proper foot positions from an 1890 Maine dance manual.

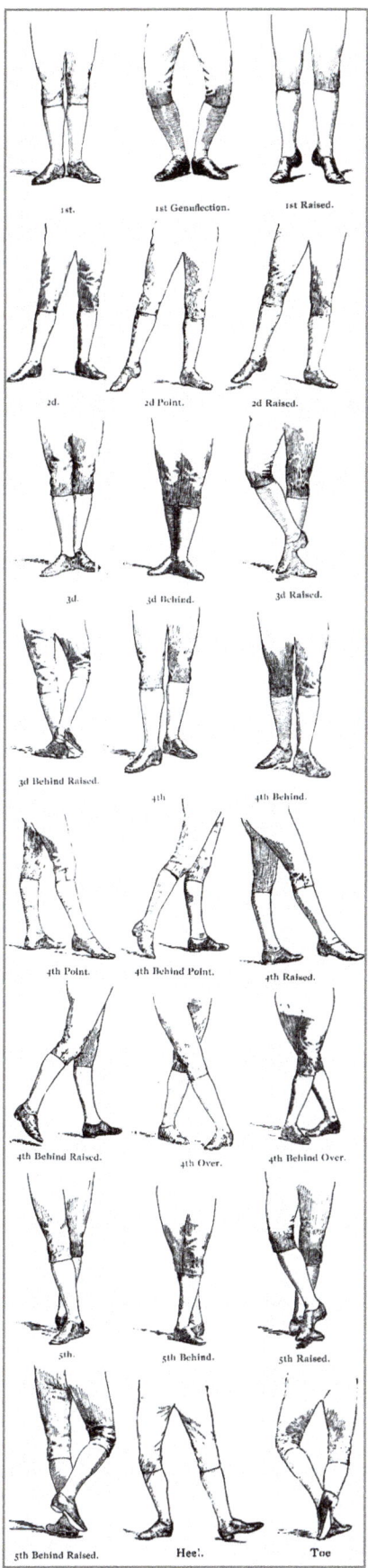

VIEW OF THE BOOTT COTTON MILLS, AT LOWELL, MASS.

It took only a decade for the Town of Lowell to become the City of Lowell as mills sprouted along the river like weeds. The Merrimack and Hamilton Manufacturing Companies opened their doors in 1826 before Lowell was even a town. They were soon followed by the Appleton Company and Lowell Manufacturing. After those came the Middlesex, Suffolk, Tremont, Lawrence, and Boott Mills, all of them established before 1835. The last of the major textile producers, Massachusetts Cotton Mills, was incorporated in 1839.[1]

The Middle Years:
Dancing 'Round Every Corner

As businesses multiplied, so did population. During the years that Lowell grew from town to city, the number of inhabitants increased seven-fold. By mid-century, it had doubled again to 33,000. More land was annexed from surrounding towns, and handsome public buildings were erected.

The latest conveniences came to Lowell. The same mill boy who wrote home so unfavorably in 1853 about his landlady's love of dance was much more impressed with the new gas lighting at Huntington Hall.

"I wish you could stop in some evening and look over the vast sea of heads as lighted by gas."[2]

Lowell was a popular stop for both presidents and politicians. And the city's own political scene was a feisty one. Again, young Anderson was impressed.

"I should think there were as many parties in Lowell as I have got fingers and toes, but perhaps not. Besides the usual parties this year there are the Temperance Party, Rum Party, Ten-Hour Party and others too numerous to mention."[3]

Politics even intersected with fashion on occasion. Historian Cowley was decidedly unimpressed with one woman's push for more practical feminine attire.

"On July 22nd, 1851, was held the famous 'Bloomer Ball,' the first practical attempt to introduce the costume originated by Mrs. Amelia Bloomer of Seneca, New York. The ball was a success, but the costume was not a success."[4]

Left: 1852 etching of Lowell's thriving Boott Cotton Mills.

Top: View of Lowell, photo from stereoscope card, c.1880.

Right: 1856 etching of Lowell's handsome new court house.

With all this rapid, unchecked expansion, it was inevitable that the utopian vision once held for Lowell would eventually fall by the wayside.

In the beginning the hours in the mill were long, but not overly long by the standards of the time. Each girl was required to tend one or two looms, a reasonable workload that left time to daydream or exchange a few words with one's neighbor. The conditions were noisy and dangerous but they were tolerable and the wages good.

As more and more mills sprang up, and as more and more New England towns turned to textile manufacturing, the price of textiles began to fall. Adding to these market woes, most of the early profits from the Lowell mills had been paid out in dividends or poured into expansion; little or none had been held back for the regular repair and replacement of existing buildings and machinery.[5] Dividends fell. The second tier of investors—those who had little to do with operations but were accustomed to the easy money of the 1820s and 1830s—were especially unhappy and leaned hard on management to cut costs and raise profits.

The work day was lengthened and the rules against talking and levity tightened. The number of looms each girl tended doubled, and then doubled again. Wages were cut and a premium system put into place where overseers were given bonuses for squeezing extra work out of the operatives.

An 1847 letter in Lowell's *Voice of Industry* pleaded: "This 'premium system' is a curse to us—it ought not to be tolerated…Often have girls been so afraid of the 'old man' they dare not ask to go out when sick, for they know he would have a great deal to say. Some girls cannot get off as much cloth as others; such ones are apt to be treated unkindly, and often reminded by the 'old man' that 'Sally and Dolly got off several cuts more the last four weeks…'"[6]

Not only were working conditions getting worse and worse, conditions outside the mill were also deteriorating. The planned city had become congested and dirty. Access to an increasingly polluted Merrimack River was now blocked by a solid wall of mills. The corporations sought to control their workers' behavior outside as well as inside the factory and kept a city-wide blacklist of "troublemakers." Those on it were turned away from every mill job in town. Strikes protesting wage cuts and demanding better conditions, or "turnouts" as they were called, became ever more common even though the leaders often found themselves unemployable thereafter.

As a result, many of the strong-willed New England women who helped make Lowell famous left the mills. They returned to their farms or found work elsewhere. By the time Michel Chevalier sought to include a group of Lowell Mill Girls at their looms as part of Paris' Universal Exposition of 1867, Lowell's operators were a motley bunch; there was no tidy group of Yankee girls left to send. A delegation was gathered from the Pacific Mills of nearby Lawrence instead. Even as this team gained praise in Paris, Lowell had another major strike.[7]

Of those who replaced Lowell's original workers, the first wave was primarily Irish. Some of these were the children of the ditch-diggers and masons who had built the city; some were the old workers themselves, no longer needed for the tasks that had first brought them to Lowell. Still others were Irish fleeing the starvation caused by potato blight during Ireland's Great Famine. And all of them lacked the option of going home; they worked or they starved.

Opposite top: Image from sheet music cover for The Bloomer Waltz, *1851.*

Opposite bottom: Lawrence, Boott, and Merrimack Mills, 1907.

Near left: "Irish Life: A Jig on the Green" from a 1909 postcard. While Irish step dances seem to have been relegated to Irish homes and gatherings, Lowell's nineteenth-century newspapers indicate that public exhibitions of the Scottish (or Scotch, as it was called at the time) Highland Fling were greeted with enthusiasm late in the century.

Across New England, these workers stepped into the roles that the locals had abandoned. A history of the mills and mill workers of Biddeford, Maine describes the Irish enthusiasm for the music and dance of their homeland.

"But dancing was the most colorful contribution made by the newcomers from Ireland. Many had come from County Kilkenny, and the more gifted are still remembered in Biddeford as 'Kenny dancers.' The Sunday evening train from Boston seems to have been a favorite with incoming immigrants and it became the custom for relatives and friends to meet that train each week for what was known as a 'greenhorn greeting' to the new arrivals. Sometimes the long wooden platform would be crowded with nearly 500 'greeters,' and impromptu dances would start while the train was awaited. Sometimes again, after the train had gone, the crowd would adjourn to a hill overlooking the river about a half mile from the mills, and there in the early dusk (and on into moonlight) the 'Kenny Dancers' would go through their lively repertoire to the music of a rollicking fiddle."[8]

Lowell's Irish may not have been dancing on some hillside in the moonlight every Sunday, but in homes, pubs, and social clubs, Irish dance and music added to the cultural tapestry of Lowell. In the ballrooms of the city, Irish jigs and reels were already part of the musical lineup that gave life to quadrilles and contras. A skilled Irish musician, one whose music and manners were good enough to overcome any anti-Irish bias, might find extra income, or perhaps even a decent career, as a member of a dance orchestra.

The 1850s and the Civil War years saw the influx of an increasing number of French-Canadians. Lowell's earliest French-speakers came from villages in New York's Adirondack region[9] but they were soon followed by the *Quebecois*.

"For their part, the French-Canadians made Saturday night mirthful, with parties held in homes throughout the city. They had their own dances and songs—the folk dances and songs of old Canada—to which many a Yankee youth tossed in wakeful envy as the parties continued late into the night."[10]

In the final decades of the nineteenth century, Greeks made their way to the City of Spindles in ever greater numbers. Following them, European Jews fleeing persecution started settling in Lowell around 1890. As the members of each group gradually improved their economic and social standing, a new group would arrive to fill the bottom rungs of Lowell's working class.

By 1912, a social survey of Lowell included elaborate maps of the different ethnic neighborhoods of the city as well as photographs showing some of the rampant squalor and congestion. The caption for the photo below reads: "Block of Thirty-Two Tenements, Corner of Elm and Linden Streets, Which Houses Representatives of Fourteen Nationalities."[11]

This diversity made for a cultural cacophony in Lowell. Music, dance, food, religion, language and holidays were just a few of the things that reflected the multi-ethnic makeup of the city.

Top: A 1939 postcard with the caption repeated in both standard French and what appears to be Quebecois. "The Evening Dance. Gaiety reigns in the house; the young people need only a bit of space, then let the music begin."

Above: Tenements of Irish and Greeks, rear view from Canal Bridge, Broadway, 1912.

Left: Tenements at corner of Elm and Linden Streets, 1912.

Right: Map of Lowell's "Foreign Districts," 1912. Although it is hard to decipher the specifics, this map makes it clear just what a melting pot Lowell had become.

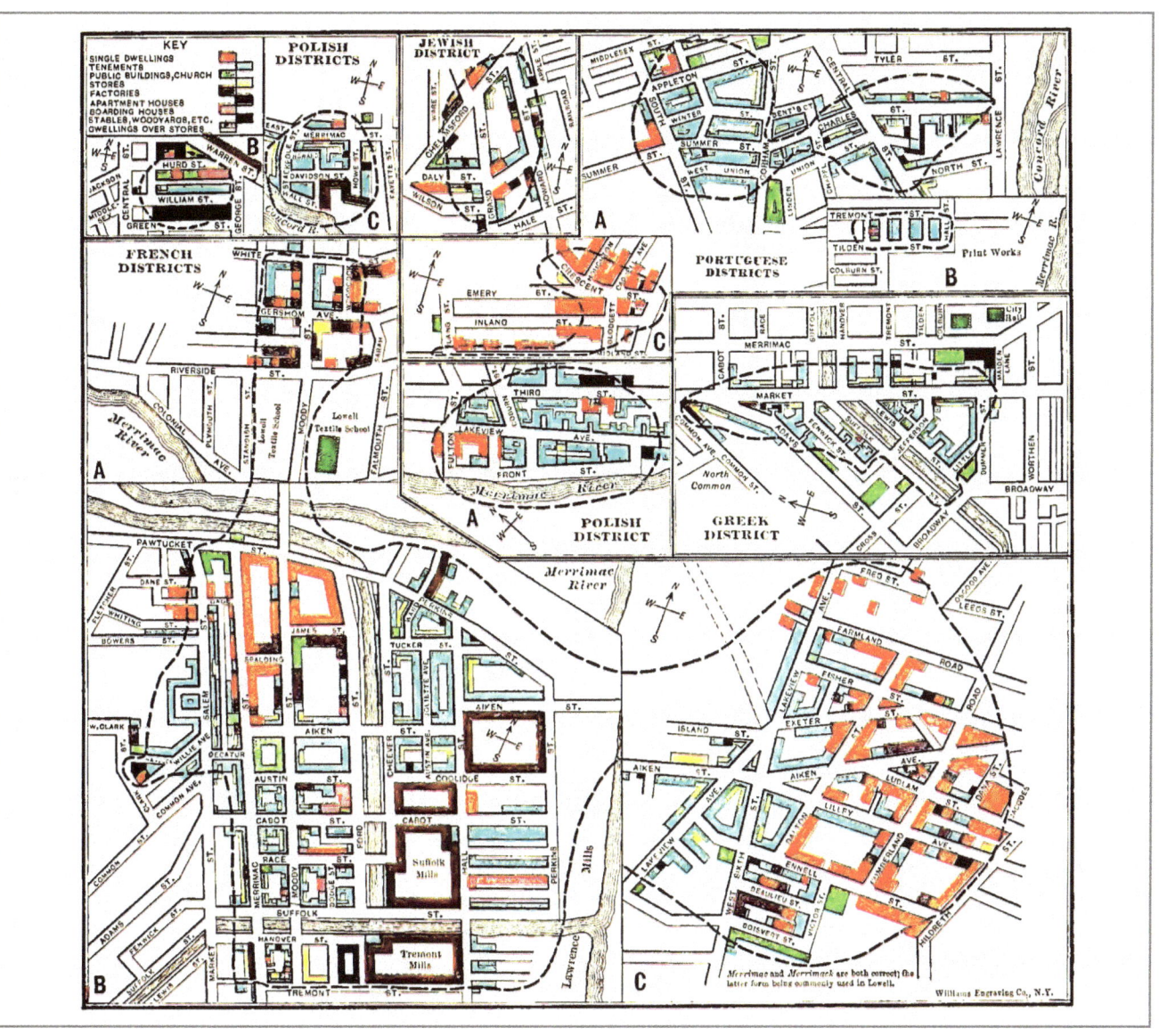

Unfortunately, cultural differences also hampered efforts to unionize and push for better working conditions.

"Solidarity of the workers was held back in Lowell by the fact that native Americans and Irish often hesitated to fraternize with French-Canadians, Greeks, and Hebrews. This lack of cohesion might conventionally be interpreted as advantageous to Lowell manufacturers."[12] "Lowell took no such leading place in the labor union movement of the post-bellum years as from its historic position in the manufacturing world might have been expected."[13]

Be that as it may, with the growth of the city and the addition of so many dance-loving nationalities, the resistance to one particular pastime was gradually being drowned out by tapping toes. Even the *Lowell Daily Courier* took note:

"JUVENILE DANCING EXHIBITION. Ganson's Hall was quite crowded last evening on the occasion of the dancing exhibition of Mr. Ganson's juvenile class. The exercises displayed a high degree of excellence—quite creditable to the pupils themselves, no less than to their accomplished preceptor. Considering the disrepute in which dancing was held by thousands, a few years ago, we can but remark what a change has taken place in the popular sentiment, in this regard, in view of the decorousness and respectability of the company present at this exhibition last evening. The parents of these Masters and Misses are so well pleased with the success of Mr. Ganson's efforts in the education of their children in this graceful art, that they have taken steps to give him a complimentary benefit." —May 6, 1854.

Yet the naysayers continued their pleas for abstinence through the latter half of the century and well into the next. An 1868 sermon at Lowell's First Congregational Church, sponsored by the Young Men's Christian Association and reported in the *Lowell Courier*, based its content on the 21st chapter of Proverbs: "He that loveth pleasure shall be a poor man; he that loveth wine and oil shall not be rich." The speaker addressed his remarks to both men and women; he firmly condemned ballroom dancing and decadent, exhibitionistic stage dancing such as ballet.

"Not all pleasure-seeking men fail in business, to be sure," the *Courier* quoted, "but the rule is destruction, the exception success. Few ladies spend the night in a heated ball-room, thinly dressed, without a cold, a fever, and often death...One play on the stage may destroy the soul; the theatre is not as it used to be; hardly a play is acted upon the stage without ballet dancing, and a lady can in no way disgrace herself so much as going upon the stage."[14]

An amusing item regarding this ongoing tug-of-war for dancers' souls graced the *Courier's* Religious News section that same year: "Mr. Jenkins, one of the ministers at Mendon, Vt., lately accepted an invitation to a ball on condition that he should be allowed to preach there; and accordingly about midnight the audience gave respectful attention while he preached a sermon against dancing."[15]

A more serious, well thought-out letter appeared in the *Lowell Courier* in 1871 questioning the wisdom of including dancing in High School Association alumni celebrations. The letter was signed "Justice for All."

"I do not in this inquiry wish to raise the question as to the right or wrong of dancing. I raise the inquiry on the grounds that there is such a difference of opinion already existing, and ask, since this is a known or acknowledged fact, if it is delicately courteous to introduce it in such a miscellaneous party? I mean miscellaneous as to religious convictions upon the subject."

"It has precluded the attendance of some worthy members, and is a source of annoyance to many more who do not wish to isolate themselves from their associates in early school life. Furthermore, the practice is extremely embarrassing to another class of community who are directly affected by it, namely: the parents and guardians of children. The children themselves doubtless have no scruples about joining in this kind of amusement; on the contrary they are scarcely restrained by the authority of the parent from so doing. The parents, therefore, are driven to one of two unpleasant alternatives, either to ostracise [their] children from the most delightful associations of their life, or to abandon convictions [they have] ever advocated."[16]

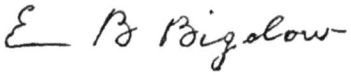

"The Peerless Morlacchi"

It is likely the plea fell on deaf ears, or at least on ears more attuned to music than morals. Not only did some of Lowell's most prominent citizens of the era embrace dancing; at least a few of them had made it part of their careers.

Erastus Bigelow, inventor of the carpet loom, (a company named after him would eventually buy up the Lowell Manufacturing Company) earned money during his younger days in West Boylston as a fiddler: "At all balls and dancing parties for many miles around his services were in request."[17]

Giuseppina Morlacchi, a classically trained ballerina from Italy, is credited with introducing the can-can to the American stage in 1868. In 1872, she met her husband, "Texas Jack" Omohundro, while playing an Indian maiden in the hit play *Scouts of the Prairie*. The pair eventually purchased a former church at the corner of Market and Suffolk streets in which to make their home, replete with an upstairs ballroom known as Suffolk Hall.[18] Her resumé was surely seen as scandalous by some of Lowell's citizenry, yet her celebrity, teaching skills, and charity work were welcomed by others.

It's hard to know just what effect the Civil War had on Lowell's dance scene, beyond skewing the male-to-female ratio and throwing a pall over life in general. Parties continued—Northern bravado demanded "business as usual"—but the war's effects on the city's residents were significant.

With the supply of cotton from the South cut off, the city's largest industry was hard hit. Some mills sold off their raw cotton at sky-high prices thinking the war would be quick; some opted to close their doors when it was not. Ten thousand mill hands lost their jobs. Other businesses suffered as the mill workers' misfortune rippled through the economy. Military paychecks cushioned the blow somewhat and the Lowell Machine Shop actually saw a surge in work. But for most, the 1860s were lean years.

For the first time in Lowell's history, the population fell. With nine of the city's mills closed, the few unmarried Yankee girls that were left went home to their farms. Other Lowell residents headed west searching for a better future. Others enlisted, many of them following Lowell's own General Benjamin Butler into the fray.

Left: Header from an 1864 Harper's Weekly, A Journal of Civilization.

Below: Also from Harper's—*"Our soldiers believe in the literal interpretation of the dictum of the Wise Man that 'there is a time to dance.' But to put their faith into works is not the easiest thing in the world, owing to the lack of partners of the feminine persuasion. However, by imagining a bearded and pantalooned fellow to be of 't'other kind,' they succeed in getting up what they call a 'Stag Dance.'"*

Below left: Patrick Gilmore, author of When Johnny Comes Marching Home, *spent a good bit of his time in Lowell and married a Lowell woman.*

Among the Massachusetts residents enlisting early in the war was Bandmaster Patrick Gilmore. Hugely influential in nineteenth-century music, Gilmore was an Irish cornetist, composer, and showman with strong ties to Lowell—but not so much to dance. Sometimes compared to John Philip Sousa, it's quite possible that Gilmore shared Sousa's indifference toward dancers, an attitude "The March King" made abundantly clear even to such world-renowned dance celebrities as Vernon and Irene Castle.

"John Philip Sousa was a bandmaster, a very famous bandmaster, and I am sure he was convinced that most of the people had come to listen to his music. He peeped out of the corner of his eye to make sure we were on the stage, then turned his back to us and began to pump away, paying no further attention to us. He ignored our frantic signals to pick up the tempo and his uniformed arms flailed away with the precise beat of a man conducting a military march, which was exactly what he was doing." — Irene Castle, on a 1916 dance performance at New York's Hippodrome.[19]

Lowell's leading politicians were as likely to indulge in dancing as anyone, perhaps more so. And the mix of sleighing and dance parties remained ever-popular.

"SLEIGH RIDING. Members of the city government for 1859, with ladies, to the number of some thirty or forty, went to Nashua, yesterday afternoon, in two large sleighs. They partook of a supper at the Indian Head Hotel, and music, dancing and jollity were the order of the evening. They arrived home about midnight, and report having had an excellent time."[20]

As Lowell grew, so did the number of balls and socials. By the final decade of the century, just about every organization in town was giving dances. Even union meetings might end with a dance!

➤ "The annual hop given by the overseers of the John Pilling Shoe Co. was held at the factory last night and, as usual, was a happy occasion. About 100 couples were present and dancing continued from 8:30 P.M. till 1 A.M."[21]

➤ "Merry Plumbers They. The fifth annual social of the Plumbers' union occurred in the Burkes' hall and some 100 couples enjoyed it. Dancing embraced an order of 10 numbers, the waltz home being executed at the stroke o' twelve. The affair was a decided success and reflected credit on its managers. A number of prominent labor men were present from out of town."[22]

➤ "The Ingrain Weavers. The ingrain weavers held a very enthusiastic meeting in the Mathews hall last night. The weavers voted to stand firm and not to return to work until the ten per cent raise in wages is restored to them. The weavers enjoyed a dance afterward."[23]

➤ "The sixth anniversary concert and ball of the Cotton Mule Spinners' union in Huntington hall last evening, was complimentary to members and friends of the union." "The dance order contained 26 numbers." "The order had this warning: 'No scabs wanted here.'"[24]

➤ "A large audience assembled in the Unitarian church vestry last evening, and applauded the efforts of the members of the Young People's club, who produced the comedy drama in two acts, entitled "A Box of Monkeys." The audience was kept in a jolly mood throughout the evening by the actions of the participants. After the entertainment, the party repaired to Mrs. Darracott's hall where dancing was enjoyed, the American orchestra furnishing music."[25]

Opposite top: Sleighing was such a popular winter theme that it appears on this train excursion advertisement!

Opposite middle: Massachusetts shoe factory worker, c.1910.

Opposite bottom: John Pilling Shoe factory—site of the overseers dance in 1896—now retirement housing.

Left: New England mule spinner and his assistant, 1909.

Below left: Postcard-style handbill. The flip side is addressed "to the public and those who we faithfully serve."

Below: Letter carriers, c.1909, with their "gray suits and mail pouches."

➤"Good news travels fast but no faster than the letter carriers as they danced at their ball last night. The hustling letter carrier put aside his gray suit and mail pouch and donned evening attire while at Huntington hall he whiled away the fleeting hours with music and the dance. It was the third annual concert and ball of the Letter Carriers' association and a large and representative attendance marked its success.

The hall was prettily decorated in the national colors and white lace. On the floor in the centre of the hall was drawn in colored crayons a large representation of the badge of the National Association of Letter Carriers and the number 25, indicating the Lowell branch. The floral decorations were also beautiful.

As is customary the American orchestra opened the event with a finely arranged concert. There was one number, a galop, complimentary to the Carriers. While the music was being enjoyed by those in the gallery, the ladies who were to take part in the ball arrived and were given seats on the floor by their escorts.

The grand march was begun shortly after nine o'clock led by Floor Manager John Ewing with Miss Elisabeth O'Connell of Lewiston, who wore a becoming gown of white gros-grain satin with pearl trimmings and Easter lilies.

An order of 25 numbers beginning with the time honored quadrille and concluding with a waltz was presented."[26]

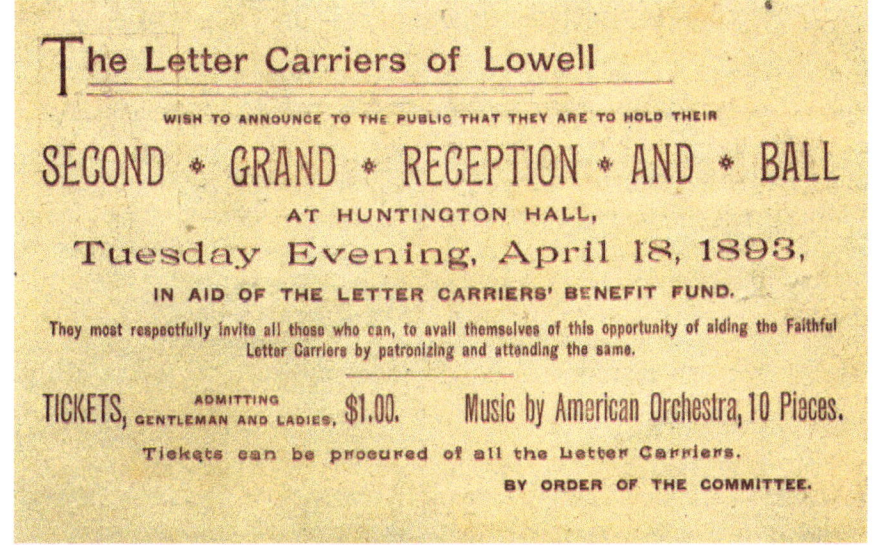

➤"CADETS' BALL Brilliant Society Event at the State Armory. Gallant Soldiers Exemplify the Blessings of Peace. The Merry Dance and the Merrier Assembly.

The armory on Westford street last evening, for the first time this season, was the scene of gayety. It was one of the very swell social events in military circles, and as usual every year it was an occasion looked forward to with great anticipation. The company was a representative one of the city and attested the popularity of the organization.

The armory was thrown open from the rifle range to the turret, and from early evening until an hour well along towards daylight, the place was thronged with guests.

The drill shed was transformed into a beautiful ball room under the direction of Messrs. Foster and Brickett of the Criterion. The colors used in draping were nile green and pink in delicate shades and pure white. The roof was hidden from view by long streamers of bunting from the center radiating to the laves. In the center was also a big, bell pendant, of the same delicate shades. The balcony was also tastefully festooned. As usual on occasions of this kind, the Mechanic Phalanx room was used as a ladies' dressing room, the Welch Guards' room as a gentleman's room, while the reception room was thrown open to the visiting military men and the reception committee.

The Salem Cadet orchestra began the concert numbers at 8 o'clock and delighted everybody within hearing with the flood of melody. Between the numbers there was a competitive prize drill for the company medal; twelve men competed.

When the music for the grand march struck up there were upward of 140 couples in line, and it was a fine looking column, for the uniforms of the many officers, the conventional dress of other men and the ladies' gowns combined to form a fine spectacle. It was a delightful dance order, and everyone seemed to thoroughly enjoy the occasion."[27]

Far left: The State Armory on Westford Street in Lowell, site of the 1893 Cadets' Ball.

Left: Main floor of Nelson's Colonial Department store on Merrimack Street. Although Nelson's opened over a decade after the Sales Ladies' dance, this photo shows how a store of the era might have looked.

Below: 1880s advertising card from Boston and Lowell Clothing Company, a business just a block off Merrimack at the intersection of Central and Gorham.

➢ "LEAP YEAR PARTY Held in Lester's Hall Last Night by Sales Ladies. The dear girls are not delinquent above assuming the duties of leap year for a delightful leap year party opened the season last night, the affair being held in Lester's hall by a party of Merrimack street sales ladies.

The attendance was large and in a short time after their arrival everyone was acquainted and a splendid time was enjoyed. At 8:15 the grand march began. After the march, general dancing was enjoyed until after midnight. Intermission was taken at 11 o'clock, when the ladies served refreshments."[28]

➢ "THE VERMONT ASSOCIATES Dance and Make Merry Over Maple Sugar. The Vermont Associates had a maple sugar party at Huntington and Jackson halls, last night, and right well the affair was enjoyed. Preparations were made to accommodate a large crowd and such it was. The decorations were tasteful and appropriate. The tables were in Jackson hall, and there all those who wished for refreshments were served. Dancing was continued in the lower hall from 9 till 12 o'clock."[29]

➢ "Such a combination of youth, grace and beauty is seldom seen in a ball room as assembled at the annual concert and ball of the Knights of Columbus in Associate hall last evening. Lowell's fair daughters were there arrayed in rich costumes and attended by gallant young men attired in evening dress. It was a gala occasion for the Knights, far excelling any previous event of a social nature conducted by the organization."[30]

➢ "The twenty-sixth anniversary of Div. 1 A. O. H. [Ancient Order of Hibernians (Irish)] was appropriately observed by a dance in Hibernian hall, last evening. The attendance was very large and all enjoyed the merry dance."[31]

➢ "For fourteen years the Mathew Temperance Institute has observed its anniversary by holding a complimentary concert and ball, and the affairs have grown yearly in popularity. The fourteenth, which was held in Huntington hall last evening, like its predecessors was a grand success."[32]

➢ The loomfixers took a night off, last night, and with their wives and sweethearts danced till early morning. It was their second annual ball and the crowd that assembled filled Wells' hall.[33]

➢ "The Emerald Base ball and Social club held its second grand social in Associate hall Patriots' eve and drew out a large crowd as they always do. Hibbard's orchestra was in attendance and furnished delightful dance music."[34]

Speaking of baseball, there were plenty of other things to do in Lowell beyond dancing—and beyond the lectures and meetings so often mentioned as pastimes for the mill girls. Local recreation areas hosted outdoor sports and races. For the less athletic, there were scenic paths such as the Canal Walk, a unique walkway that extended out over the junction of the Merrimack River and the Northern Canal.

Top: Sheet Music Cover from the 1860s. This tune is clearly at the intersection of two great loves of the period: Baseball and Polka.

Right: Lowell's Canal Walk was once a popular place to stroll out over the water where the Northern Canal meets the Merrimack River.

Opposite top: Ice skating at Shedd Park, from a 1912 postcard.

Opposite middle: Taking a dip in the pond on Lowell's South Common, from a 1910 postcard.

Opposite bottom: Willow Dale Park, owned by the Bower Brothers.

76

In the winter there was, as always, sleighing, plus a number of skating parks for amusement. In the summer there was boating and swimming; some people might even sneak a dip in the pond on South Common. Around the city, landscaped parks and cemeteries doubled as picnic grounds.

Or people could travel four miles northwest of Lowell by carriage or barge or, in later years, by trolley to Willow Dale on the shore of "Tyng's Pond" (Lake Mascuppic).

"For forty years the delightful summer resort 'Willow Dale' has been known to the people of Lowell and each year its opening is hailed with much pleasure. Each year the proprietors endeavor to make 'Willow Dale' more and more inviting and this year they have spared no expense. They have enlarged the cafe, have erected a new open air theatre; also added to the many attractions a roller coaster, new swings, new pleasure and fishing boats. They have launched on the lake a new and commodious steamer the 'Willow Dale,' which will accommodate 150 passengers."

—And yes, they also had dancing: "Dancing will begin this week Saturday and there will be a fine band concert Sunday afternoon and evening."—*Lowell Sun*, May 1896.

"The horses now with nimble tread
   Along the streets resounding,
And o'er the river's rocky bed
   Toward Willow Dale are bounding.
More harmless mirth and frolic now
   Are needed without question;
The best—as doctors now allow—
   Specific for digestion.
If there is one whose cheerless turn
   Demands a kind adviser,
Go to a Willow Dale and learn
   To be a little wiser."
     —*old advertising copy*.[35]

More urban amusements abounded as well. Social clubs were common. Those with their own buildings would sometimes install bowling alleys and gaming rooms alongside the usual library and assembly hall.

For the teetotalers, there were multiple temperance institutes in town. For the drinkers, there were any number of bars, often patronized by a specific ethnic group.

Theaters came and went, often replacing one another in the same building: The Lowell Museum, Savoy Theatre, Casto Theatre, People's Theatre, Star Theatre, Bijou Theatre, Wonderland Musee, and The Music Hall were some of the names. Vaudeville arrived in Lowell and became increasingly popular as the century waned.

"American vaudeville, like the English music hall, was an outgrowth of the Industrial Revolution. As our society became more industrialized toward the close of the nineteenth century, the average American working man sought entertainment and relaxation of a nature different from that offered by saloons and beer halls. And he now had the money to pay for it," wrote Charles Stein in his book about vaudeville.[36]

Early in the twentieth century, Lowell even had one of the more important of the country's fledgling automobile race tracks. The Merrimack Valley Course ran along what is now Route 113; its dips and curves offered drama and diversion to Lowell's residents.

Roller skating caught on following the Civil War and had plenty of local fans. The Lowell Skating Rink stood at the corner of Gorham and Union Streets in the 1870s and early 1880s. Bands were hired to supply music by which to skate.

But roller skating could be as controversial as dancing. An 1884 column in the *Lowell Weekly Sun* states a skating rink "is in its effects the most immoral licensed institution that we have. It is the cause of more and worse immorality—yes, ten times more,— than the worst conducted rumshop in the city. The theatres are a Sunday school compared to it."[37]

As in dancing, the exposure of naive girls to wicked persons who might lead them astray seemed to be the big concern. But roller skating had one drawback of which dancing was rarely accused.

"Does it improve a young girl's modesty or morals to fall in a heap on a skating rink floor, in the gaze of hundreds, with perhaps her feet in the air and her clothes tossed over her head? Is it good for her proper training to even see other females in such plight?"[38]

Regardless of all the other activities going on in nineteenth-century Lowell, dancing was a perennial favorite for many. And it didn't require special equipment or special facilities, or even a whole lot of room. In the latter half of the century, spontaneous bouts of dancing seemed to sprout in parlors all over town. In particular, they often followed the surprise presentation of a gift.

"Mr. and Mrs. Hugh Gildee were the happy subjects of a surprise party…about fifty friends calling and presenting them an elegant black walnut chamber set. Supper and dancing were among the pleasures of the occasion."—*Lowell Weekly Sun,* Dec. 30, 1882.

"A surprise party assembled at Mrs. Kehan's…and presented that lady a handsome bed lounge. Refreshments and dancing were also enjoyed." —*Lowell Weekly Sun,* Dec. 16, 1882.

"Mr. Thomas Linscott's friends visited him at his home…and presented him a beautiful gold ring. During the evening there were singing and dancing, and a general good time." —*Lowell Daily Sun,* Jan. 3, 1896.

"Mr. James Sparks…was favored with a surprise party Saturday evening, when he was presented a fine easy chair… Dancing, singing, etc., were enjoyed until midnight." —*Lowell Weekly Sun,* Feb. 3, 1883.

Mr. and Mrs. Hood were presented a valuable range by a company of friends Friday night of last week. The usual festivities were enjoyed, including dancing. —*Lowell Weekly Sun,* Feb. 17, 1883.

A large party of friends invaded the new home of Mr. and Mrs. W. H. Jones Tuesday evening and made them the happy recipients of a beautiful carpet. Refreshments, dancing, etc. followed. —*Lowell Weekly Sun,* Oct. 21, 1882.

It seems these groups of "invaders" were in the habit of bringing along a few musicians, back in those days when recorded music wasn't an option. Much like nowadays, an evening without music would hardly have been considered a proper celebration. And, if one had gone to the trouble to supply music anyway, why would one *not* dance?

Top left: Young Men's Christian Institute bowling alley, 1902.

Middle left: Merrimack Valley Auto Race Course from postcard, c.1910.

Bottom left: Advertising card from Lowell Skating Rink, c.1880.

Top right: Comic postcard, 1916.

There are any number of dance manuals that offer descriptions of nineteenth-century ballrooms, but it makes sense here to turn again to Massachusetts native, Elias Howe, and his co-authors for information.

"Ball-rooms, like tastes, vary so much, that it is impossible to describe the particular form that prevails. But that which gives the greatest satisfaction has a form nearly square, one side being only a little longer than the other."

"The head or top of the ball-room is that end of the room where would be the head of the table, were the room converted into a dining-room. Where there is an orchestra at one end, the orchestra end is the head, and will be found in general farthest from the principal *entrée,* or staircase. It is always of importance to know and remember the head of the ball-room, as ladies and couples at the head always take the lead in the dance."

"Good flooring is indispensable for a ball-room; but when the floor is rough, the evil may be remedied by covering it with holland, tightly stretched—a practice which is now much in vogue. This adds greatly to the comfort, and improves the appearance of the floor. The holland may even be stretched over the carpet. The room ought to be well lighted and well ventilated. Those who give private parties should carefully attend to these two particulars." [Holland is a tightly woven cotton or linen fabric, often heavily finished.]

The Ball Room:
Its decorum, dimensions, and delights

"Good music should also be provided; for bad music will spoil the best dancing, and destroy both the beauty and the pleasure of the entertainment."[1] —Howe's *American Dancing Master,* 1862.

The preceding instructions seem to be primarily for well-to-do homeowners throwing private balls. In 1868, the owners of French's hall were promoting a different approach, as shown in the *Lowell Daily Courier* article below.

"**A New Idea**. Quite a new plan of having large parties without trouble to housekeepers and without injury to furniture is coming into vogue here. It is to invite one's guests to French's hall, where there is ample room for dancing and other amusements, and where Messrs. Nichols and Hutchins are prepared to supply refreshments in elegant style. Where one's house is not large enough—as few houses are—to accommodate several hundred guests, or when for any reason it is desirable not to use one's house, as on account of sickness, &c., we think this plan is an admirable one, and it is likely to be extensively adopted. Several such parties have already been held, and those who have given them are delighted to be able to get up the next morning and find their domestic arrangements undisturbed."[2]

Opposite: This photograph from a stereoscope card depicts a turn-of-the-century New England ballroom.

Right: Ballroom image from a 1907 postcard.

But French's hall on Central Street was only one of several mid-century venues downtown. Just around the corner, Patrick Lynch had added to the building that housed his liquor store and was advertising new halls in 1871.

"**HALLS TO RENT.** The Three Splendid Halls, 80 Feet by 40, with gas, water closets, ante-rooms, wash rooms, and steam heating apparatus, in Lynch's Block, on Market street, are offered to any organizations for rent on reasonable terms, the block being now nearly completed, and one of the finest in the city. Application must be made to me at my office, adjoining the block on Market street, or my residence, 74 Cross street. Patrick Lynch."[3]

Also just opened was the Urban Block over on Middle Street. The *Lowell Courier* wrote about its halls in detail:

"**Urban Hall.** Hundreds of persons interested in the announcement that the new Urban Hall would be thrown open for inspection last evening found their way thither and looked and admired. We went through the several rooms, and give the results of our observation for the benefit of those who were not there to see. A general description of the new building has already been printed, and an account of the interior must suffice."

"On the second floor are, (besides Burton's) two large rooms, named, respectively, 'Banquet Hall' and 'Russian Hall.' 'Russian Hall' is 54x20 feet, fronts on Middle street, has three convenient ante-rooms, and is connected with 'Banquet Hall,' which is of very nearly the same size. Both rooms are plainly but very neatly finished, and are just the thing for use at parties not wholly devoted to dancing, or for which the larger hall would be too extensive. A smaller room, opposite the 'Banquet Hall,' is intended for private suppers, or may be devoted to other and general uses."

"On the third floor is 'Urban Hall,' 76x40 feet, and 23 feet high in the center, fronting on Middle street. This, the principal room in the building, is also the most elaborate in decoration and finish. A peculiarity is noticed in the ceiling, which in the center rises into an arch extending the length of the hall, and adds greatly to its general appearance. At the Middle street end are a platform and desk, the latter containing a self-registering thermometer, and also a clock, upon the face of which in small gilt letters are the words 'A time to dance. Eccl. III:4.' Opposite is a gallery, intended to accommodate spectators to the number of one hundred. The walls and ceiling are tinted a pale green; and around the sides are fixed seats, upholstered in red enameled leather, for about one hundred and fifty persons. Movable and folding settees for four hundred are to be provided, making the capacity of the hall six hundred and fifty." —*Lowell Daily Courier*, November 15, 1871.

Left: This 1874 advertisement for Lynch's liquor shows the expanded dormers on the fourth floor that were part of the building's 1871 remodel (see page 100 for a pre-remodel photograph).

Top right: The galleries of the White City Dance Hall in Worcester (just a trolley ride away from Lowell) display how space for spectators was considered an important part of a venue's design.

Right: Streamers radiating from the ceiling's center were a popular way of dressing up a hall, as seen in this photo of a Huntington Hall exhibition (Lowell Historical Society).

Galleries—also referred to as balconies—were present in most of the major halls, and there was a good reason for them. Dancing was not just a social activity; it was a spectator sport. It was the reality television of the day. Just imagine all the buzz among the watchers...

Who was dancing with whom? Who was wearing what? Was her dress too tight? Too loud? Too low? (Particularly easy to see from above.) *Did they know their steps? Were they showing off too much? Were they dancing together too often? Too close? Was she too tall for her partner? Was he too low class for her? Did she really let him put his hand* **there?!**...

And the beauty of it was that one could watch without violating one's own morals by actually dancing! A ball was very often preceded by a concert; the spectators might already be in place before the dancers even arrived.

At Huntington Hall in 1895: "While the music was being enjoyed by those in the gallery, the ladies who were to take part in the ball arrived and were given seats on the floor by their escorts."[4]

Society balls could be formal for the dancers while much less so for the onlookers. The Cadets' Armory ball in 1893 was a "dressy affair," yet "spectators in street dress" eagerly filled seating set aside for them.[5]

The opening number at a ball was invariably the "Grand March" which was, as the title implies, more of a procession than a dance. The March might be led by the organizers, by an honored guest, or simply by whoever joined the line first. The evening's floor managers directed the line of marching couples this way and that, often separating the columns of men and women

> *Hubby and I like to dance just about anywhere there's live music, whether anyone else is or not. Apparently, people enjoy the "show" and we tend to get a reputation, especially at regular events near home.*
>
> *Once, when we visited our old neighborhood for an event with a live band, we overheard some fellow on his phone: "Yes, Mom, they're here." He then turned to us and declared: "She's coming right over!"* —Author

to weave about in various patterns before pairing everyone up again. Or perhaps the managers would reconfigure the dancers to walk two couples abreast, or even four. All that meandering allowed participants to check each other out as they passed by, for the opening march was a display of finery to be admired by both dancers and spectators alike.

The Grand March at an 1895 ball given in Associate's hall by the Alpine club was described as follows:

"At the sound of the bugle the participants entered the hall from the reception room and the Alpine march was on. It was a gem. The costumes of the young ladies were elegant and attracted considerable attention from those seated in the galleries. All the young men were attired in evening dress, and their conventional suits blended nicely with the gayer gowns of their lady friends. In the march the participants started off in fours and went through many evolutions, which made a very pretty showing."[6]

To get the full effect of all this, one needed ample lighting. The best ballrooms made every effort to illuminate the hall properly. Those first steps from the outside darkness into the brightly lit world of the ball were steps into a new realm: *"As they enter the ball-room she is quite charmed and dazzled by its splendor and the gaiety of the scene, which is so novel to her."*[7]

When Major Emery, the owner of the Merrimack House, remodeled the building in 1848, the lighting of the hall was an important feature.

"**THE NEW HALL.**—The grand fete by 'The Old Line,' in honor of opening Emery's elegant new Hall, takes place tomorrow night, and will be a brilliant affair. The Hall is the finest dancing room in the city, built with express regard to making it all that such a place can be, for pleasure seekers. The building is 67 1/2 feet, by 47. The first floor is built for a wood, coal, and store house. The second contains the Hall, beautifully and tastefully finished, 60 feet by 44 feet 8 inches in dimensions, lighted by two splendid and costly chandeliers, of ten solar burners each, and admirably adapted for balls, concerts, and lectures. There are two entrances; one from Dutton street, and the other through the Hotel."[8]

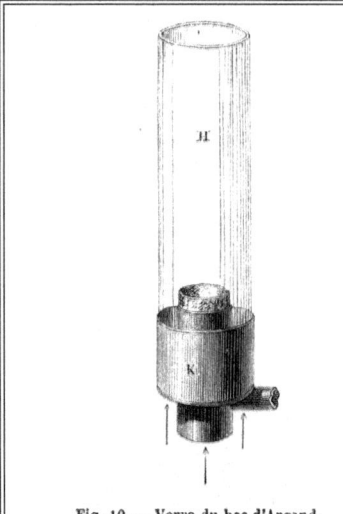

Fig. 10. — Verre du bec d'Argand.

"Solar" nowadays refers to light sources that draw their power from the sun but two centuries ago the term was used for flames that burned "as bright as the sun." Solar burners, or lamps, made their appearance in the 1840s and would have been cutting edge technology when Major Emery remodeled in 1848.

Based on the earlier Argand lamp, solar burners used a sleeve-shaped wick that allowed viscous fuels to reach the flame more easily by traveling through the open center of the wick; whale oil, vegetable oils, or lard could be burned more efficiently. In addition, solar lamps had an all metal construction that transferred the flame's warmth to the fuel and prevented it from congealing. The tall, narrow chimney steadied the flame and improved the flow of air, thus creating a high, extraordinarily bright flame.[9]

In decorative, flame-based lighting, such as the chandeliers at Merrimack House, a clear chimney was often used together with a frosted, outer globe. In the case of solar lamps, the chimney would have protruded well above the top of the globe.

A wide variety of decorative light globes can be seen in the display at far right.

Just a few years later those costly chandeliers became obsolete when gas lighting arrived in Lowell. The long newspaper description previously cited of Urban Hall's 1871 open house also included information about the hall's modern lighting, heat, and ventilation. The balance of that article follows:

"Steam-pipes extending completely around the wall will supply a summer temperature; and sixteen ventilators would seem to be sufficient to keep the air fresh and healthful. The mode of lighting is unique. There are five brackets, each holding a cluster of twenty-five jets, arranged in pyramidal form; and two large golden wheels fixed against the sides of the hall, each blazon with sixty-one jets; two hundred and seventy-two in all. The result is, of course, very brilliant. The remainder of the third floor is devoted to a ladies' room, and elegantly fitted reception room, and a clothing room, not to mention Mr. Rawson's apartments."

"On the fourth floor are a gentlemen's room, the entrance to 'Urban Hall' balcony, and 'Highland Hall,' 43x28 feet, very prettily finished and intended

for the use of dancing classes and teachers. Throughout the whole building are all the conveniences of arrangement and furniture necessary to completeness, and the first floor is provided with a first-rate cook-room of ample dimensions besides the three unfinished stores."

"So elegant and convenient accommodations were never before offered to the pleasure-lovers of Lowell; and they cannot fail of full appreciation. The new block is centrally located, easy of access, and the only one in the city especially devoted to the wants of the public in the line of social amusements."[10]

The question of ventilation—as mentioned in the article—was no small thing. The dance "season" in Lowell lasted from September through May, at which time the rich fled the heat of the city for cooler venues,

Opposite top: Gas chandeliers at an 1860 ball in Manhattan have "clusters of jets" arranged in (inverted) "pyramidal form."

Opposite bottom: Diagram (c. 1869) of lamp with glass chimney and hollow wick designed by Ami Argand in 1784; it is the forerunner of Merrimack House's solar burners.

Above: 1907 advertisement for Lowell Gas Company.

Left: Gas fixtures in the Y. M. C. I. hall on Fayette Street, Lowell, c. 1907.

Below: Gas chandeliers exhibit, Philadelphia, 1876.

and everyone else tried to find open-air settings for their "social amusements." But even so, good ventilation mattered, and one needn't be dancing to appreciate it, or to suffer from the lack of it. An 1868 review of a November concert in Huntington hall made this fact abundantly clear:

"The want of a thorough system of ventilation, was most seriously felt last evening, and we desire to ask our City Fathers if some plan cannot be adopted whereby Huntington Hall may be improved in this respect, without the exposure occasioned by opening windows indiscriminately. The air was most oppressive and foul last night, and detracted greatly from the evening's enjoyment, so much so as to excite general remark and dissatisfaction. This is a matter of much importance and should have immediate attention from the proper source."[11]

One has to wonder what the modern nose would think of these elegant halls of times past. In the days when the well-to-do rarely bathed more than once a week, and common people bathed hardly at all, body odor was the norm.

> *I always remember the smell of the rural dances I attended as a teen: woodsmoke, a touch of Old Spice after-shave, and Woodsman's Fly Dope (to ward off hungry mosquitoes ever-eager to join the throng).*
>
> *I never noticed the smell of sweat, or anything much unpleasant, although I do recall a friend noting that the air at a Thanksgiving evening dance—after all that rich food—did get a bit "ripe."* —Author

Antiperspirants and deodorants did not yet exist, but among the upper classes scented hankies and small bouquets of flowers—known as nosegays—might be used to hold back the olfactory assault of the great unwashed masses. In the ballroom, a *judicious* use of cologne was acceptable:

"Perfumes should be avoided as effeminate; if used at all, for the handkerchief. They should be of the very best and most delicate character, or they may give offense, as persons often entertain strong aversions to particular scents, as patchouli, eau-de-cologne, &c."[12]

Eli Hoyt of Lowell made his fortune from the manufacture and sale of his "German" cologne during the latter half of the 1800s. Hoyt's advertising assured customers that his perfume should not be confused with "trashy" substitutes. Perhaps this meant it had the required "delicate character."

When it came to the inevitable perspiration of the dancers, a pair of white kid gloves was essential, particularly for the men. Gloves not only spared the lady contact with damp, male hands, they protected the back of her gown from sweaty palm prints. But they were only one part of the proscribed evening wear.

For men, *Howe's Complete Ball-Room Hand Book* lists: "a black superfine dress coat, well-fitting pants of the same color, white vest, black or white cravat (tie or stock), patent leather boots, low heels, white kid gloves, white linen cambric handkerchief slightly perfumed, and the hair well dressed, without being too much curled."[13]

Above: Hoyt's German Cologne advertising card, 1891.

Right: This couple wears middle-class dance attire of the late 1800s. Society might reluctantly give the young lady the option of dancing gloveless, but no proper gentleman went without.

Above far right: Dr. J. C. Ayer's advertising cards helped build the kind of fortune that allowed Mrs. Ayer her grand party in 1871.

Far right: The latest ball gowns from Paris as seen in an 1865 magazine.

For the ladies, there were more choices, but there were also more rules. Here are a few specifics from *The Ball-Room Guide*, published in 1866:

"A lady, in dressing for a ball, has first to consider the delicate question of age; and next, that of her position, whether married or single."[14]

"As everything about a ball-room should be light, gay, and the reverse of depressing, it is permitted to elderly ladies to assume a lighter and more effective style of dress than would be proper at the concert or opera."[15]

"Young unmarried ladies should wear dresses of light materials—the lighter the better; such dresses should be worn over a silk slip."[16]

The Guide goes on to say that "there is no restriction as to colours" but does caution that, "arsenic green should be avoided as injurious to health."[17]

"Silk dresses are, as a rule, objectionable for those who dance."[18] (Perspiration and cleaning would be a problem.)

Of course, some of these rules were only for high society balls. Mill girls and mechanics could hardly be expected to be able to meet the same standards of dress when they gathered for a dance.

One fashionable Lowell party where dress and manners were of the highest order was Mrs. J. C. Ayer's house party in February of 1871. Her home was the former inn once known as the Old Stone House.

An account of the event appeared in the *Boston Post* and was reprinted in the *Lowell Daily Courier*. Excerpts appear below; the entire article is available in the appendix.

"It is very probable that there is no other city of its size in New England, or for the matter of that, outside of it where there is so much social gaiety as in Lowell. All winter long one entertainment follows another in rapid succession with scarcely a lull in between…and life in the city of mills, as so many persons see and experience it there, is not at all an unpleasant phase of existence. Every building is not a factory, nor every block a colony of operatives' boarding-houses."

"Although it was snowing steadily and persistently outside, the scene inside was like a peep into fairy-land. Carriage after carriage rolled up to the door, and deposited its precious freight underneath the broad awning, which stretched from the gate to the steps. Dainty feet stepped lightly over the carpet put to shield them from the ground, which was kept clean and dry by busy hands, which brushed away the snow as persistently as it fell. Through the spacious doorways they flitted, mysterious bundles done up in multitudinous wraps, through the brilliantly lighted hall, up the broad staircase into the dressing-rooms, where presently from each dull chrysalis would emerge a brilliant, bewildering butterfly."

"Off from plump, pretty shoulders heavy wraps were removed, trains were adjusted, gloves drawn on, one last parting glance at the long mirror was stolen, and down stairs they swept, wave after wave of bright-hued sylphs in billows of tarletane and lace, into the drawing room where Mrs. Ayer received her guests. Mrs. Ayer was elegantly attired in a pink silk dress, with a court train trimmed with an exquisite point lace flounce. The overdress was of point, looped up with bunches of pink rosebuds. The body was low and pointed with puffed sleeves, and a berth of point. The bouquet de corsage was of exquisite French roses and buds, while bunches of the same ornamented each shoulder. Around her neck was a heavy gold chain, to which was suspended a magnificent diamond cross, while large solitaire diamonds glistened in her ears. In her dark hair, which was arranged in long, loose curls at the back, with puffs on the top, was a bunch of pink rosebuds."

> *There is a difference between an event with dancing and a dance event, a difference that still exists today. Mrs. Ayer's party was the former; only some of the attendees would be subjecting their gowns to the stress and sweat of dancing. At a full-fledged dance event, where dance was the primary activity, there would probably be considerably less silk rustling about the scene.* —Author

The reporter's description went on and on about silks and flowers and china and sparkling champagne, about rooms filled with rare bronzes and costly pictures, and about "merry feet and chattering tongues" keeping time to "Strauss waltzes and wild galops."

"Between two and three hundred people must have been present from ten until twelve, when they began to retire, the older ones first, leaving more room for the dancing, which was kept up until two o'clock, when the still unwearied dancers gave a sigh as the last notes of a galop died away and the musicians closed their books, and all bade Dr. and Mrs. Ayer a reluctant good night. To say the ball was a success, is but simple truth."[19]

How did the mill hands reading this account feel about it? Were they jealous? Angry and disgusted? Resigned to such inequity? Fascinated, in awe, admiring, or all of the above?

Mrs. Ayer's ball was strictly high society, but there were other situations where different classes of dancers might mix; the most common one being at a dancing school. Yet, even there, there was often conflict between the haves and the have-nots. One little story that has survived the years comes from northwest of Lowell, in Keene, New Hampshire, but one can imagine the actions and reactions happening almost anywhere that the classes mingled.

The tale goes that in 1840, one Mr. Weaver of Boston arrived to teach several terms of "dancing and deportment." At the close of his school, a grand ball was held which was attended by all levels of society. Some of the upper crust women caused a fuss when they declined to dance with the farmers and mechanics; one of their male peers caused a stir of his own when he left the party with the indignant remark that "turkeys and dunghill fowl can't mix."[20]

The snooty comment was widely repeated, and when an exclusive ball was later held at the same hall, the event was sneered at by those not invited as a "turkey ball." The attendees were labeled "turkeys." Perhaps this was the beginning of the turkey's fall from grace, the point at which the name of a bird long considered noble became a derogatory term.

Upper class balls tended to be by invitation; middle class ones were more likely to be public. Howe's manual describes how such balls were arranged.

"There are various ways of originating Balls. The most common one is for several persons, interested in dancing, to meet together and choose a Committee of Arrangements, or Managers as they are sometimes called, whose duty it is to procure a hall, engage a quadrille band, make arrangements for the supper, and issue cards of invitations to such persons as they may wish to have attend. The number of the committee varies from five to twenty, according to the amount of services to be performed."

"On the evening of the ball, two or more of the committee should be chosen as floor managers, to see that the sets are full, and that all persons wishing for partners are supplied, and also to direct the music when to commence, as well as to decide any questions that may arise in the ball-room."

"Military and fire engine companies, clubs and associations, often give a single ball, or perhaps a series of parties—the same committee officiating during the different evenings."

"It is the custom for teachers of dancing, in connection with their schools, to open their rooms to the public after nine o'clock in the evening, and any proper person may for a small sum, (usually fifty cents,) join in the amusements. These parties usually close about twelve o'clock, while balls are generally continued some hours later."

"Sometimes balls are got up by some speculator, who generally manages the whole matter himself. Balls of this class are not always select, as the invitations are given to the public in general, and improper persons too frequently gain admission."[21]

Lowell papers made little attempt to provide detailed descriptions of the crowd at working class events, but an 1872 magazine article paints a lively picture of a public dance elsewhere in New England:

Many years ago, at the behest of the Park Service, I created a pattern for their 1830s Mill Girl dress. I also made three replicas, the dress itself being too delicate to be displayed.

Examining the original made it clear how frugal the girl had been; she could not afford to waste fabric. Two back bodice pieces had been cut with the print flowers pointing down, and one of them was stitched together from scraps. —Author

Top left: The Ayer home as it might have appeared lit up for an evening party (from a 1912 photo).

Bottom left: Turkeys used to be highly regarded, so much so that the upper class once identified with this noble bird.

Left: Mill workers often went from the mill to the dance hall with no time to change. The dress style worn by these Lawrence doffers would have been pressed into service as dance wear.

"Strolling down thither as soon as my repast was ended, I found the low open building filled with young people, and quadrille sets nearly formed. The very dirtiest master of ceremonies I had ever seen was hurrying through the crowd in his shirt-sleeves, and vociferating, 'One more couple wanted here,' while the couples he had already mated were standing up, with some shamefacedness of manner, and looking as if they would be better acquainted when once in motion. They were neatly enough dressed, though generally gloveless, and looked like young Americans of the working class."

"Presently the violins struck up, the dirty manager began to shout the familiar figures, and the young people plunged into the dance with an old-fashioned energy that amazed me. Even the young men did not walk their steps evasively, as of yore, but danced the soberest 'forward two' with a waggish vivacity that almost shook the hats upon their heads. It was not a solid German heartiness, but there was a suggestion of almost French volatility about it, and one almost expected that there would presently be something improper, though there never was. This in the quieter passages; while the slightest suggestion to 'swing partners' was received with a vehemence that shook the platform, and must have materially encouraged the motion of the earth upon its axis."[22]

There were, in certain settings, truly low class dances, totally lacking in both rhythm and decorum. Historian Page wrote that "the old style of square dancing made it a very stately and polite form of the dance, where ladies were treated like ladies and the men themselves acted like gentlemen. The dances then were quadrilles, lancers, contra dances, etc. with the heel and toe polka, waltz, galops, etc. for the round dances." But then he added a caveat:

"To get the story straight though, you must know that even then there was a style of dancing very common in low class dance halls known as 'hoe-down' dancing, where most anything went. It made no difference if anyone was in time with the music or not, or if they did a promenade in a certain number of beats, or how many measures it required for a grand right and left. Roughness prevailed, very little thought was given to other people who were dancing; if anyone bumped someone else it was just a common occurrence. Many people knew no difference, and few cared anyway. This 'high, wide and handsome' style did a lot to spoil square dancing for many people."[23]

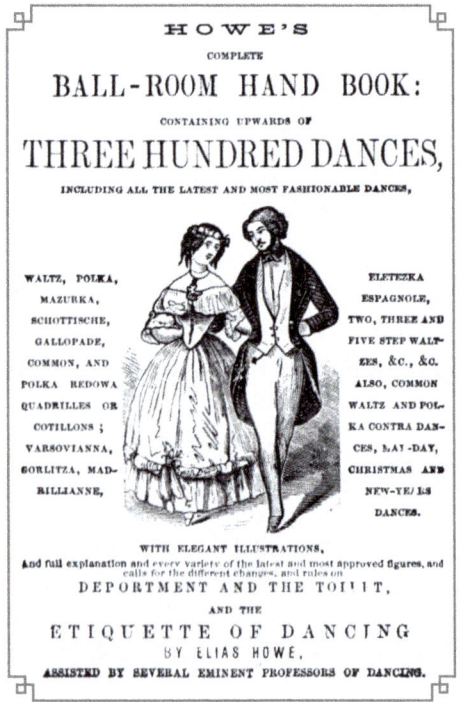

But for those people who cared what society thought, or who just wanted to enjoy themselves without being bruised and buffeted, there were a great many books to which they could turn. *Howe's Complete Ball-Room Hand Book* covered the minutiae of dance decorum in 1858:

"The following hints on Ball-Room Etiquette may be of use to persons unacquainted with dancing, or who have not been accustomed to attending balls with ladies. In calling for the lady you have invited, be punctual at the hour appointed; if you order a carriage hand her in first, and sit opposite to her unless she requests you to change your position. In leaving the carriage you will precede the lady and assist her in descending, you will then conduct her to the ladies' dressing room, leaving her in charge of the maid, while you go to the gentlemen's apartments to divest yourself of overcoat, hat, and boots, adjust your toilet, draw on your gloves, (white or colored). The lady in the meantime, after arranging her dress, retires to the ladies' sitting-room, or awaits your arrival at the door of the dressing-room, according as the apartments may be arranged."

"Your first duty is to procure a programme for your partner, and introduce your friends, who place their names on her card for the dances engaged. You should always dance first, with your own partner, afterwards you may exchange partners with a friend or dance again with her, should she not be engaged. The floor-managers give the order to the orchestra to commence; they also take the lead in entering the ball-room. You either join in the promenade, or conduct your lady to a seat. Before taking your place in the set, await the signal from the managers or the call of the trumpet. Avoid rushing for places, which we regret to say is so prevalent in our public ball-rooms of the present day."[24]

"Should you wish to dance with a lady with whom you are not acquainted, apply first to your friends, should you have any present, who may be successful in procuring for you the desired introduction. If not, make application to one of the floor managers, who will introduce you, should he be intimate with her, otherwise he may not present you without first demanding the consent of the lady."[25]

"An introduction at a public ball affords you no claim to an intimacy with your partner afterwards."[26]

"In requesting a lady to dance, you stand at a proper distance, bend the body gracefully, accompanied by a slight motion of the right hand in front, you look at her with complaisance, and respectfully say, will you do me the honor to dance with me, or shall I have the pleasure of dancing with you, remaining in the position you have assumed, until the lady signifies her intention, by saying, with pleasure sir, or I regret I am engaged sir."[27]

Top left: Detail from an 1897 cartoon showing the common people's version of a society ball.

Far left: Elias Howe—a musician originally from Framingham, later of Providence, RI and of Boston—did well for himself publishing music instruction books. Also among his publications were a few dance manuals, including this one.

Left: Successfully asking a lady to dance meant being versed in proper manners.

"You ought not to engage a lady, for more than four dances during the evening, as it may deprive her of the pleasure of dancing with those of her friends who may arrive at a later hour; besides excessive familiarity is out of place in a ball room."[28]

"A lady cannot refuse the invitation of a gentleman to dance, unless she has already accepted that of another, for she would be guilty of an incivility which might occasion trouble; she would, moreover, seem to show contempt for him whom she refused, and would expose herself to receive in secret an ill compliment from the mistress of the house."[29]

"Ladies should avoid affectation, frowning, quizzing, or the slightest indication of ill-temper, or they will infallibly be marked. No loud laughter, loud talking, staring or any act which appertains to the hoyden [a girl or woman of saucy, boisterous, or carefree behavior], should be seen in a lady's behaviour."[30]

"As it is considered a violation of etiquette, for man and wife to dance together, they should avoid doing so."[31] [To do so would be seen as snubbing one's friends; the author and her husband admit to being rather rude on this count.]

Howe's manual also offered tips about the music: "A good Band is indispensable, one that can play in perfect harmony, and time, the most approved selections from the latest and best composers."[32]

"Fashion and custom usually determines the kinds of instruments to be used for dancing, but what is fashionable is not always the best."

"Brass instruments and most of those which go to make up a military band would be highly improper in a small parlour or drawing-room. If but one instrument is used for dancing, the Violin is unquestionably the best, if two are used, a Violin and a Clarionett, the third instrument if in a small or medium sized room, should be another Violin, Harp, or Flute; if in a large hall it should be a Cornet, Sax-horn, Post-horn or a E♭ Bugle."

"If five instruments are used in a large hall, a Violin, Clarionett, Cornet, (Sax-horn or Post-horn) Harp and Violoncello will produce the best music for dancing. For a sixth instrument, add another Violin, and for any larger number add any of the instruments used in military Bands."

"The Piano-Forte well played, will alone produce good music for dancing, the Violin, Clarionett, Flute or Harp for a second instrument would be the most proper, for a third add one of the Brass instruments named above."[33] (Another manual warns that if using a solo piano, "the hostess should secure the attendance of a professional pianist, because the guests ought not to be left to the mercy of those who happen to be present and can be prevailed on to play."[34])

"The musicians should not be elevated too much, especially if the ceiling of the room is low, as the heat and unwholesome air that arises from a crowded room, is not only injurious to the musicians, but it has a very bad effect on the instruments. The prompter or caller should however, be elevated enough to be able to see all parts of the ball-room."[35]

There were certainly plenty of music groups offering their services for dances in Lowell; several of those groups had offices downtown (as the reader will see in the next chapter).

Above: 1901 Lowell Sun *advertisement.*

Left: Fiddle and piano were the preferred instruments for small parties.

Right: The frontispiece from The Ballroom Companion *shows an 1866 ball room scene.*

Top far right: 1907 advertisement for the Lowell Cadet Orchestra.

Bottom far right: Salem's Cadet Band was popular in Lowell's ballrooms. They are said to still haunt their bandstand at the Salem Willows in Salem, Mass.

One popular group from outside of Lowell was the Salem Cadet Band. Made up of woodwinds, brass and percussion, they were both marching band and dance orchestra.

"GRAND CONCERT AND BALL. Centralville Odd Fellows say their concert and ball at Huntington hall on Thursday, Feb. 7, will be the event of the season. They have secured the Salem Cadet full brass band, 24 pieces, and as a special feature will have a grand exhibition drill by the Centralville Rebekahs' degree staff. The hall will be beautifully decorated."[36]

Another event with the Salem Band at Huntington hall was described in the *Sun* as follows:

"Huntington hall, the scene of the festivities, was transformed into an immense bower. Over the ceiling was a canopy of pink, white and nile green colors, rendered brilliant by the lights behind it, while a large number of streamers from the centre chandelier to the balcony, in the same, delicate colors, added greatly to the beauty of the scene. The boxes were tastefully and profusely decorated, while suspended from the centre of the ceiling was a mammoth bell."

"On the stage, almost entirely hidden from view by many hot house plants, the Salem Cadet band, Jean Missud leader, discussed its sweetest music giving an enjoyable concert previous to the grand march which began about 9:30 o'clock. The grand march showed the beautiful costumes of the ladies to great advantage. The joy of the dance was unconfined until 11:30 o'clock, when intermission of an half hour was taken, during which supper was served by Caterer McCoy in Jackson hall. After supper, dancing was resumed, and kept up till 2 o'clock."[37]

In Salem, Massachusetts today, the Cadet Band is rumored to haunt their old bandstand at the Salem Willows; there are some residents who claim they can still be seen playing on foggy nights. If only that were so, and the ghosts could speak, this author could get all the first-hand information about those old balls she wanted!

Lowell had a cadet band of its own, although it never reached the popularity of the Salem group. One local ensemble that was kept very busy playing for city events was Joe Hibbard's Orchestra. The Honorable Joseph H. Hibbard was a violinist, manufacturer (of potato chips), member of the Massachusetts House of Representatives, and an all-around involved citizen.[38]

Both the Lowell Cadet band and Hibbard's Orchestra were present at one turn-of-the-century ball for a fireman's association. Headlined "Fire Laddies in Red Shirts and Ladies in Gorgeous Gowns Made the Scene One of Great Beauty," the article describes the hall in detail and then tells of the evening's musical program:

"From 8 till 9 o'clock the Lowell Cadet band gave a complimentary concert." "Joe Hibbard was there, too, with his full orchestra and as might be expected, the music was one of the finest features of the evening. The hall was packed when the engine bell sounded for the grand march."[39]

Using an engine bell to indicate the start of dancing was a unique touch appropriate to the crowd; the more common signal was a brief fanfare by coronet, trumpet, or bugle.

The same article also tells of a wall of greenery on the stage and at one point mentions Hibbard pulling something from "the mysterious depth of the forest in which his musicians were hidden."[40]

The Honorable Joseph H. Hibbard

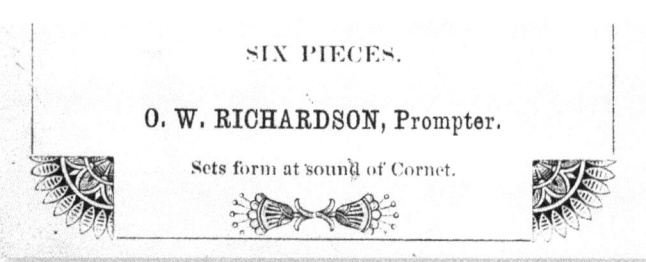

That wall of greenery screening the orchestra turns up over and over again at balls in the latter 1800s and early 1900s. What follows is a description of an 1899 event at Lowell's Colonial Hall, but it could just as well be describing the New York City ballroom at left, circa 1914. Although the New York hall is more elaborate than Colonial Hall, both have similar architectural styles with generous lighting, a divided ceiling, arched doorways, and moderately elevated stages.

"The scene in the ball room was rarely beautiful, the handsome gowns and bright faces of the ladies greatly enhancing the golden and white beauty of the hall, while myriads of lights brought out in grand effect the general attractiveness of the scene. The floral decorations were of the choicest plants from the tropics in the dance hall, the orchestra stationed within a leafy bower, while in the reception room was a wealth of rare cut flowers."[41]

The custom of hiding the orchestra was intended to make the music seem as if it wafted out of nowhere; it was, essentially, a way of keeping the nuts and bolts of the "sound system" out of sight so as to not mar the beauty of the scene. But with the arrival of recorded music, a hidden sound system came to mean cheap, recorded music, and a live orchestra was a luxury to be put on display. For a dancer today, experiencing the energy generated by any half-decent live band is a real treat, superior to the best recorded melodies.

Mid-page left: Dance cards sometimes specified a signal that would begin the ball, a way to quiet the crowd and to get everyone's attention without benefit of a modern sound system.

Left: Tropical plants filled this c. 1910 ballroom and concealed the orchestra.

Top: Although captioned "Interior of Women's Club," this hall was most likely Colonial Hall on Palmer Street. Note the gallery visible at left.

Above: Once recorded music began to replace bands, orchestras became something to show off, not to hide.

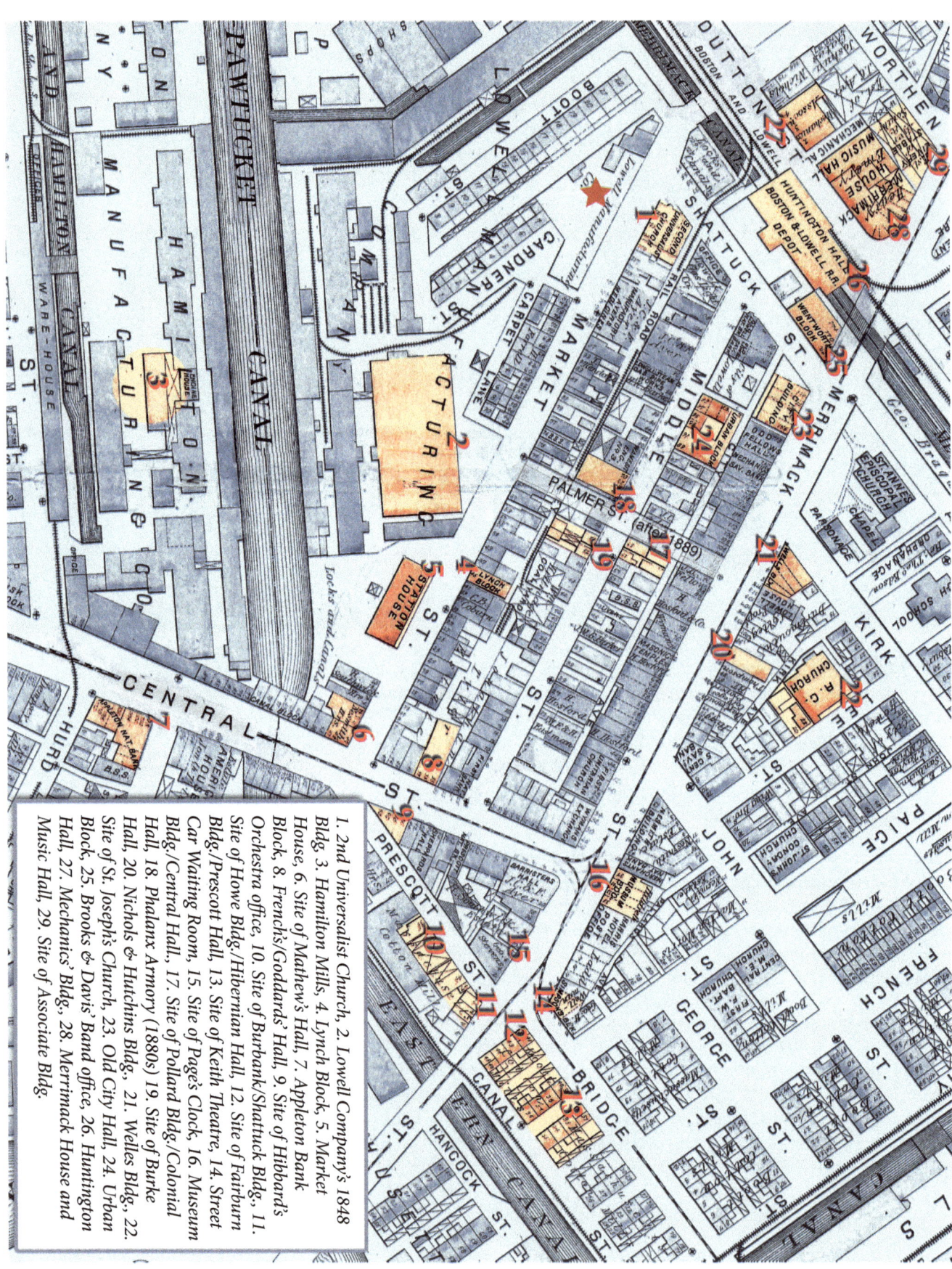

1. 2nd Universalist Church, 2. Lowell Company's 1848 Bldg. 3. Hamilton Mills, 4. Lynch Block, 5. Market House, 6. Site of Mathew's Hall, 7. Appleton Bank Block, 8. French's/Goddard's Hall, 9. Site of Hibbard's Orchestra office, 10. Site of Burbank/Shattuck Bldg., 11. Site of Howe Bldg./Hibernian Hall, 12. Site of Fairburn Bldg./Prescott Hall, 13. Site of Keith Theatre, 14. Street Car Waiting Room, 15. Site of Page's Clock, 16. Museum Bldg./Central Hall, 17. Site of Pollard Bldg./Colonial Hall, 18. Phalanx Armory (1880s) 19. Site of Burke Hall, 20. Nichols & Hutchins Bldg., 21. Welles Bldg, 22. Site of St. Joseph's Church, 23. Old City Hall, 24. Urban Block, 25. Brooks & Davis' Band office, 26. Huntington Hall, 27. Mechanics' Bldg., 28. Merrimack House and Music Hall, 29. Site of Associate Bldg.

There were halls in abundance in Lowell throughout the nineteenth century. The public gatherings of the times—lectures, plays, concerts, political rallies, meetings, celebrations, banquets, and yes, dances—required them. What follows is a short walking tour of some of the downtown halls that history tells us hosted one type of dancing or another. It begins and ends at Lowell's National Historical Park Visitor's Center. ★

Stepping out of the Visitor's Center complex and onto Market Street, the first thing one sees is the parking lot of the Athenian Corner restaurant across the way. This was the site of the Second Universalist Church, one of the churches that hosted discussion groups for the mill girls. The church was best known for its pastor, Abel Thomas, who in 1840 edited and published a pamphlet titled *The Lowell Offering, a Repository of Original Articles written by Females employed in the Mills*. More issues would follow, and *The Offering* would often be pointed to as proof of the virtue and intelligence of the factory women of Lowell.

A Short Tour:
The Victorian Dance Halls of Downtown Lowell

Less well known is that the congregation eventually moved elsewhere and the church became a theatre, the Savoy, later re-dubbed the Casto. The stage regularly offered dance acts, often to good reviews. Although the Casto is gone, its outline remains visible on the wall of the neighboring building.

"THE CASTO THEATRE— The dancing Howards present an act in which the variety of terpsichorean evolutions offered will set the lover of the intricacies of the mazy into rapt delight. It is an excellent act and won many favorable comments." —*Lowell Sun*, Dec. 2nd, 1902.

"The third week of the Casto vaudeville season opened yesterday and judging from the pleased countenance of those who trooped out of the theatre last evening it will be a record breaker...Armstrong and Wright are seen in an act replete with travesty singing and dancing. Bernard Williams, the man of melody, mirth and mystery, an old Lowell favorite, scored heavily in his neat and original art and the Mannings round out the bill with a strong singing and dancing act that was heartily appreciated." —*Lowell Sun*, October 21st, 1902.

Opposite page: Composite map of downtown Lowell from 1879 city atlas. Items listed as "site of" weren't yet built in 1879.

Upper right: 1882 etching of the Second Universalist Church.

Lower right: 1905 photo of the Savoy/Casto Theatre.

Lower left: A 2013 photo of the adjoining building with the church-turned-theater's outline imprinted on it.

Turning right and heading toward Central Street, one passes several former mill buildings and comes to the Leo Roy garage. This entire area, including the Visitor's Center, was originally part of the Lowell Manufacturing Company. Behind the garage and across the canal are the surviving buildings of the Hamilton Mills complex. In 1848, both companies had major dance events. On March 20th, Lowell Manufacturing celebrated the completion of a new building that once stood at the site of the garage. On the Fourth of July, Hamilton Mills held a large picnic and dance.

Left: The Leo Roy garage, standing on the approximate site of 1848's Blowing Out Ball (or Blow Out Ball), can be seen in the background. On the right is one of the Lowell Company's remaining buildings, now converted to condominiums.

Below: The low building in the left foreground of this 1868 etching is Lowell Manufacturing's 1848 Ingram and Axminster Weave Mill where the ball was held. It covered 38,000 square feet of floor space and was lit by numerous skylights.

Right page: Advertisements from the 1866 Lowell Directory.

It is interesting to note that the people writing about these events knew that a significant portion of their readers considered dancing immoral, and reassured them accordingly.

Prior to the March event, flyers were posted around town announcing the "Grand Annual Blow Out Ball," an old tradition celebrating the approach of spring and the putting away of the foul oil lamps that lit the mills during the short days of winter. But, held in Lowell Manufacturing's huge, new, not-yet-equipped Ingram & Axminster Weave Mill,[1] the 1848 party was, according to the *Lowell Courier*, a-one-of-a kind bash: "It was the greatest event of the kind that ever took place in this or any other neighborhood—it was great, good, glorious…a sight for a life time."[2]

The party was referred to as a "Pic Nic," despite being indoors, for the food was served cold: "Cold corned beef, cold ham, bread, cheese, pies, tarts, apples, oranges, raisins, &c., were provided in abundance." The guests dined in three or four shifts and the leftover food was distributed to the poor.[3]

"The room in which the Pic Nic was held is two hundred and thirty two feet long, and one hundred and thirty-eight feet wide—large as some half dozen Faneuil Halls, and any quantity of ordinary dancing rooms. This vast floor was all open, no partition—no obstruction but the one hundred and twelve iron posts which support the roof. It was lighted by three or four hundred hanging and side lamps. The sides were beautifully ornamented with the fabrics of the Carpet mill; splendid carpets and rugs were displayed all around, while parti-colored yarns were interwoven

LOWELL CO. MILLS.

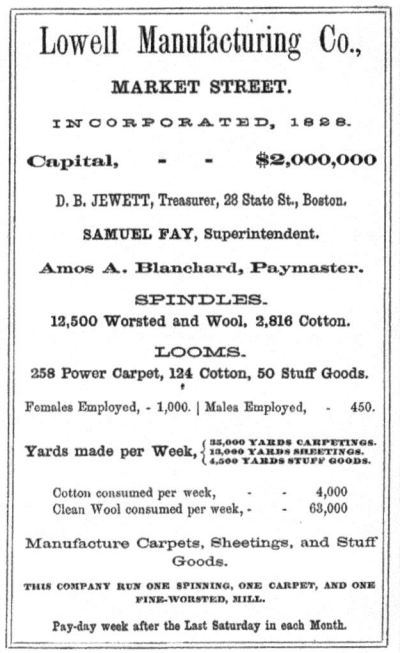

in the most tasteful manner between the windows at the side, and hung from the windows in the roof. A platform upon one side, for the band, was handsomely decorated. The scene upon entering, say about 9 o'clock, was the most magnificent one we ever beheld. The settees, which extended around the hall were occupied by ladies, and some three or four thousand ladies and gentlemen were promenading about the room in all directions, for the space was ample. The blaze of light, and the blaze of beauty, the rich decorations and rich dresses—the ensemble—was superb."

"About ten o'clock the dancing commenced. Two bands were in attendance. The Washington Band performed for the promenade, and Smith & Lovejoy's Cotillon Band for the dancing, which was under the direction of Mr. G. P. Kitteredge. The dance was kept up with much spirit until about half-past one o'clock, when the company broke up, large numbers having retired before that time. Indeed, there was a complete progress of carriages, to and from the pic nic, during the entire evening."[4]

The Golden Threads quotes a description from an unidentified source: "Every one in this vast assemblage, clad with extreme neatness, and conducting themselves with good breeding and decorum, afforded but another proof of the superiority and refinement of the class of operatives in Lowell."[5]

And a few Midwest newspapers ran a travel article, "*Lowell, A Pleasant Adventure*," which also mentioned the event:

"My guide first showed me into the building just erected, to enlarge operations in the carpet manufacture…When roofed and floored, the Company gave out invitations for a small dance by candlelight. The company amounted to the pleasant parlor full of 5000, and at one time the band was giving out music for no less than one hundred cotillon sets on the floor at once."

"—Now, my dear sir, I do not want to unhinge your steady head by dancing, nor encourage your readers to dance, but we sometimes are compelled to illustrate the good by the bad. And besides, if you can so heartily forgive Martin Van Buren his past sins on slavery, you can forgive anything, and I therefore ask you just to imagine one hundred sets of waltzers flying rapid as cotton jennies, into all the wheelings and contortions, and devious circles to be thought of, all on one floor, with room enough left on the sides and in the spaces for near 5000 spectators. It is an immense room, soon to be appropriated to the more profitable occupancy of power looms."[6]

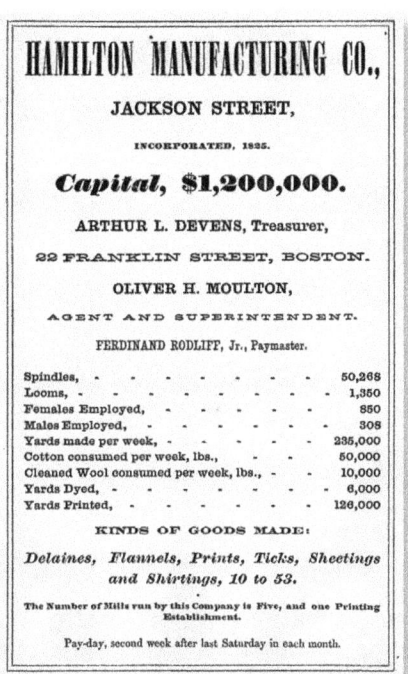

As for the Hamilton Mills 1848 event, a newspaper on July fifth reported:

"After all, the crowning affair of the day was the Pic-Nic at the Hamilton Mill—where some twelve hundred young girls, beautiful in person, elegant in dress, and graceful in manners, were gathered for a social celebration of the day, with invited guests. We have never seen a more beautiful or gratifying sight than the hall presented when the whole company was assembled; and the world could not gather a more ladylike, refined appearing body of females, from whatever station or occupation they might be chosen."

"The Nashua band was present, and gave life to the scene by its stirring music. Previous to the collation, addresses were made…; after which the company moved to the immense hall where a double row of tables was set, and most bountifully covered with a variety of refreshments…In the meantime, the dancers were getting ready, and an hour was spent in this merry, and most invigorating, as well as innocent, recreation."[7]

Next along Market Street in our tour is the Carleton and Hovey Company's building, makers of Father John's Medicine. This structure was not erected as a single entity. Instead of investing in new construction, existing buildings were combined and a new facade added.[8]

One of those older buildings was the Lynch block; it once held Patrick Lynch's Ale & Porter Depot. Mr. Lynch was a business man and made the most of his property; the upper floors included halls for rent.

It was common in the 1800s for a single hall to have multiple names depending on which regular user of the venue was hosting an event. Yet everyone seemed to know where to go. Events taking place over the Ale & Porter Depot were promoted as being at "Lynch's Hall," or, sometimes at "Hibernian Hall," given Mr. Lynch's Irish heritage and connections. Lynch's was not the only "Hibernian Hall" in the latter half of the century; announcements for Hibernian Hall events often specified Market Street, Merrimack Street, or the Howe Block on the corner of Merrimack and Prescott. Regardless, there's no question that dancing went on in the Market Street building—at least it did if a group could scrape together the rent!

"A dance will be held in Lynch's hall on Market street, Saturday evening, Nov. 18, for the benefit of Frank A. McCaffery, who is now seriously ill. This is a very worthy charity and should be well attended."—*Lowell Sun*, Nov. 4, 1882.

"An exhibition in walking, club-throwing, dancing, &c, advertised for Lynch's Hall Saturday evening, as a benefit to James Haydock, pedestrian, did not take place, the hall rent not being forthcoming."—*Lowell Courier*, Jan. 27, 1873.

Above: The Carlton and Hovey (or "Father John's") building today.

Left: The Lowell Mechanics Phalanx drills in front of the Lynch building, c.1870 (Lowell Historical Society). By November of 1871, Lynch had expanded the dormers to make a full fourth floor and was advertising halls for rent (see page 82).

Opposite top: The Market House served as the Phalanx's headquarters during the 1870s. It also held the police court where a couple was tried for suggestive dancing in 1914.

Opposite middle: 1853 Newspaper announcement for a series of dances sponsored by the Phalanx.

Opposite bottom: Mansur building, once home of Mathews Hall, seen from the corner of Market and Central. Entrance to hall was at lower left.

Across the street from Father John's is the Market House, intended to be the supermarket of its day.

"In 1837, The city government committed its first great blunder—in building the Market House. It is the fixed habit of the people to have their meat brought by butchers to their doors. To expect to change their habits by merely building a market house, was grossly absurd. Of course the experiment failed."[9] —Cowley's *History of Lowell*, 1868.

The Market House served various government purposes over subsequent years, one of them being to hold the police court and another to house the offices of the Mechanics Phalanx, a local volunteer militia. No formal dances took place in the building (although one sensational dance trial did) but the Phalanx itself frequently hosted dance parties elsewhere, often at French's Hall around the corner on Central. In 1883, the Phalanx moved its headquarters to Middle Street.

There were also multiple bands headquartered in the Market Building. The 1855 Lowell directory gives the following listings under "**BANDS OF MUSIC**."[10]

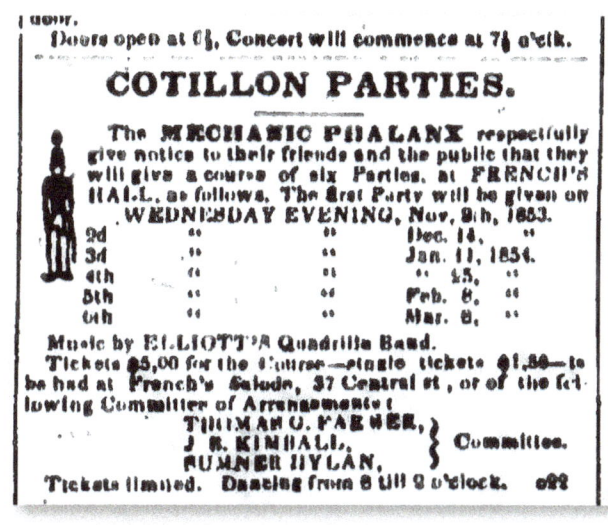

"Marble's Lowell Cornet Band. Office, over City Market. Are prepared to furnish music for any appropriate occasion, at short notice and on reasonable terms. Apply at the office or to D. Marble, East Merrimac street, or to William O. Brooks, 10 Market Street.

"Lowell Brass Band. Office, City Market. George Brooks, Leader."

Mr. Marble was also connected with another band—Eastman & Marble's Waltz & Quadrille Band—that could be engaged by applying to "D. Marble, at F. Coburn's, corner of Central and Market Streets."

Past the Market House is the New Mansur Building—what's left of the old one abuts the southern side and fronts on Central Street. When the Ingrain Weavers' meeting ended in a dance in 1894, it was in Mathews Hall in the New Mansur. The hall entry was at 97 Central.

From the intersection of Market and Central, one can see the still-ornate 1879 Appleton Bank building a block down Central. This structure replaced an older Appleton Bank at the same site. When the earlier building opened, the bank held a dance, much the way a business today might woo new customers with an open house.

"**GRAND OPENING BALL**. Messrs. Fusree & Gee would most respectfully announce to the citizens of Lowell, that they will give a GRAND OPENING BALL, at their new and splendid Hall in the Appleton Bank Block, corner of Central and Hurd streets, on THANKSGIVING EVENING, Thursday, Nov. 30th, 1848. Music by Pushes & Bend's Cotillon Band. For further particulars, see bills."—*Lowell Daily Journal & Courier*, Nov. 23, 1848.

Notice the name of the band in the announcement above. While "this guy" and "that guy" was a very common name for a dance orchestra, this group chose to name itself after either the exertions of the musicians or the moves they inspired in the dancers!

Returning our attention to the intersection of Market and Central and looking north, one is roughly at the spot from which the circa 1870 photograph at right was taken. The third building on the left side of the photo once housed French's bakery and catering service. The bakery had a dance hall upstairs, the site of many balls in the 1850s and 1860s. By the time of the photo, Benjamin Goddard had taken over the business, and the hall had become known as Goddard's Hall.

At far left in the photograph, hangs a sign for Knowles Brothers "trunks and fancy goods" store. Prior to the Knowles' occupancy, this was F. Coburn's grocery, the handy place previously cited where one could not only engage Eastman and Marble's band, but from which one might send "Drafts, notes, bills of exchange &c." via "Tuck & Co.'s Lowell & Boston Express."[11]

Goddard's was at 37 Central; Knowles Bros. was at 45. In the 1870s there was a band office between the two, that of the American Brass Band at #41.

Lastly, visible at the far end of the street in the 1870 photo is the building that held Central Hall—more on that building later.

Above: The 1879 Appleton Block today viewed from the south-west corner.

Below: That same building—midway up the right side—flaunts its original flashy roofline in this c. 1900 image.

Opposite top: An 1866 advertisement for French's Catering, and an 1855 dance card from an event at their hall (Lowell Historical Society).

Opposite middle: Looking north on Central Street, c.1870, from a stereoscope card (Lowell Historical Society).

Opposite bottom: An 1876 dance card from Goddard Hall (Lowell Historical Society) and an 1874 advertisement for Goddard's Catering.

A. B. FRENCH & CO.,

WHOLESALE AND RETAIL DEALERS IN

CONFECTIONERY AND CAKE,

37 Central Street, Lowell, Mass.

☞ Particular attention given to the MANUFACTURE of **Ice Creams, Jellies, Wedding and other Cake.**
☞ Parties supplied with **Oysters**, Scalloped, Stewed, or Raw, on the most reasonable terms. Orders promptly attended to. Strangers visiting the city can find Refreshments at every hour of the day.

UNION BALL,
— AT —
FRENCH'S HALL,
MONDAY EVENING, MARCH 5TH, 1855.

MUSIC:
GERMANIA SERENADE BAND.

Butchers' Dress Ball,
GODDARDS' HALL,
THURSDAY EVENING, DEC. 11, 1856.

Benjamin Goddard & Son,

Wholesale and Retail Dealers in

CONFECTIONERY and CAKE,

No. 37 Central St.,

LOWELL, MASS.

Particular attention given to the Manufacture of

ICE CREAMS, JELLIES,
WEDDING AND OTHER CAKE.

☞ Parties supplied with OYSTERS, Scalloped, Stewed, or Raw, on the most reasonable terms. Orders promptly attended to.

Strangers visiting the city can find Refreshments at every hour of the day.

BENJ. GODDARD.   BENJ. F. GODDARD.

The postcard image above is from three or four decades later than the preceding photo—same angle, wider view. By that time, the wedge-shaped building at center would have held the offices of Hibbard's Orchestra and American Band. The Hon. Joseph H. Hibbard was a politician, businessman, and active member of the community; his orchestra played in local ballrooms for years.

Bearing right and walking up Prescott Street, one sees a modern building sandwiched between two older ones. This structure replaced the earlier Burbank building—also known as the Shattuck building after the owner—which had a dance hall on the top floor.[12] An 1893 newspaper item also mentions the hall's use as a dance studio.

"There are three well known dancing academies in this city, first, that of Professor D. C. Lester in the new Shattuck building on Prescott Street, next that of Professor Wells in the Runels building, and third Mrs. Darrocott's academy in the same building."[13]

The hall in the Burbank/Shattuck building was commonly known as Shattuck, Burbank, or (Prof.) Lester Hall. It was replaced with rooms for rent after a 1903 fire.

Beyond the Burbank site is the Howe building, once home to Hibernian hall and frequent dances. It's likely that the hall was positioned much like the neighboring halls—that is, on the top floor. Around the turn of the century the building also housed Merrimack Square's streetcar waiting room, an important way-stop for party-goers.

Opposite top: Intersection of Central and Prescott Sts looking north, c. 1900.

Opposite middle: Band advertisement, 1907.

Opposite bottom: The Burbank building, from an 1893 advertisement.

Top: By the time of this parade on Central Street, c. 1914 (likely a Fourth of July event), the building that once held French's/Goddard's hall had been replaced by the imposing Central Block. The building at left had survived from earlier years but it—and Central Block—are now gone.

Right: Recent photo of the Howe building, once home to both Hibernian Hall and a streetcar waiting room. The modern building just barely visible to the rear of the Howe sits on the Burbank building's old site.

105

Left and below left: Postcard image of the Fairburn, c. 1900, followed by a recent photograph.

Bottom left: Looking down Merrimack Street with the Fairburn in the distance. The Fairburn's prominent spot made the roof perfect for advertising signs in the 1900s.

Right: The Keith Vaudeville Theatre with the Fairburn just beyond. (Lowell Historical Society). Although the theater has minimal frontage and looks tiny, it actually wrapped around behind the building on the left and seated in excess of 1660 patrons.

The Runels building—mentioned as home to both Prof. Well's and Mrs. Darrocott's dance academies—still stands across the intersection from the Howe. Its facade says "Fairburn," after a later owner, but it was first named for owner George Runels.

The Fairburn didn't just host dancing classes; it hosted plenty of full-blown balls in its fourth floor hall, known variously as Prescott Hall, Darracott's Hall, and Wells' Hall. One 1895 dance card gives the location as "Well's Hall, Runel's Building" in order to distinguish it from *Welles* Hall down the street. Whatever the name, the Fairburn building was a popular dance site for years. Today, the upper levels hold condos, but it's easy to picture dancers twirling past the arched windows of the top floor.

"Last evening, Prescott hall was the scene of one of the prettiest social events which has taken place in Lowell this season. It was the occasion of the annual ball of the Phillips Literary Institute and only tended to add in the laurels which the organization has already earned in the way of

entertaining. The hall was well filled with the members and friends of the institute, and the beautiful costumes of the ladies together with the conventional dress of the young gentleman made the scene a brilliant one."[14] —*Lowell Sun*, 1893.

Almost a century later, Grace May Burke, a mill worker from a family of mill workers, recalled: "That place at the corner of Merrimack, of Bridge Street now, up on the top floor there, there use to be a hall, a dance hall they called the Prescott Hall. That's where my mother and father use to go to dance years ago!"[15]

The Fairburn had another dance connection after B.F. Keith got hold of it in the early 1900s. Mr. Keith built both an office/retail building and a Vaudeville theater directly adjacent to the older building. The Fairburn itself held the theater's business offices while the new office building's primary function was generating rents.[16]

Although the structures on either side still stand, the B.F. Keith Vaudeville Theater was replaced by a parking lot in the 1970s. But for a time, the stage hosted all manner of dance acts.

"Marshall and Trebble sing and dance for twenty happy minutes and the Three Musketeers unravel a line of nonsense that simply twinkles. The Zola sisters, reflection dancers, have a real novelty entertainment and the Rolando brothers, hand balancers, round out two solid hours of enjoyment." —*Lowell Sun*, September 20, 1912.

"Boyle and Brazil, singers and dancers,… do things a la machine. They dance, giving an imitation of the famous soft-shoe dancers, Primrose and West, in an exceptionally clever manner. They finish their act with the 'lunatic dance,' which makes a very lively wind up." —*Lowell Sun*, October 8, 1912.

One can only guess at what these acts comprised. Did the Zola sisters' act include mirrors? Or did they mimic each other as if one were the other's reflection? And does "a la machine" mean in that jerky, robotic fashion that entertainers sometimes use today? Alas, the author could find no further details.

The roof of the Fairburn also offered the perfect spot for Keith's eye-catching electric sign, visible from several blocks away. *The Sun* described it as "the biggest illuminated sign that Lowell has ever seen…12 feet long by 21 high." Over twelve hundred bulbs adorned the proclamation: "B. F. Keith, high class vaudeville."[17]

Across Bridge Street from the Fairburn, is Simpson's Block, built in the late 1840s. In 1902, a new streetcar waiting room for Merrimack Square opened up in this building. It may not have been a dance site, but it most certainly saw plenty of dancers passing through. During the hot summer months at the turn of the century, the trolleys offered an economical way for residents to escape the heat of the city for the dance pavilions of Lakeview Park and its many sister resorts.

Looking back across Merrimack from Simpson's Block is Page's Clock. Installed in 1914, it became a convenient meeting place for young people about to head out for a night on the town. Anita Wilcox Lalecheur, another mill worker, explained the custom.

"Downtown, that's where we would meet. If you were going to meet anyone to go to the C.Y.A. Dance, or to take the bus to go to Lakeview to dance, that's where you met, at Page's."[18]

Street Car Waiting Room, Merrimack Square, Lowell, Mass.

Moving down Merrimack, next door to Simpson's Block is the stately Hildreth building with its distinctive bay windows. But before the Hildreth was built, it was the Lowell Museum that stood there. The museum property also housed a dance venue for some years, one known as Central Hall.

In the 1800s, the term "museum" was routinely used to make a theatrical sort of endeavor sound respectable. In actuality, such a business had more in common with a carnival sideshow or a vaudeville theater than a modern museum. The Lowell Museum is of particular interest because the building began as the Freewill Baptist Church, constructed with funds donated by the mill girls and often touted as proof of their piety.

Historian Cowley tells the story of the Freewill Baptist building as follows:

"The Freewill Baptist Church was organized in 1834. The proprietors were incorporated in 1836. The spacious edifice on Merrimack street, opposite Central street, was erected in 1837, at a cost of $20,000, which was largely

Hildreth Building, Lowell, Mass.

Left: Streetcar waiting room in the Simpson Block at the corner of Merrimack and Bridge.

Far left: Page's clock, a favorite meeting spot for young people.

Bottom left: Postcard image of the Hildreth Building that replaced the Lowell museum.

Right: Ticket to an 1875 ball held at Central Hall in the Museum building.

Below: The Lowell Museum and former Freewill Baptist Church stands in the foreground of this photograph of Merrimack Street taken about 1880.

FIFTIETH ANNIVERSARY BALL

Lowell Mechanic Phalanx,

At Central Hall, Wednesday Evening, Oct. 27th, 1875.

Admit .... with Ladies.

NOT TRANSFERABLE.

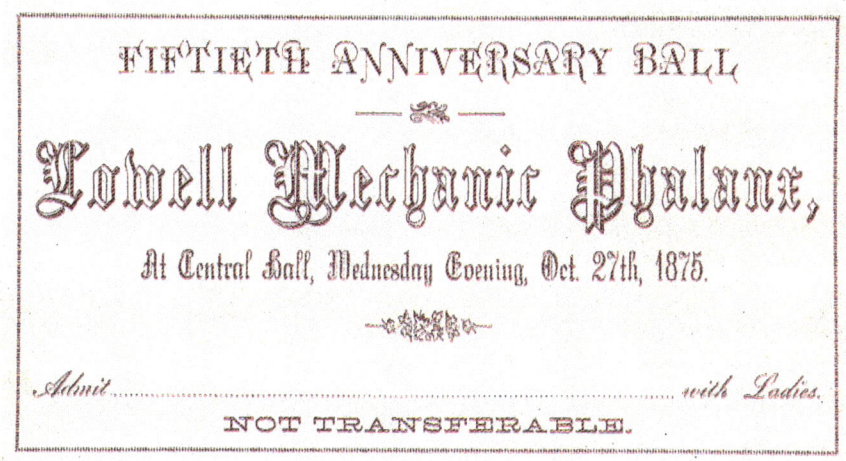

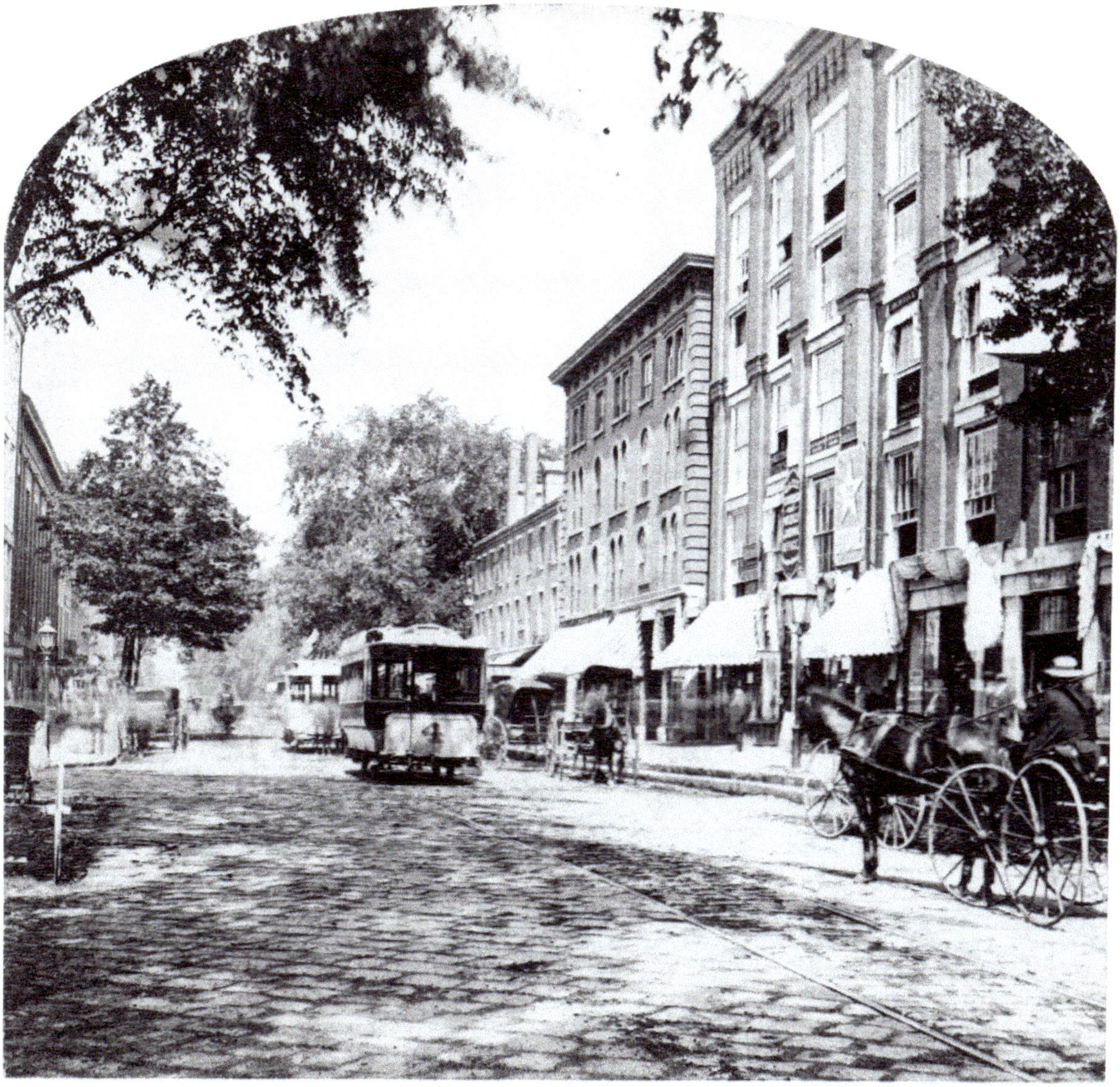

contributed by the factory girls. There preached the somewhat famous Elder Thurston, now no more; an honest man, and popular as a preacher, but incapable of managing important matters of business…Through his incapacity, more than ten thousand dollars was lost, in the course of six years, and a tremendous panic ensued…Then arose controversies about the church property…and on July 29th, 1846, the deacons were forcibly ejected…That comedy might follow tragedy, the new proprietors, Benjamin F. Butler and Fisher A. Hildreth, converted the church into a museum and theatre. After being used thus for nine years, once struck by lightning, and three times burned, in 1856, this ill-starred edifice was fitted up for a dance-hall, a bowling alley, lawyers' offices, a newspaper office, an exchange, etc…"

"More than twenty years have now elapsed since the perversion of this edifice into a museum. Let us hope that before another twenty years have rolled by, this church—the monument of the piety of the factory girls of Lowell—will be restored to its original purposes, and reconsecrated to the worship of the everliving God."[19]

A block beyond the Hildreth on the opposite side of the street is Palmer Street. Palmer was a late addition to the downtown street grid; it was cut through from Merrimack to Market in 1889.

In 1898, the four story Pollard Building, including Colonial Hall, was constructed on the east side of Palmer Street.[20] The hall was regularly used by the Middlesex Women's Club; *The Lowell Book* commented in 1899 that "by the erection of Colonial Hall in the building adjacent to the club-rooms, the Middlesex Club came into possession of an exceptionally fine auditorium."[21]

Above: Image of the Freewill Baptist Church from the September 1841 issue of The Lowell Offering.

Left: The remaining two stories of the Pollard building as they appear today.

Opposite top: This 1889 fire station was built after an earlier station and the Mechanic Phalanx's Middle Street armory were lost to fire.

Near right: 1891 architect's drawing of how the Burke Institute's Middle Street building would look when the planned remodel was complete.

Far right: Photograph of the Institute Building, home of Burke Hall, 2014.

The *Lowell Sun* described an event held in the building in 1911:

"The non-commissioned officers of Co. K. Sixth regiment, held a select dancing party in Colonial hall last evening and it proved to be one of the prettiest events of the season. The decorations were simple and of a military nature. They consisted of a line of stacked rifles with palms screening the orchestra. The ball room scene was of rare beauty, all military men in full uniform and all civilians in evening attire, while the ladies without exception were charmingly gowned."

"Hibbard's orchestra furnished an order of 20 numbers, including all the latest operatic and dance hits. The dance began at 9 o'clock and was continued until a late hour."[22]

Colonial Hall was also known as Forester's Hall—since it was regularly used by the Forester's Club—and may have sometimes been called Middlesex Hall. At some point after 1924, the upper two stories of the Pollard building were removed and with them went the hall. During Lowell's long downturn, it was not unusual for owners to demolish sections of underutilized properties to cut their tax burden; Colonial Hall may have fallen to this trend. A look down Palmer Street today reveals the remaining two stories still standing.

Diagonally across the street from the Pollard building is the former Central Fire Station, the last in a series of fire stations at the site. Part of this structure covers the footprint of what had been the Mechanic Phalanx's armory following their move from Market Street. Not surprisingly, the Phalanx celebrated their 1883 move with a dance.

"**PHALANX ARMORY DEDICATION**. The completion of improvements in the interior finishing and furniture of the armory of Co. U, Mechanic Phalanx, on Middle street, was observed Monday evening by a formal dedication, supplemented by a supper, music and dancing. About 200 guests, including many of our prominent citizens, were present by invitation, and members of the company appeared in uniform. The American orchestra furnished music, beginning with a concert from 7 to 8 o'clock, and ending in a dance lasting till 1 o'clock."[23]

The armory burned down in 1888.

In the opposite direction on Middle, around the corner from the Pollard building, is the Institute Building, once home of the Burke Temperance Institute. After the Burke organization purchased the structure from the Electric Light Company in 1891, they completely remodeled it.[24] The fourth floor held Burke hall, the site of both temperance meetings and dances.

The hall, with its twenty-three foot ceilings, still exists but is in poor shape and kept closed.[25]

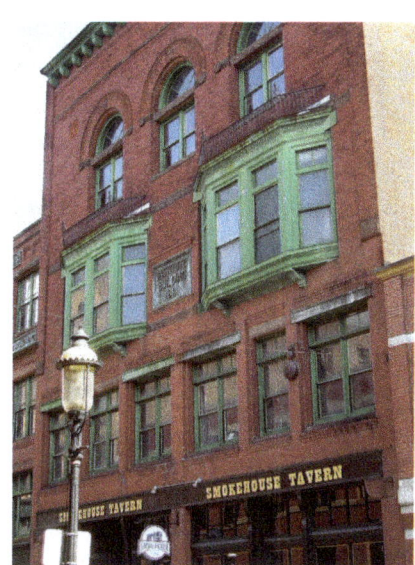

Back on Merrimack Street, right across from Palmer, is the Bon Marché Building. The right hand end of this structure was once the Railroad National Bank,[26] but before that it was the Nichols and Hutchins Building.

From the *Lowell Daily Courier*, May 8, 1873: "**Large Real Estate Sale.** Messrs. Levi Nichols and Melbourne F. Hutchins (formerly Nichols and Hutchins) have purchased the lot of land on the northerly side of Merrimack street, above John street, occupied by a ten-foot wooden building. The lot is 31 feet front by 107 deep and was purchased of the Lowell Five Cent Savings Bank. Upon it Messrs. Nichols and Hutchins design erecting this season a splendid four-story brick building, with all the modern improvements. Upon the first floor they design establishing a saloon and confectionery establishment. The price paid for the lot and building was $16,000."

Nichols and Hutchins, once employees of A. B. French & Company, had gone into business on their own and their new building included a ballroom as had French's. In the years following the purchase, rave reviews of the events held at the Nichols and Hutchins establishment began appearing in the local papers:

"One of the most enjoyable social gatherings of the season was held under the auspices of the 'J's' at Nichols & Hutchins' Hall last Wednesday evening, where about 100 young couples and many of the more elderly and staid men and matrons of our city assembled, and throwing off all restraint, joined heartily in doing honor to 'Terpsichore.' The American orchestra furnished exquisite music, and at 9:30 the grand march, headed by Floor Director John P. Quinn, was formed, and circled around the hall to the entrancing strains of the orchestra. From that time the cry went up, 'On with the dance, let joy be unconfined,' and quadrilles, waltzes, polkas, redowas, mazurkas, and galops followed in quick succession. At 12:30 an intermission was held, when the party retired to the banquet hall, where the wants of the inner man were amply satisfied by the genial caterers, Nichols & Hutchins. Returning to the ball room, the happy throng resumed the pleasures of the dance until the "wee sma' hours," when all retired to their homes with the unanimous opinion that there was a splendid time, and a desire to attend more of the 'J's' parties."—*Lowell Weekly Sun*, Feb. 18, 1882.

Above: Recent photograph of the Bon Marché building, in particular, the section that was the Nichols & Hutchins building. Despite being built in 1874, that section's facade bears a date of 1831, the year that the Railroad Bank, a subsequent owner, was incorporated.

Left: Advertisement from the 1874 Lowell Directory.

Next door to the Bon Marché is the Welles Block. Constructed in the 1840s, this building once had a third floor assembly hall[27] that housed numerous dances over the years. The event described below took place in May of 1893:

"**Alpine Ball.** Welles' hall has been the scene of many select parties, but none have been more brilliant than that of last night. The ballroom with its decorations presented a pretty sight. The walls of the room were hidden from view by pink and blue draperies; above each window and the doors the pink and blue were blended into one large rosette, from which white lace was suspended, hiding the windows from view. The ante rooms were furnished and used as reception rooms. The costumes worn by the ladies were beautiful and unexcelled on any previous occasion. The whole scene as the dancers glided over the waxed floor was really entrancing."

"Music for the dancing was furnished by Hibbard's Orchestra and 'Joe' outdid himself in his efforts to please all."[28]

Around the corner from the Welles Block, at the intersection of Kirk and Lee Streets, is St. Joseph's. This church's dances came to the attention of the author in a rather ignoble fashion when she found the following 1895 news item:

"**Latest.** Costello's Case. Now on Trial at the Superior Court. …The Vose girl was cross-examined at great length by Lawyer Henry S. Courney, the cross-examination bringing out several facts not mentioned in the direct examination."

"She said she had known Costello two months before the night of the [sexual] assault. She had met him at dances in St. Joseph's, Highland and Associate halls."[29] (More on this case can be found in the "Trolley Parks" chapter.)

Top: The Welles Building as shown on a 1916 postcard and as it looks today.

Right: Saint Joseph's Church as shown on a vintage postcard and as it looks today.

Returning again to Merrimack Street, one can look across the way to Old City Hall, built in 1830 and remodeled in 1895. *A History of Lowell and Its People* tells us "An old-time dance card of this era gives a sense of the social liveliness of the thirties. It invites to a 'Union Ball' to be held in the town hall on January 3, 1833. …One who attended this ball said in later years that it began at four o'clock in the afternoon and ended at six the next morning. He remembered that 'the bakers who carried out bread early in the morning returned with their frocks on and finished out the dancing.' The tickets were six dollars each, regarded as a stupendous price in that day and generation."[30]

To the left of Old City Hall is an empty lot that allows one to see right through to Middle Street. There were once three buildings filling up that gap along Merrimack Street and, behind them, facing Middle Street, was the Urban Block. An advertisement from 1873 reveals that not only did the Urban Block contain Urban Hall, but three smaller halls as well: Highland Hall, Russian Hall, and a banquet hall. Evidence of balls at Urban Hall can be found in local newspapers and surviving dance cards of the 1870s and 1880s, including at least one masquerade. The smaller halls were available for dance classes and private parties. The building remained standing well into the twentieth century.

And then, there is another mention of the popular and "notorious" Urban Hall in this amusing 1881 letter to the editor. Though rather long, this letter is worth quoting in its entirety for the images it offers, ranging widely from attitudes to attire, and all discussed with tongue planted firmly in cheek.

Top left: 1833 invitation to the Union Ball (Lowell Historical Society).

Above left: Recent photograph of Old City Hall flaunting its 1895 remodel.

Above right: Circa 1870 photograph looking east on Merrimack Street with Old City Hall in right foreground.

Right: Postcard image, c. 1900, with remodeled Old City Hall in foreground.

Opposite top: 1873 Advertisement for the remodeled Urban Block.

Opposite bottom: 1865 Advertisement for Brooks and Davis' Quadrille Band.

Far right: Wentworth Building, 2013.

"Editor of the *Sun*: Dear Sir, -- A few aesthetic ladies of local habitation, whose fine tastes, by too frequent contact with metropolitan chips, have been whittled down to waxen-floor prancing, are busily engaged organizing a terpsichorean society to be known as the 'Catch On' club. The name is a good one, and, although somewhat indelicate, expresses the sentiment of the originators."

"It is refreshing, in this progressive, liberal nineteenth century, to find that a woman is not considered too fine a dancer to be virtuous, as in the days of Horace; though it is as freely conceded that a woman can be virtuous without being even a good dancer. Be that as it may, novelty without morality is ofttimes fascinating, and if there is anything in a name, novelty would seem to be the force and the attraction of the 'Catch On' club."

"At present, over two dozen ladies, including some awfully nice school ma'ams, and as many gentlemen of no small account in the aesthetic docket, constitute the membership of the club. Of course, as is usual, piles of haberdashery and bushels of paint and false teeth are on hand for the grand opening of the dancing school. Everything, down to a hair pin, is in readiness, except the dancing master and the hall. The former they might get along without, but their disappointment in procuring a hall must be galling to their pride. It was hoped that Nichols & Hutchins' could be procured, but to no purpose; Urban hall was tried, but 'no go;' less notorious places were negotiated for, but with the same results. The ladies evidently suspected that financial obstacles were the principal ones in the way, for the leader, whose fertile brain conceived the enterprise, was heard to say that she believed the gentlemen's clothes were so very tight that there was no room for 'loose change' in their pockets. Be that as it may, the ladies have taken the matter into their own hands, and while they allow the gents to spend the forenoon drowning their hair in castor oil and cologne they are busy beeswaxing the floor of some fifth story attic on Central street, where they hope to 'catch-on' and trip the light fantastic toe before the winter is out. —Old Morality."[31]

Still on Merrimack, just west of Old City Hall, the Wentworth Block once housed the office of Brooks and Davis' Quadrille Band. It would have been a convenient location for the band since the building is only a stone's throw away from the intersection of Merrimack and Dutton Streets, the site of multiple dance venues.

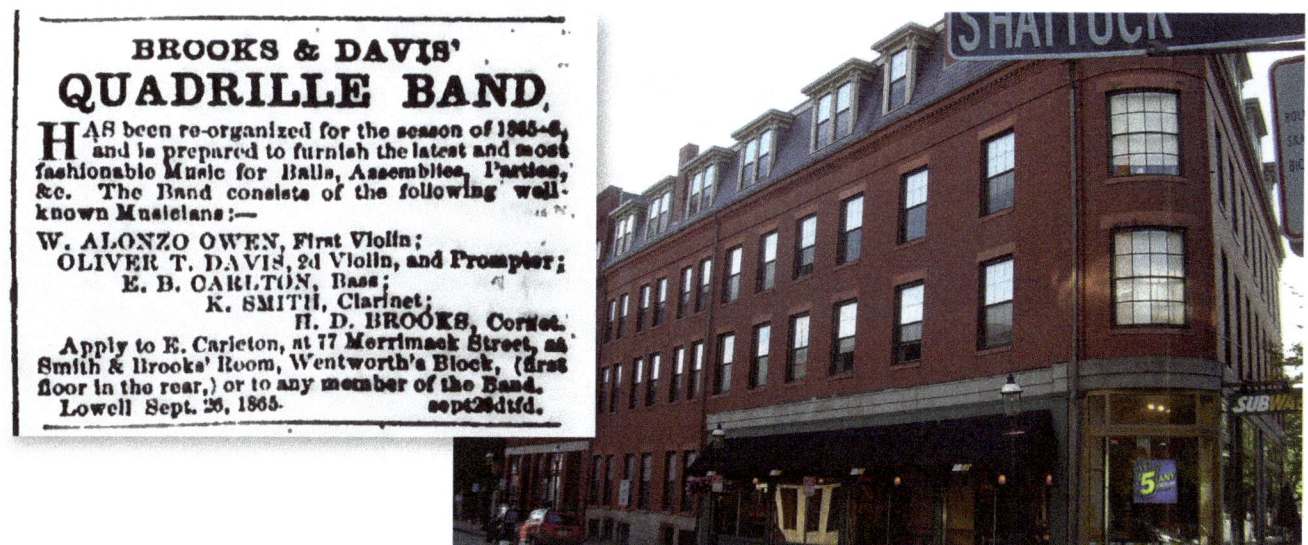

Left: Huntington Hall was over the train depot that once occupied the southeast corner of the intersection of Dutton and Merrimack Streets. The depot is shown here in 1905. Today, its facade is represented by a free-standing brick wall which is just visible through the trees at the left end of the wide modern photo below.

Middle of page: The Mechanics Hall building—shown today and in 1904—still stands a little way south on Dutton Street, although both the facade and the interior have been significantly remodeled. It can be seen just beyond the Hess station in the panorama.

Left: Merrimack House, on the southwest corner of the intersection, hosted a great many parties and dances for almost a century. A gas station is currently located at the spot. This photo is from around 1870, before the fourth floor of the hotel was added.

Right: The Associates Building with it's popular dance hall is visible on the far left of this vintage postcard image. It once stood where the Goodyear Tire store sits (to the right of the Hess station—now a Speedway station) in the center of the photo below.

Below (this page and facing): 2013 panorama of the intersection of Merrimack and Dutton Streets.

Left: Dance card for an 1890 Huntington Hall event.

Immediately below: Arches representing the front of the old Merrimack Street train depot at the intersection of Dutton and Merrimack Streets, complete with ticket window.

Below: 1856 etching of the Shattuck Street side of the depot. From all appearances, this was the public entrance to the upstairs halls.

The Merrimack Street depot was built in 1853 through a joint effort of the City of Lowell and the Boston and Lowell Railroad. Upstairs from the depot were two halls. The larger was Huntington Hall, named after the lieutenant governor at that time, and the smaller was Jackson Hall, after one of Lowell's founding fathers. Huntington was in particular demand and held concerts, lectures, strike meetings, sporting events, exhibitions, and many balls.[32]

It appears the building may not have been up to the task of hosting all those events. Cowley's *History of Lowell* tells us: "On October 28th, 1856, while that great magician, Rufus Choate, was delivering one of his most powerful appeals for the Union, in Huntington Hall, the floor suddenly settled; and Lowell narrowly escaped a catastrophe ten fold more appalling than that which Lawrence afterward suffered by the fall of the Pemberton Mill. There were assembled, not only nearly all the Lowell politicians of all parties, (whose loss would have been an infinite gain,) but more than three thousand people of either sex—as many as could stand in the hall when all the settees had been removed. The consequences of the fall of the building under such circumstances are too dreadful for contemplation."[33]

Iron trusses were used to bolster the floor, and the hall continued to be used without further incident. The building was heavily damaged by fire in 1897, rebuilt over the course of two and a half years, dedicated anew in 1900, and then reduced to ruins by a 1904 fire.

The Middlesex Mechanic Association was incorporated in 1825 as a trade guild for local craftsmen. Their building on Dutton Street was dedicated in September of 1835 and remained in the Association's hands until the end of the nineteenth century.[34] From the hall's earliest years, it was used for dancing. Both dance teachers and party organizers took advantage of the large, centrally located space.

From an 1837 newspaper: "**Messrs Stimson & Denchar**, Professors of Dancing, from Boston, would most respectfully announce to the inhabitants of Lowell, that they will commence a Day School at the Mechanicks large Hall, for the instruction of young ladies and gentlemen in the accomplishment of Dancing. In their academy will be taught Gymnastics, Quadrilles, Waltzes, Mazourkas, Gallopades, Contra Dances and Medley."[35]

And sixty years later, in 1898:
"**FINE PARTY HELD IN MECHANICS HALL**. The mid-winter German [or cotillion] conducted in Mechanics hall last evening by a party of young ladies of the Lawrence hosiery was a most enjoyable affair... There were in attendance 100 couples and the scene was inspiring and beautiful as they glided over the floor in the waltz and two-step. The decorations were not profuse, still an elegance and beauty were obtained by the tasteful arrangement of evergreen and pretty streamers of various hues. The dance order had 16 engagements, with four extras, and the dance continued until one o'clock this morning. The cake walk feature created much amusement."[36]

Some months after that party, the property was sold to the First Trinitarian Congregational Church. By 1923, it was in the hands of the Knights of Columbus who again hosted dances in the building. Damaged in the Associates Hall fire of 1924, the building was rebuilt with the current Greek revival exterior. The Knights remained owners for some years after.

Above: 1904 image of Mechanics Hall.

Left: 1912 image of the Mechanics Building when it was a church; note the decorative, sectioned windows, likely of stained glass.

The Merrimack House was one of the first hotels in downtown Lowell and opened in 1832. Built by the Locks and Canals Company as a business hotel, it played host to many visiting dignitaries including Presidents Jackson, Polk, and Pierce and future Presidents Lincoln and Van Buren. Its balcony served as a reviewing stand for processions and ceremonies.[37]

From Coburn's *History of Lowell and its People*: "One of the most celebrated of American tourists was President Andrew Jackson, who was in Lowell, June 26-27, 1833. His welcome was most cordial. The striking feature of the parade arranged in his honor, was one of 2,500 mill girls, all tastefully clad."[38]

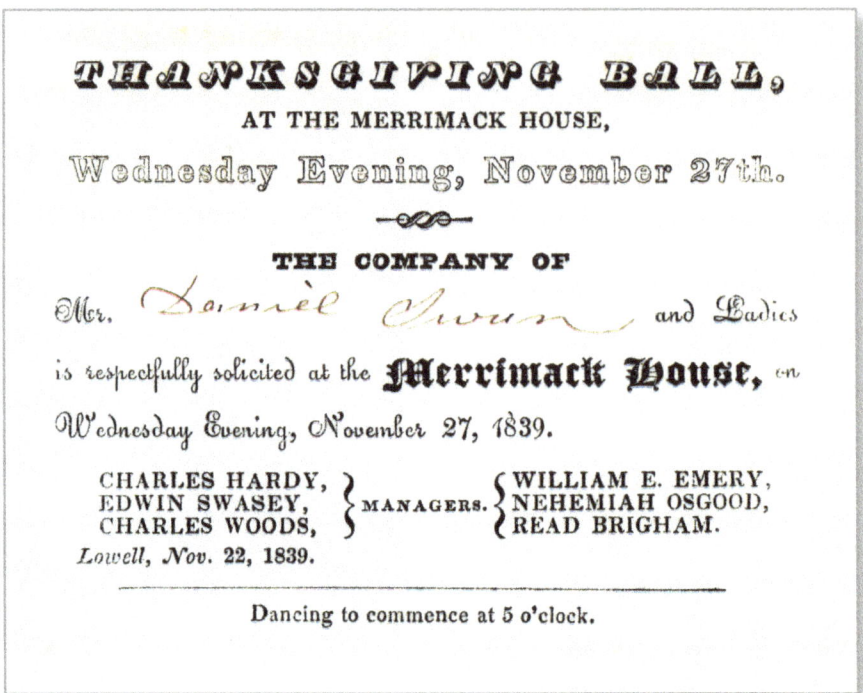

And from Cowley's *Illustrated History of Lowell*: "Clothed in white, these Lowell factory girls looked like 'liveried angels.' They walked four deep, and their beauty and their elegance of dress were greatly admired. The procession passed in review before the President, with drums beating, cannon booming, banners flying, handkerchiefs waving, and nine times nine hearty cheers of welcome."[39]

As a center of elegance and entertainment, the hotel hosted a large number of balls over several decades. In 1866 an adjoining theatre, the Music Hall, was opened offering plays, concerts and vaudeville performances. In 1872 the building was further remodeled and the fourth floor added. Around this time the "K" was dropped from the name and it became Merrimac House.

After the destruction of Huntington Hall and the depot across the way, Merrimac House gradually lost its standing as the city's premiere lodging. Converted to retail and office space in the early 1920s, then seriously damaged in 1924 by the Associate Hall fire and rebuilt, the building was finally razed in 1955.

The Associate Building was the late comer to the dance scene at this intersection. Completed in 1893, the third and fourth floors held a huge hall with all the amenities:

"The stage of considerable area is in the southerly end. There is a large balcony on three sides in which are three rows of seats, the balcony being supported by iron trusses, thus doing away with the inconvenient posts. The hall is well lighted, finely ventilated and high studded, and the seats on the floor moveable, so that the hall may be let for social purposes."[40]

Those seats were removed fairly often. One 1895 event was the Barber's Ball:

"It came naturally to the barbers to say 'you're next,' when forming sets at their dance in Associate hall last evening, for even during the happy hours of the dance they couldn't shake the cares of business although they shook their legs to the inviting music of Hibbard's orchestra."

"The feature of the intermission was to have been a shaving contest. There were many nervous people waiting to see the heroes who should submit to be shaved in a lightning contest where the hirsute adornments were to be removed in double-quick time. The contest was omitted as the Boston men who were to compete [against the Lowell barbers] did not show up. Dancing was enjoyed till one o'clock."[41]

By the time the Associate building was gutted in a spectacular 1924 fire, it was apparently holding regular, public dances. In photographs of the wreckage, the letters D-A-N-C-I-N-G can still be made out on the huge, vertical sign mounted on the front of the building.[42]

Opposite top: Invitation to an 1839 ball at the Merrimack House (Lowell Historical Society).

Opposite bottom: A vintage postcard image of Merrimac House after the fourth floor was added and the porch removed. Also, a 1907 advertisement.

Top right: A souvenir program from a 1909 Elk's Club ball at Associate Hall.

Above: 1894 advertisement from the Lowell Sun.

Right: A 1900 photograph of the Associate Building taken from in front of Lowell's current City Hall.

This brings the reader just about back to where this chapter started. To the left of the Huntington Hall arches are a few steps down to a walkway. This walkway runs next to a brick vault that once separated the Merrimack Canal from the depot straddling it.

A few steps further, past the trolley stop and through a little park, and one has returned to the Lowell National Park Visitor's Center.

In all likelihood, an old hall or two has been overlooked. There were certainly other halls in the few blocks covered—Barrister's Hall at the corner of Merrimack and Central, Sheppard's Hall at the junction of Prescott and Central, and Wentworth Hall upstairs at the corner of Shattuck and Merrimack to name a few—but the author has found no evidence that they were used to host dancing. Nor was it uncommon for hotels of the era to offer dancing, so perhaps Lowell House on Merrimack and American House on Central should have been included but, again, specifics are lacking. These sites can all be located on the 1879 map of downtown.

> *After reading a number of old newspaper stories, one realizes wryly that every ball is "the prettiest," "the most brilliant", and the women attending the most "elegant," "proper," and "charming" to be seen anywhere.*
>
> *Such P.R. nonsense!*
>
> *It reminds one of the quaint lie: "Only men perspire on the dance floor; women glow."*
>
> —Author

And there were plenty of dance halls outside of this radius, some of which are discussed elsewhere in this tome. For whether one believes dancing to be an art or a sin (or both), there was certainly a lot of it going on in old Lowell!

Above: Recent photograph of the brick arch over the Merrimack Canal that was once hidden under Huntington Hall. The Lowell National Park trolley is visible in the background.

Right: Detail from an 1856 etching showing the Lowell Museum—once the Freewill Baptist Church—a few months after one of its all-too-frequent fires. This bout of rebuilding included adding a dance venue known as Central Hall. An 1850 advertisement for the Museum appears below.

Following pages: Photos taken from City Hall tower, 1900 and 2012. The 2012 photograph is courtesy of Corey Sciuto.

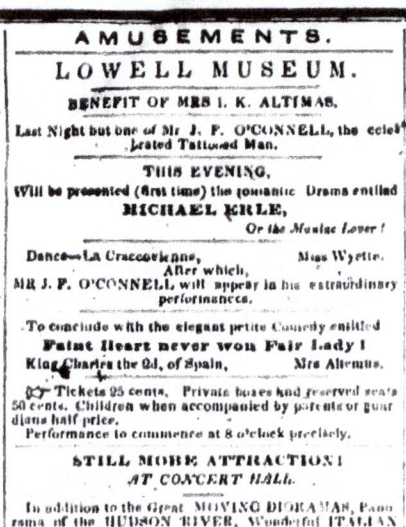

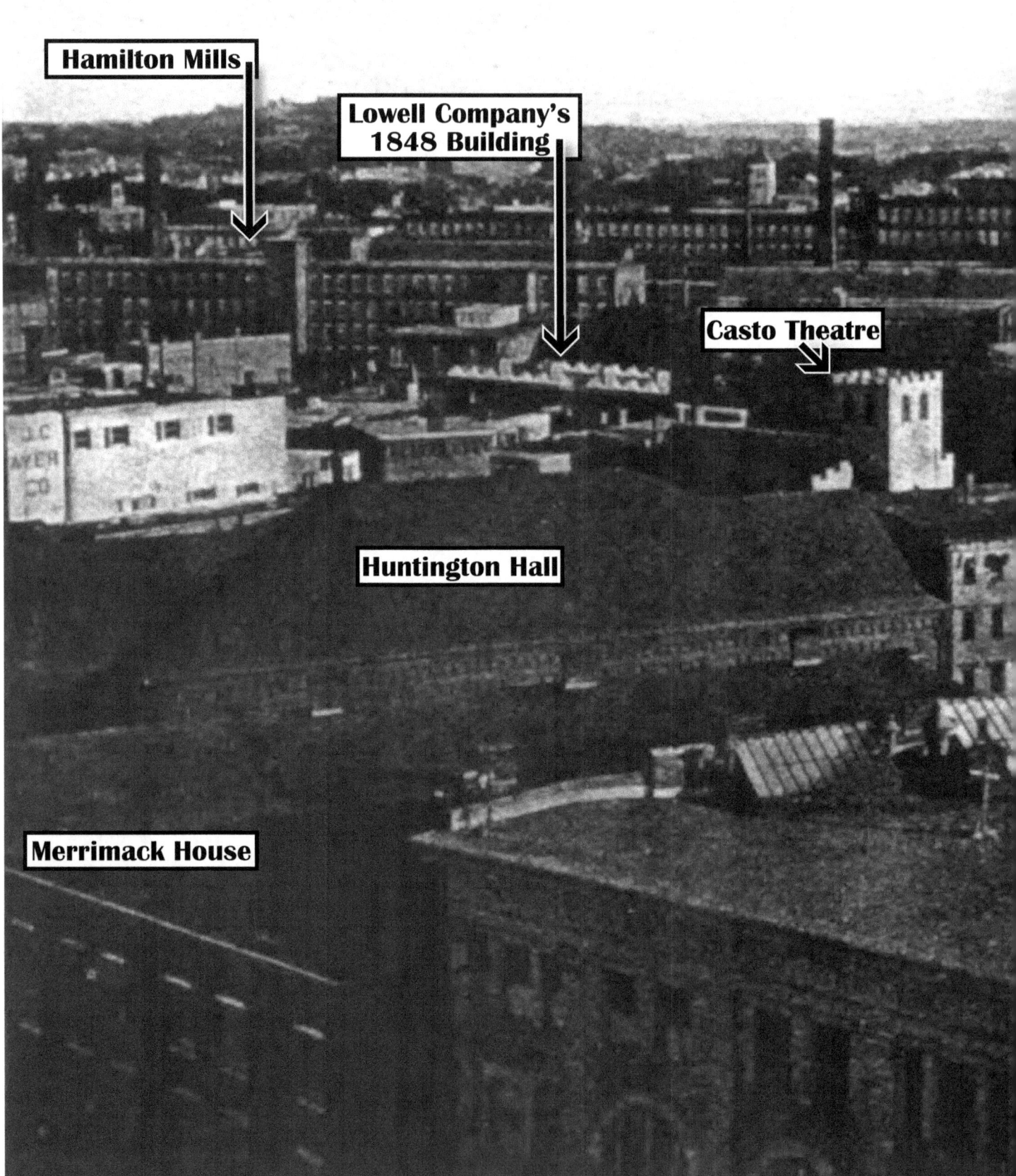

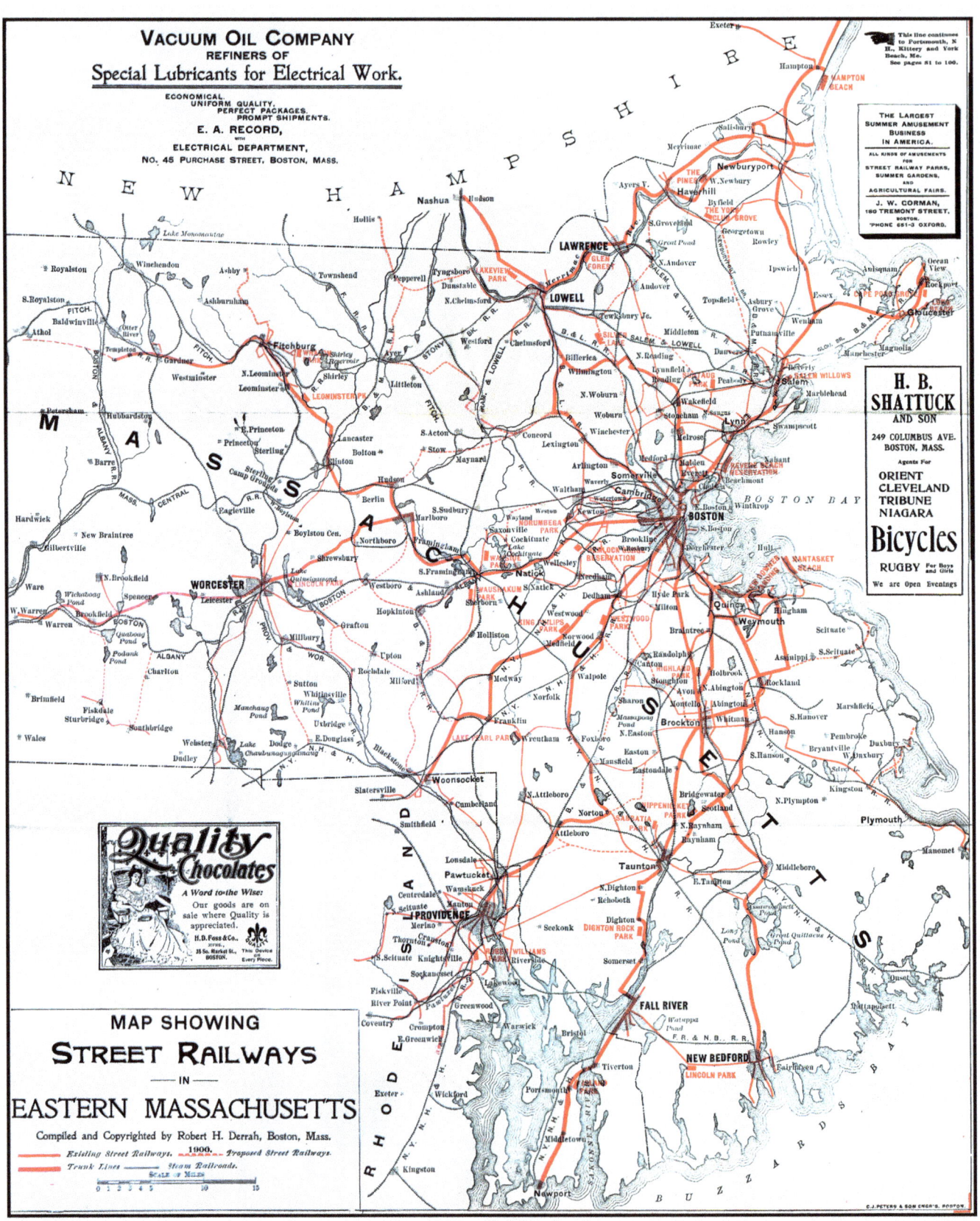

By the turn of the century a trip from Lowell to the suburbs no longer required a horse-drawn carriage or sleigh; the electric trolley had come to town. The 1900 edition of *Derrah's Official Street Railway Guide for Eastern New England* had this to say:

"In 1889, when electricity was introduced in street railway transportation, there were less than five hundred miles of street railway lines within a radius of fifty miles of Boston, carrying about 131,000,000* passengers annually. The street railways then were operated only in large cities and in their congested portions." [*Yes, six zeros is correct.]

The president of one street railway saw potential for expansion and took action:

"Building lines into the sparsely populated districts, he enhanced the value of Massachusetts realty by millions of dollars. Electric transit made homes in the suburbs possible to those of limited means and soon, from being used exclusively for business purposes, the electric cars became the means of affording country outings to those in the city at a small expense. [This] led to the construction of country lines in every direction. The cities were brought together and the farms were closer bound to the towns and cities."

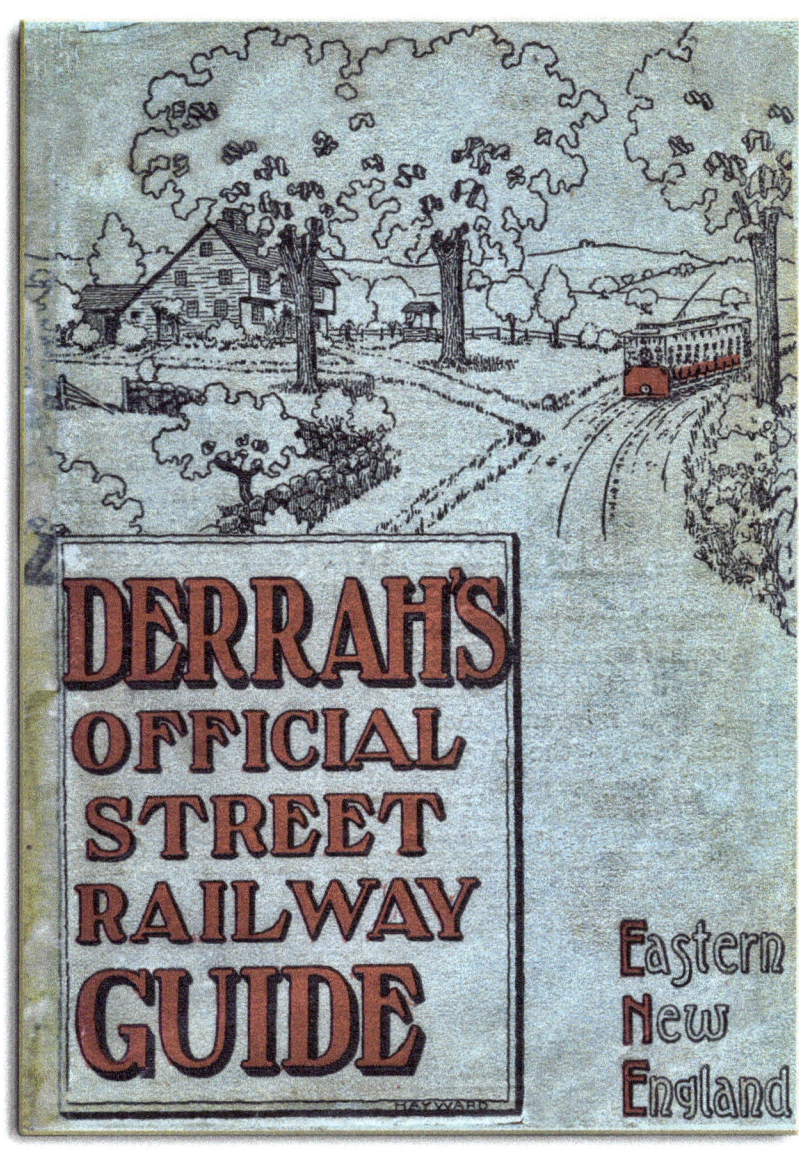

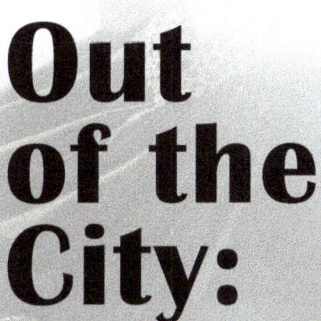

Out of the City:
The Trolley Parks

"Today 1700 miles of electric lines are directly connected with the city of Boston, running into four of the six New England States. Last year the street railways contained in this *Guide* carried over 435,000,000 passengers, and there is not a town in Massachusetts with a population of more than 3000 that has not an electric railway in operation or under construction. Many of these lines run through country districts where there is little local traffic, but where an immense income is derived purely from the pleasure travel."[1]

Ah yes, pleasure travel. In order to keep the trolley cars generating income on the weekends, and to make the rural lines more profitable, rail companies began purchasing land for recreation areas along their train routes. Picnic groves and dance pavilions were staples of these leisure destinations.

Opposite page: Fold out map from inside cover of Derrah's Official Street Railway Guide *showing street car and steam railways.*

Above: Cover of 1900 railway guide for Eastern New England.

For the residents of Lowell, Lakeview Park in Dracut was the nearest of the trolley resorts. Derrah's guide describes Lakeview Park as "a popular summer resort, among the attractions of which are a spacious pavilion, a fleet of boats, and a steamer which plies regularly to Mountain Rock Grove, a part of Lake Mascuppic, which has been richly endowed by nature. In addition there are the usual park conveniences and a rustic theatre."[2]

Articles about Lakeview appeared in local papers regularly, as well as advertisements touting its wonders:

From the *Lowell Sun*, August 24, 1894: "HIGH TIDE IN PATRONAGE. Yesterday was the banner day for a crowd at Lakeview, and the principal reason was the return of hot weather. Almost continuously from 11 A. M. till 8 P. M., the cars were crowded, and between 6:45 and 7:45 P.M., the rush at the square was almost too great for handling by the cars available at Lakeview, the crowd overflowing everything, the theatre, dance hall and bowling alleys, and as it was a delightful day and evening the grove and pavilion plazas were favorite places of resort."

The *Lowell Sun*, Aug. 12, 1918: "LAKEVIEW PARK. Where is the best dancing floor in Lowell or vicinity? Where is the best dance music to be found? Where is the best time to be had at the least expense? Ask Johnny Onestep. He knows; It's at Lakeview park that you'll find this pleasing, trouble-chasing combination, and don't let old Bill Bay State chase you away from it."

"Where are ideal picnic grounds, woodsy, yet with all conveniences? Where is the best place to take the children away from the hot sun and muggy weather? Ask any mother. It's Lakeview park, with its stately trees, its shady paths, its safe and sane amusements, its comforts, its accessibility."

"Line up for the end-of-the season frolic, now being prepared by the Lakeview management. It'll be worth going to."

Recollections of the dance hall at Lakeview Park—and the trolley ride it took to get there—appear frequently in oral histories gathered from Lowell's mill workers.

From Valentine Chartrand: "When I first started to go out I was always going out with girls. …I used to go out with them once a week to the dance at lake, at the Lakeview. They had a big ballroom there."

"I only went out once a week and I had to be home at 10:30. And I can see my dad even today. He's been gone over forty years. I can still see him. He had a stick in his hand and he was sitting near the stove. We had a coal stove, a big house, and we heated up by coal. And he'd be sitting near the stove in the winter time, and he'd be looking at the clock. …You go to the dance, and the dance started at 8:30 then, I think, [and at] 9:30 I had to decide to come back to Lowell to get the trolley to go home near Tewksbury. And it was hard to do… [after only the] one hour you could have up there."[3]

From Edward Hart: "You know where Lakeview is out there, way out? You went out there for a nickel. We went to Lakeview to a dance hall. And you bought six checks for a quarter. Check dancing, you know."

"…you never went with a girl. A guy taking a girl out there was unheard of. You met them out there even if you were going with them. She went with her friends and you met them out there. And you'd dance with them and then take her home, but you never [went out there with her]. Never went, and you knew where every girl was. If she wasn't in that section, she wasn't there.."

"[As for the trolley to] Lakeview,…they'd let anybody on there, to make money. It was overcrowded. And the [conductor] would go from one set of seats to the other and you would be hanging on and he'd be getting on the outside of you. And he'd try to remember who just got on the last stop so he could collect. And coming in from Lakeview, why the only place they weren't on was on the roof!"[4]

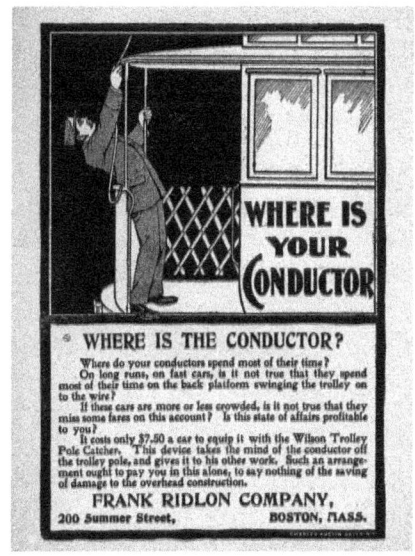

And from Edward Harley: "There was an amusement park there at the time too, and a very large dance hall that was very, very popular. And the amusement park had a roller coaster, and bobby horses and dodgeums, eating spots, drinking spots. The dance hall was a very, very attractive place. In the summer you were right out on the lake."

"You would mingle, you'd go with people from your own neighborhood, but you would go out and dance with the people from other neighborhoods. You would meet people from other neighborhoods. …there was no turf here. You'd be neutral… There was fights of course, but those came about just because of the arrogance of youth."[5]

Oral histories aside, there were other, less favorable opinions of Lakeview and its sister trolley parks. Ms. Chartrand's strictly enforced curfew and Mr. Hart's insistence that a man never, *ever* took a woman with him on a jaunt to Lakeview hint at what might have been going on beyond the welcoming glow of the dance pavilion.

When Patrick Costello was charged with "carnal abuse" in 1895, one of the headlines stated "The Testimony Shows the Influence of Lakeview." As mentioned in the Downtown Halls chapter, the woman making the accusations had met Costello at various dances around Lowell, but it was the trolley park connection that rated headline status.

The rape was reported to have occurred in Costello's room at the Shattuck Building (a.k.a. the Burbank Building and one of the downtown dance sites). The victim and her friend claimed to have gone to his room willingly but then had been locked in. Once Costello appeared to be asleep, they, too, lay down—one would think that that would have been a good time to try to escape instead of napping—and that's when the assault occurred. Despite their odd story and some question about their reputations, the jury deadlocked with a 6–6 split.[6] Some months later while awaiting a retrial, and after almost a year in jail, Costello pleaded guilty. He was sentenced to the Concord reformatory for an unspecified term.[7]

Far left: Flyer handed out on the Lowell Highlands trolley car, Friday evening, August 12, 1892.

Left: Lakeview pavilion, as seen on a 1908 postcard.

Top right: Advertisement for a Trolley Pole Catcher, a device that allows a conductor to focus on collecting fares instead of monitoring the trolley wire.

Above: Lowell Sun *advertisement, June 14, 1902.*

But the Costello case only involved the park's *influence*. Much more damning of parks like Lakeview than being associated with a rape was this statement from the Massachusetts Commission for the Investigation of White Slave Traffic in 1914:

"The dance halls of many recreation parks in the suburbs of the cities as well as in the country—with no effective supervision, with the near-by fields and woods and the darkness—are freely used for purposes of prostitution. Not only do well-known professional prostitutes ply their trade in these dance halls at parks and recreation resorts, but here also pimps and procurers and other immoral men resort to take advantage of innocent, pleasure-seeking young girls. The evidence is indubitable that the seduction of many young girls occurs in recreation parks as at present conducted. The investigators actually witnessed the most gross and open immorality at several parks and seashore resorts."[8]

In the end, the downfall of the trolley-linked recreation parks was not the misbehavior of patrons. It was the automobile. As car ownership grew, trolley ridership fell, and pleasure-seekers had a vast landscape to explore away from the confines of the rail routes. Not only that, but to the newly independent drivers, the 10–15 mile per hour pace achieved by the trolleys with their frequent stops—similar to the speed of today's city buses—seemed insufferable. Lakeview and most of its kin are distant memories now.

But in the trolley parks' heyday, the sites dotted the landscape and were linked by a network of street railways and steam railroads. If revelers from Lowell got tired of Lakeview's dance hall, there were plenty of other facilities in Eastern Massachusetts and Southern New Hampshire to choose from. If they didn't mind a bit of a ride, that is!

Left: Page from Derrah's Guide *showing several Merrimack Valley attractions.*

Above: Image from vintage corset advertisement.

Above: Recent photograph by Meyer Billmers of a dance pavilion at Pinewoods Camp, Plymouth, MA.

Below: Image from vintage postcard.

> There is at least one dance camp in Massachusetts that still has the open dance pavilions that the parks favored in the days before air conditioning. There, the well-worn path through the trees to the pavilion is full of dancers coming and going, and beneath the sloping roof there is light and music, warmth and camaraderie. Between sets, when the fiddles are silent—and if the talk and laughter aren't too loud—one can hear the wind rustle in the trees; one feels cool air wash across warm skin. And the primal darkness beyond the railings tingles with mystery.
>
> It's easy to see how girls were led astray in such a setting. A relaxing stroll away from the crowded dance floor could turn into something else entirely—whether wanted or not. It happened in the mill girls' day; it happened in mine; and I'm sure it will keep happening as long as humans are humans.
>
> But some things *have* changed. It's been decades since a woman's "honor" referred to her virginity, at least in the United States. And birth control has come a long way in the past century. My peers might have found a bit of pine needle caught in their hair the morning after the dance and smiled fondly at the memory. A hundred years ago, a young woman might make a similar discovery and feel her stomach knot—for the bit of pine only served to remind her that both her reputation and her prospects for the future were now irreparably damaged.   –Author

Fifteen miles north of Lowell—easily accessible from Lowell, Lawrence, Haverhill, and Nashua—is Salem, New Hampshire. Trolley lines arrived in Salem in 1902 (Salem was not yet a stop on the 1900 time table at right). Within eight weeks of the first Salem trolley, the Hudson, Pelham, and Salem Railways opened Canobie Lake Park. Originally, the resort included canoeing, sporting events, the Circle Swing, picnics, and the Penny Arcade.[9] But by 1912, the park also had the dance hall shown below.

During the 1920s the railways lost increasing numbers of riders to the automobile. The Salem rail line was abandoned in 1929, and the park closed shortly thereafter. In 1932, a new owner refurbished the park, brought in a roller coaster, and reopened Canobie Lake Park.[10]

Despite some lean years, more ownership changes, a hurricane, robbery, and the demise of so many other amusement parks, Canobie Lake Park has managed to survive and, in recent years, thrive. The park still boasts a Dancehall Theatre down by the lake—presumably evolved from the old Dance Hall—but without the public dancing that once defined it.

Dance Hall, Canobie Lake Park.

In Lunenburg, about 25 miles west of Lowell, was Whalom Park, established by the Leominster and Fitchburg Street Railway in 1893. *Derrah's Guide* extolls: "No higher tribute can be paid to the park than the fact that picnic parties return there year after year." The park included halls, rides, boats, picnic tables, a bandstand and stage, and "other attractions of a kindred nature."[11] The popularity of the dance hall is clear in this circa 1900 image.

Alas, picnickers did not keep returning forever. Whalom closed its doors and was dismantled in 2000.

Dance Hall, Whalom Park, Mass.

The Grounds & Skating Pavilion, at the Pines, Groveland, Mass.

In Groveland, well northeast of Lowell, was a "great pleasure ground on the banks of the [Merrimac] river known as The Pines. Here [were] boats, swings, a dancing hall, a pavilion, an electrical fountain and other attractions."[12] One might guess that the skating pavilion shown at left doubled as a dance hall, a common occurrence at the time.

Originally developed by the Bay State Street Railway, the area was purchased by the town in 1950 and today includes sports facilities, nature trails, and picnic sites.[13]

To the southeast of Lowell, and a bit of a trolley ride away, was Suntaug Lake Park. The park itself was one of the simpler recreation areas, consisting mostly of tennis courts, picnic areas, and a boathouse, but Suntaug Inn on its northern edge was another story. The Inn boasted lavishly furnished rooms,[14] open-air dining, and a ballroom; it was South Lynnfield's largest structure during the nineteen-teens.[15]

The Inn was popular through the 1920s, 1930s, and 1940s, but its last American Hotel Association's guidebook listing was in 1956.[16]

Also appearing on the railway map is Lake Pearl Park in Wrentham. Although too far away for Lowell residents to have visited much, it was another active trolley park known for its ballroom. Today, the Lake Pearl site is a 25-acre function facility popular for weddings.[17]

Interior of Dance Hall, Lake Pearl.

If it was a day at the ocean that a vacationer from Lowell wished, there were numerous spots along the coast from which to choose. In 1880, the Naumkeag Street Railway Company opened an amusement park in Salem, Massachusetts that became known as "the Willows." The park offered a wide variety of activities and kept its reputation wholesome by banning alcohol.[18]

Salem Willows has undergone plenty of changes over the years but is still a favorite summer spot for many. The Dancing Casino shown below is today an arcade.

134

The Hampton Beach Casino in New Hampshire ("casino" then being a highfalutin' term for social hall or building) was built by the owner of the Exeter, Hampton and Amesbury Street Railway Company. First opened on July 4, 1899, the second floor held, among other things, a large hall for dancing and other entertainments. The building was remodeled in the 1920s with a ballroom big enough for 5,000.[19]

The Casino remains the centerpiece of Hampton's boardwalk today. The 1927 ballroom lives on as a concert and comedy venue.

While Hampton Beach was the northern-most of the area's ocean-side trolley resorts, Nantasket Beach was the southern-most. Its Atlantic Park was built in 1868 but was later replaced by the stunning Paragon Park.[20] Built by the Eastern Park Construction Company, Paragon Park opened June 10, 1905 as a mini world's fair with everything from Japanese temples to Wild West shows, and arcades to fun houses. The park also had a zoo with bears, monkeys, apes, waltzing mice, kangaroos, pythons, pheasants, parrots and peacocks.[21]

And there were dance halls. Palm Garden's hall eventually became known as the Chateau Ballroom. A story about opening day reported: "In the big dance hall, where the veranda is fanned by the ocean breezes, merry sessions hold forth from the opening of the park until the last boat leaves, at 10:30 P.M."[22]

A second dance hall was built around 1917 as shown in the postcard at left.

Much of the park was destroyed by fire and rebuilt in 1963. The park finally closed for good in 1985. Today, only the carousel remains.

135

At Salisbury Beach in northern Massachusetts, there were multiple dance pavilions; the 1908 postcard at right shows Columbia Dance Hall (Round Hall) to one side of the trolley stop and Montgomery Dance Hall (Square Hall) to the other. Columbia was built to house a carousel but served some time as a dance spot.[23] The image below of Montgomery makes it clear just how in-demand dance space was!

Another dance pavilion was Ocean Echo. Covering almost an acre and jutting out over the water,[24] it hosted free dance lessons for children.

In 1931, Massachusetts set aside Salisbury Beach State Reservation "in order to give the people of Lowell, Lawrence, Haverhill, Newburyport, and the entire Merrimack valley, a place where they might recreate amid surroundings of natural beauty...with clean amusements furnished by chic business men at the beach."[25]

Today, nothing remains of those "chic businesses;" the state park's main amusement is the beach itself. Rides and arcades outside the park's boundaries eventually fell on hard times and they, too, are all but gone.

For trolley excursions in the Cape Ann area, *Derrah's Guide* offers: "Another branch to Long Beach affords a popular trip. Here are found, in addition to sea bathing on a beautiful sandy beach, a pavilion and dancing hall, bowling alleys and other popular attractions."[26]

It seems that that Pavilion was also a hotel—or at least it was by the time it burned in the mid-1960s—but it included a ballroom right to the end.[27] The Cape Ann Motor Inn currently stands on the spot.

Closer to Boston, development of Revere Beach as a summer resort began in the 1830s; the spot was accessible via the Eastern Railroad as early as 1838. The Boston, Revere Beach, and Lynn railroad built their own spur in 1875. After the Great Ocean Pier was built in 1881—and a dancing pavilion built upon it—ferry service to Boston and Nahant ran every thirty minutes.[28]

The Metropolitan Park Commission took control of Revere Beach in 1896. After some improvements, it was reopened as the nation's first public beach on July 12, 1896.[29]

By 1918, dance sites at Revere Beach included the Ocean Pier Dancing Pavilion, Condit's Dance Hall, Crescent Garden Dance Hall, and the Nautical Ballroom.[30]

The Revere Beach of the past faded gradually until many of its remaining structures met their end during the Blizzard of '78. Revere Beach Reservation was declared a National Historic Landmark in 2003 and the site has since undergone major revitalization.[31]

By the beginning of the twentieth century, Lowell faced challenges on several fronts. Water power may have made the city great, but coal-produced steam had become Lowell's primary power source, a source equally available elsewhere. The northeast no longer had a monopoly on textile manufacture. Benefits such as ease of access to ocean shipping, proximity of raw materials, cheap labor, and lower tax rates began to draw companies away. The Trade and Labor Council of Lowell expressed their concern for the future in *Lowell: A City of Spindles*:

"It is early yet for any one to say that manufacturing [in Lowell] has reached its declining turn, and it is hoped that such may not be the case for years to come, if ever; but, in this rapid going age, with unforeseen developments springing up mushroom-like, our solidity may at any time be shaken and our future rendered unstable. This city, once called the 'Manchester of America,' has been fairly outstripped in the cotton enterprises of sister cities. Remembering our fair name of the past and present, let us hope and trust that these large enterprises may live long and prosper."[1]

Others dismissed the "Menace of Southern Competition" as "fantasy" and claimed that southern factories had "propagandists" who extolled the benefits of southern locations so insistently that it became fashionable to predict that Lowell was doomed. In response, these Lowell supporters argued that certain factors "favoring continued prosperity of the cotton industry in New England" had been overlooked.

The 1900s Arrive:

Ragtime Dances Come to Town

"They ignored the truth that with millions of unclad and half clad people in the world there was room for all the factories of both sections. The value of experience passed on from generation to generation of textile workers was not always properly appreciated. Pessimism, likewise, failed to take into account the larger reservoirs of quick capital which are available in thrifty New England."[2]

An article in the *Lowell Sun* on January 1, 1901 went even further denying that hard times might lie over the horizon, predicting instead a glorious future for Lowell.

"Our city has been dependent mainly upon the mills for support but in the coming century we anticipate an influx of new industries to bring about a healthy diversity."

"The population, now 95,600, will undoubtedly be 200,000 at the end of the next century" [the actual population in 2001 was just over half that] "and by that time Lowell will have absorbed all the suburban towns, such as Dracut, Chelmsford, Tewksbury and Billerica. The work of building up this greater Lowell has already begun [with the proposed] annexation of Wigginville."

"After the annexation of Wigginville, will come that of Dracut, Chelmsford, and other towns: and this will lead to the laying out of new parks, wider streets and in general better public thoroughfares. It will also result in the development of land now vacant. Some streets thickly settled at the present time will be occupied by a different class of people while the present

Left: Vernon and Irene Castle, the best known American dancers of the Ragtime era, doing the Castle Polka.

Right: One of a number of mill buildings constructed even as Lowell's textile industry was beginning to slide; this 1910 cotton picker and power house on Market Street is today slated to become high-end condos.

139

residents will move outward to the more healthful suburbs. This migration of population has been going on for some years past. As the residents of Lowell move outward they promote the conditions that will eventually bring about the absorption of the outlying towns for miles around."

"This will be the greater Lowell, the Lowell of the 20th century, extending far beyond the angle enclosed by the confluence of the Merrimack and Concord rivers, yet using both for drainage and water power."

With such wildly differing opinions regarding the future of Lowell's textile industry, management strategies varied widely. When Bigelow Carpets bought up Lowell Manufacturing's property on Market Street in 1899, they invested heavily in new construction, as if building for a bright future. Meanwhile, new managers at the Boott focused on lowering labor costs and did little to update buildings or machinery, deciding instead to squeeze out every penny possible for as long as they could.

Even as the cotton business was moving south, other textile industries were taking up some of the slack. Woolen and worsted operations became central to Lowell's mills. Both silk and artificial silk—more commonly known as rayon—joined the local manufacturing landscape.

Other changes were taking hold in Lowell, just as they were across the nation. Prohibition inched closer to becoming law, as did women's suffrage. In nearby New Hampshire, Democratic Chairman Carr went on record in favor of a women's right to vote.

"Believing that whatever adds to the intelligence of the ballot makes for good government, I believe that we should declare that the right to vote should be extended to our wives, our mothers and our sisters, under the same restrictions that should apply to us, to be exercised by them as unites of duty and public advantage." —*Lowell Sun*, September 10, 1902.

When the suffragists gained ground in the Granite State, the *Lowell Sun* declared: "Massachusetts and other neighboring states would like to see woman suffrage given a fair trial in New Hampshire." —February 5, 1903.

Above: After being purchased by Bigelow Carpet in 1899, the Lowell Manufacturing site on Market Street underwent major remodeling in the first decades of the century. The 1909 spinning mill above—now condos— was only one of a half dozen buildings constructed during that period.

Left: Bigelow moved its operations to Connecticut in 1914 and the buildings were gradually sold off. Lowell Silk Mills set up shop in the former Bigelow Weave Mill for a time; today it houses the Lowell Visitor's Center, among other things.

Right: Victrola advertisement, c.1915.

Social upheavals aside, the new technologies available to Lowell's citizens were a source of wonder!

"...the invention of the electric telegraph, the telephone, the phonograph, and last and most wonderful of all, wireless telegraphy. Who will deny after witnessing such marvellous inventions as these that the flying machine is a certainty of the near future? With steam and electricity, we have annihilated space and overcome the law of gravity."

"At present we know that [liquid air, as it was earlier called,] is one of the most subtle and potent elements yet wrung from nature's treasure house. When Ben Franklin drew electricity from the clouds, he knew that the element existed, but what raptures would have filled him could he have foreseen the multiplicity of wonderful developments that have ensued and have been given to the world, mostly through the genius of our own Edison."

"With such a record for the past century, no human mind can conceive the possibilities of the coming century." —*Lowell Sun*, December 31, 1900.

To the dancers of Lowell, the phonograph must have been a particularly welcome innovation. No longer did they have to engage a professional musician, or be at the mercy of whichever amateur present might be able to squeeze out a tune. For those who could afford such a machine, the latest music by the best artists was there at the turn of a crank any time the mood struck them.

By the time Lowell's well-to-do were investing in phonographs for a little "impromptu dancing," the elaborate patterned dances popular in the late nineteenth century had fallen from grace. The old Valse à Deux Temps—sometimes called the "Ignoramus Waltz" because of its lack of fancy footwork and its appeal to the less disciplined—was not only the waltz of choice, but had also become popular in two-quarter time.

Lloyd Shaw, a mid-twentieth century dancer and dance historian, says of the Valse: "...done to 2/4 time, it becomes a simple two-step. It was a step with the left, and a close with the right on the first beat, and a step-hold on the second beat. Then a step with right and a close with the left on the next beat and step and a hold with the right on the next."[3]

The same author writes that "the two-step is nothing more nor less than a Galop or Gallopade, with a change of direction or lead for each measure."[4] In other words, very much like a tamped-down Polka.

Mr. Shaw also writes: "In discussing the history of the two-step, it is necessary to point out that by the beginning of this century it had taken the field. It had crowded almost everything else off our dance floors. In my own college days I remember that the dance program alternated two-step and waltz, two-step and waltz and nothing else. When the musicians played a waltz, we all did a two-step to 3/4 time—we didn't waltz. Of course, we didn't know it. We thought we were waltzing. Then the orchestra played a piece in duple rhythm and we all two-stepped. Our whole evening was nothing but two-step, regardless of what the orchestra played and we pushed the girls around, stiff in their heavy corsets, and I didn't like dancing at all. I hated it. I think now I know the reason why. No one can survive a steady diet of nothing but two-step."[5]

Lowell's dancers may have fared a bit better, being part of staid New England with its Yankee fondness for all things tried and true. The Lowell dance programs of the period always seem to have a few contras, quadrilles, or schottisches tucked in amidst all those two-steps and so-called waltzes. The program at the bottom of this page is from the Lowell Elks' 1909 concert and ball at Associate Hall.

But, despite Shaw's two-step overdose, the two-step had its advantages. In 1914, Vernon and Irene Castle called it "the biggest romping dance that we have ever had."[6] Fifty years earlier, French Dancemaster Cellarius had defended the two-step's predecessor, the Valse à Deux Temps, as particularly enjoyable for the dancers:

"...they spring with that fascinating vivacity—which the waltz à deux temps alone permits—relaxing or quickening their pace at will, promenading their partner in every way, now obliging her to fall back, now themselves retreating, going to the right, to the left, varying their pace almost at every step..."[7]

Although it still was not a true lead-follow dance, once this less-structured waltz morphed into a two-step, and the two-step became widely popular, the door was open for the lead-follow dances that came after. The music for dancing was changing, as well. When the two-step first became popular, it was often danced to march music.

"Then came the vogue of the Two Step, with its Sousa music and its swift tempo," wrote the Castles. "There was neither dignity nor beauty in the fast Two Step; but every piece of music that lived to be whistled and hummed in those days was set to Two Step time."[8]

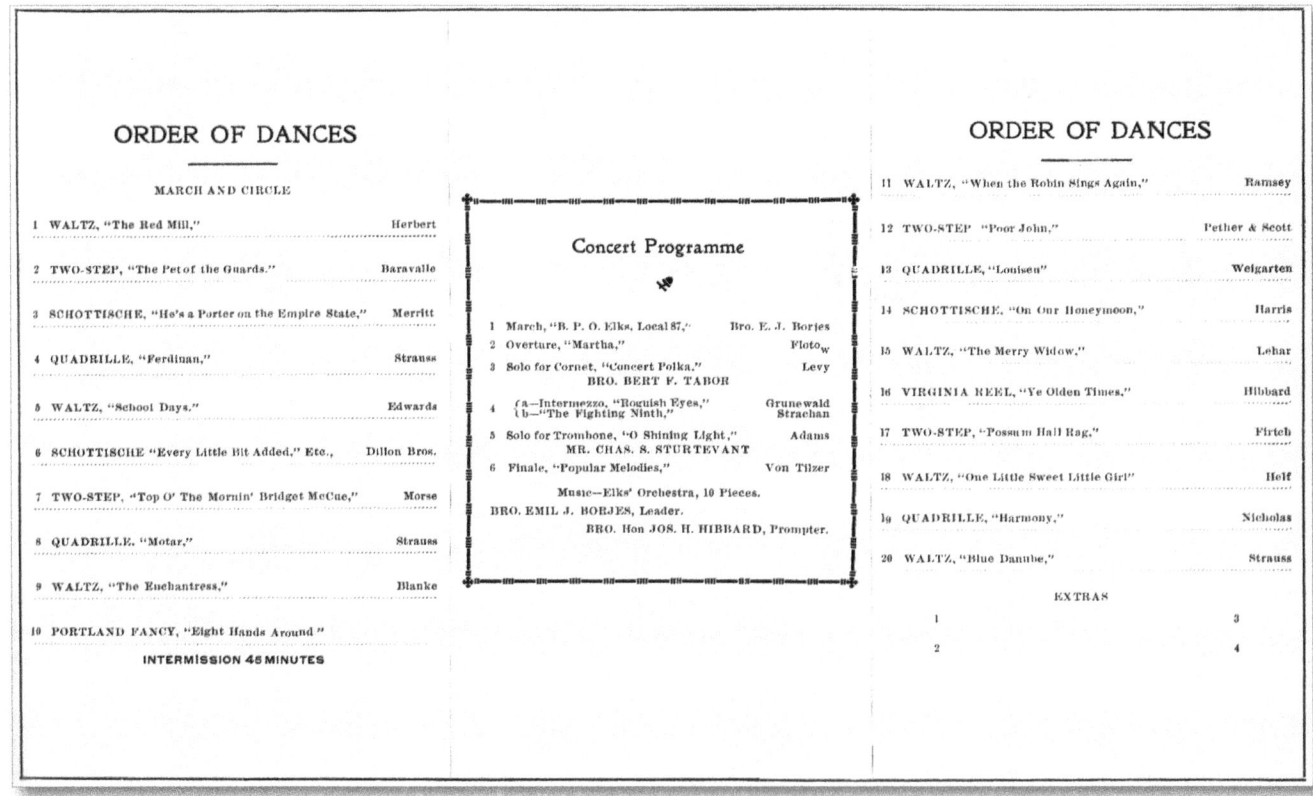

The Castles continue: "Then came the rag, the rag with its syncopated tempo and its subtle phrasing."

Originally associated with itinerate black piano players,"ragtime" music first caught the attention of the wider public at Chicago's 1893 World's Fair. By applying intricate African rhythms to more familiar tunes, such as Sousa's beloved marches, musicians produced a uniquely American style of syncopated—or "ragged"—music.

Scott Joplin's famous *Maple Leaf Rag* (excerpt below) offers a clear example of traditional versus rag rhythms. The bass line moves along with the notes falling on evenly spaced beats. The melody line, however, starts just *after* beat one. And the longer notes, which receive added emphasis by virtue of their length, are in totally unexpected places.

Ragtime swept the nation, and for the next two decades it was the defining music of the era. The style was warmly embraced by the dancing public—the vast majority of rags were perfect for two-stepping!

Not everyone loved Sousa *or* ragtime. The *Sun* ran a letter in 1902 slamming the Lowell Orchestral Society's playlist.

"A leader who held to the highest ideals would never make room in his repertoire for such inanities as Sousa's stuff—Sousa, who has done more harm to the cause of legitimate music than any one in America, not even excepting the manufacturers of 'rag-time.'"[9]

Interestingly enough, one mill worker in Lowell's sister city, Lawrence, offered a totally different use for the term "rag-time." This operator wrote to the local paper complaining bitterly about politicians who spoke only of profits and prosperity while mill employees were losing pay through repeated shutdowns.

"Between you all, you must have forgotten that there is a city named Lawrence on the map of Massachusetts, or else you would get those republican mill managers to keep their mills running and give their operatives a chance to feed and clothe themselves instead of being on rag-time." —*Lowell Sun,* Nov. 1, 1900 (reprinted from *Lawrence News*).

As far as dancing goes, the term "ragtime," as it's used today, encompasses several dances that were rarely done to music with the defining "ragged" rhythm; they were simply popular during the right time period. The ragtime favorites still remembered from the decades leading up to the Great War were true lead and follow dances—dances where the leader not only steered the couple about the floor, but chose the step patterns and could wordlessly convey those choices to his partner with subtle body movements.

As the new dances came in and the two-step took a back seat, the one-step with its quicker tempo became the next favorite. Like the two-step, the one-step was often danced to actual "rags." In the eyes of many—including the Castles—this made it irresistible.

"People can say what they like about rag-time. The Waltz is beautiful, the Tango is graceful, the Brazilian Maxixe is unique. One can sit quietly and listen with pleasure to them all; but when a good orchestra plays a 'rag' one has simply *got* to move. The One Step is the dance for rag-time music."[10]

Mr. and Mrs. Castles' 1914 dance manual, *Modern Dancing*, stresses that the new dances are smoother and more graceful than those recently gone by: "Shuffles and twists and wriggles and jumps are no longer words to be used in connection with dancing."[11]

Even the bright and up-tempo One Step (of which they had their own version, the Castlewalk) must be done smoothly:

"When I say *walk*, that is all it is. Do not shuffle, do not bob up and down or trot. Simply *walk* as softly and smoothly as possible, taking a step to every count of the music. This is the One Step, and this is all there is to it. There are very many different figures, but they are in this same strict tempo. It is simply one step—hence, its name."[12]

There's no need to bore the reader here with all the details of exactly how one *leads* all those different figures—such details as shoulder angle, foot placement, hand pressure and such—but *Modern Dancing* offers a description of how to guide one's partner around a corner that paints a picture even a non-dancer should find clear.

"To turn a corner you do not turn your partner round, but keep walking her backward in the same direction, leaning over slightly—just enough to make a graceful turn and keep the balance well—a little like a bicycle rounding a corner. If you like, instead of walking along in a straight line, after you have rounded your corner, you can continue in the same slanting position, which will naturally cause you to go round in a circle. Now continue, and get your circle smaller and smaller until you are walking around almost in one spot, and then straighten up and start off down the room again. It sounds silly and is silly. That is the explanation of its popularity!"[13]

THE CASTLE WALK
The correct way to start the Castle Walk.

THE CASTLE WALK
Taking a corner.

THE SPIN
To spin very rapidly the right foot should never leave the ground.

> *About 30 years ago, long before I'd ever imagined Charles as my soulmate, I found myself dancing the One-Step with him at a vintage dance event. Mid-dance, I started laughing at the absurdity of it all. Here I was, stepping backward at high speed (2 steps/sec ±), never looking at my feet, smiling pleasantly, and I was magically supposed to know what to do and where to go! Yet, somehow, his strong lead made it work.*
>
> —Author

Right: Vernon and Irene Castle demonstrate three moves from the Castlewalk, their own version of the One-Step. Their "Spin" seems to be identical to the buzz-step swing described on page 43.

Opposite: This 1914 advertising preview for sheet music promised that directions for the appropriate dance would be included with the score.

The Castles' book makes another One-Step figure, the Spin, sound the same as a buzz-step swing (page 43), a move which was starting to appear in contras and quadrilles during the same period.

"It is absolutely necessary for both lady and gentleman to use the right foot. Now both these feet must be close together. With the left foot you propel yourself round—the gentleman holding his partner closely and bringing her round with a steady pull."[14]

Did the older dances steal the move from the Castles, or vice versa? Some sources say the buzz-step came from a similar Scandinavian dance step, but who can say now for certain?

In the years leading up to the Ragtime era, the waltz had been simplified further and further until it had been cleansed of the footwork and patterns that had first made it interesting. The two-step version of the dance merely involved steering about the room; there was no lead-follow to it because there were few figures to be led.

"It was against this pitiful, sterile condition of the ballroom that the Vernon Castles rebelled. They shocked the world, but the corsets came off and the stiffness went out, and a new life was breathed into the ballroom. So successful was this onslaught against the two-step that they chased it entirely from the floor."[15] —Lloyd Shaw.

So the Castles—and others—began to come up with variations; step patterns simple enough to be led on the fly but different enough to put both artistry and a bit of play into the dance. One of these was the Hesitation Waltz. This dance included graceful pauses rather than a step on every beat. The pause could be highlighted with pivots, pointed toes, rondés (an elegant little circle drawn with one foot) or other stylish enhancements appropriate to the music.

"...try to do the hesitation when the music seems to 'ask it'—if you know what I mean. Nearly every good Waltz has certain strains which, if you have a good ear for music, you will not fail to recognize as calling for some sort of hesitation or pause."[16]

Mr. Castle adds a caution to the preceding instructions:

"In my opinion it is much better to hesitate when the music hesitates, and, when it does not, simply do the ordinary Waltz movement or steps to that tempo. Avoid always the terrible schedule which obliges you to waltz, hesitate, waltz, hesitate, etc., no matter what tune is being played or who is in your way. That kind of dancing belongs to the people who count to themselves, looking up at the ceiling, 1, 2, 3—1, 2, 3—1, 2, 3."[17]

The Castles go on to describe a half-dozen waltz figures. Other sources of the period offer dozens of step sequences, stringing together turns, walks, and hesitations, all of them designed to be leadable.

Another form of waltz, the Boston, had been introduced in the 1870s; it included a little dip in the step to spice it up. Declared childish by some, it took hold in eastern Massachusetts before gaining wider popularity. The name hung on for several decades, even as the dance mutated. During ragtime's reign, "the Boston" could mean almost any trendy sequence done in ¾ time.

Above: This film-strip style Hesitation Waltz illustration from 1914's Modern Dancing *shows the Castles doing a "Waltz Walk" in the left-hand column and a "Hesitation" in the right. The third frame down on the right shows the actual pause with toes pointed to the side.*

Left: This postcard image (c. 1914) is labeled "Tango," but many dips were used in multiple dances. This one was a common Ragtime Waltz move.

> *In today's athletic world of competitive ballroom, lead-follow is akin to signaling a runner to switch direction mid-stride using the subtlest of clues. With a novice follower, it can feel like guiding a rusty push mower. As the beginner improves, the "mower" gets some oil, maybe new ball bearings; cast iron becomes carbon steel. A good pro is a top-of-the line, self-propelled mower, ready to sail off in the right direction at the lightest touch.* —Author

The Tango has, perhaps, the most interesting history of all the ballroom dances. An Argentinian dancer, Señor Juan Barrasa, offers one of the more likely versions in a discussion with the author of 1918's *Secrets of the Tango*.

"The original name of the dance was Milonga, because it was danced to the Milonga songs in the Argentine. The gauchos, or cowboys, brought the Tango into existence under the name of Milonga. Subsequently, through some remote suggestion of the Spanish Tango, a dance which may be, and probably is, very old, the Milonga became the Argentine Tango."[18]

The gauchos were often of mixed race, making African influence likely.

Other sources in *Secrets* finish the story: "From Latin America it was brought to Paris, where it found its first welcome in quarters sufficiently Bohemian not to be afraid of it in its native shape. In Paris finally was invented the Tango of our ball-rooms, a dance suggested by the South American Tango, but thoroughly reconstructed to suit the usage of polite society."[19]

Vernon Castle says that "It is not only a dance, it is a style; to master the Tango one must first master its style, absorb its atmosphere."[20]

That atmosphere derives from South American history. After Argentina gained independence from Spain in 1810, promoting immigration was seen as key to the future of the fledgling country: "To govern is to populate," stated one politician.[21] Immigrants were often single men hoping to make their fortune, only to find themselves trapped in poverty instead. The male-to-female ratio became wildly skewed. The Tango of the barrio was as likely to be a preening competition between two men as it was a "negotiation for sex" (as it's sometimes described) between a man and a woman.

Thus, the feeling of the Tango was—and is—a haunting mix of sorrow, pride, and desire; a dance where the man may puff out his chest with arrogance, but the all-too-rare woman has the power to cast him aside if she chooses, with a dozen other suitors ready to make sure he goes quietly.

From *Secrets*: "The delicately sensuous spell in which it envelopes one is as pleasant as the vaguely opiumised tobacco of a good Egyptian cigarette."[22]

The jolting, clichéd image of tango—common in the minds of people who've never danced it—bears little resemblance to Mr. Castle's description.

"The most important thing about the Tango is its tempo. You must, before you can dance at all, understand and appreciate the music, and the best way to learn this is to walk (with or without a partner) in time to it. By doing this you impress upon yourself that it is a slow dance, and that it should be simple, and not full of jerky and complicated steps. This walking to Tango time is not as easy as it may seem; it should be practised frequently, so as to make it smooth. The shoulders must not go up and down, the body must glide along all the time without any stops. It is correct either to walk on your heel and toe or just on the ball of the foot; but the Argentines nearly all seem to walk flat-foot, or else they step out on their heel first. I advise dancers to do what is the easiest for them, for when one is walking comfortably it is easier to do the steps naturally. The first step to master, and one of the most difficult, is the Cortez."[23] [also spelled Corte or Corté]

Above: A couple perform a Tango figure called the Corte con Cruzado.

Below: The Castles dance a Scissors step as part of the "Innovation," their own hands-free version of Tango. The lead-follow in the Innovation was done entirely with visual cues.

Above: The Castles illustrate a cortez.

Above right: The Corte con Cruzado as done with an unusual open hold.

Below: Cheryl Burke and Chris Jericho perform a modern Paso Doble on ABC's Dancing With the Stars. *Copyright 2011 by Taylor/ABC.*

Opposite page: This 1914 sheet music came with Maxixe directions.

Secrets of the Tango stresses the importance of the Cortez, as well.

"Before you do anything else, you must know how to do the *corte*, because it gives you the correct rhythm, and from it you can do any step of the Tango. And you must always go back to the *corte* after each figure, so as to give the gentleman time to consider which figure you will do next. There are eight standard figures in the Tango, but from these eight can be developed endless variations of steps. The whole secret is in getting the steps to the correct time of the music and knowing exactly what figure your partner will do next."[24]

Not surprisingly, there's some disagreement on what those basic steps might be, but here are a few candidates (plus descriptions) for the interested reader: The *Media Luna* resembles a box step done with *cortes*. The *Tijeras*, or *Skating Step*, is a gliding step done side by side. The *Scissors* involves crossing the ankles in a "lock" step. In the *Ring*, or *Rueda*, the woman walks around the man. And the *Corte con Cruzado* requires the woman to step first to one side of the man and then across to the other.

Several Ragtime tango figures—among them ones similar to the Corte con Cruzado, ones that sweep the woman across as if she were a cape—appear today not as tango moves, but as modern Paso Doble figures. The image at left shows a couple finishing up a "caping" move (the Chassé Cape) before stepping into a Grand Circle, a move virtually identical to the earlier Rueda.

Other Tango figures from the Ragtime era survived into modern Tango, the Promenade being one of the more obvious. In recent decades, the modern Tango has been joined in ballrooms by a re-exported version of the South American dance that started it all, one truer to its origins, and known specifically as the Argentine Tango.

Ragtime boasted a second dance referred to as a tango, one also with South American roots: the Maxixe, or Brazilian Tango. Vernon Castle had this to say about it:

"The Maxixe Brésilienne is, up to the time of writing this, the latest modern dance. I know how to do the dance, but the name I have not yet quite mastered. The Brazilians themselves pronounce the word Ma-shish, with a slight accent in the second syllable."[25]

Mentel's Maxixe

La Mattchiche Brésilienne

BY
LOUIS H. MENTEL
COMPOSER OF
MENTEL'S HESITATION WALTZ
MORE MUSTARD - ONE STEP
MENTEL'S TANGO, ETC

Directions for Dancing The Maxixe

1. Take the same position as in an ordinary Two-Step. Two-Step for 16 counts. (The above takes 8 Bars of Music.) This Two-Step is the same as the old-fashioned Two-step, except that when you Two-Step to the left you sway the body to the right a little, and when you Two-Step to the right sway the body to the left. (Illustration No. 1.)

2. (Single Step.) Take position as in Illustration No. 2; advance the heel of the outside foot, count 1; draw the inside foot up to the outside foot, count "and"; advance the heel of the outside foot again, count 2; draw the inside foot up to the outside foot, count "and". (1 Bar.)

Repeat all of No. 2 three times. (3 Bars.)

3. During the Single Step the gentleman releases the lady's right hand and she places it behind her back where he takes it in his right. He takes her left hand in his left and holds it above her head (Illustration No. 3). In this position they do an ordinary Two-Step for 16 counts. (8 Bars.)

4. (Skating Step.) Take position as in Illustration No. 4 and Two-Step towards the left, count 1, "and" 2; then Two-Step towards the right, count 3, "and" 4. (2 Bars.)

Repeat No. 4 three times. (6 Bars.)

5. The gentleman steps behind the lady and they do the Single Step towards the left. The gentleman holds both of the lady's arms by the wrists and while "Single Stepping" to the left he makes a circular movement with the lady's hands. He moves the lady's hands up slowly in a circle, bringing them together over her head, down the center and out, then up again, down the center and out, making two complete circles. (4 Bars.) Illustration No. 5.

For more explicit directions, and for other steps to be used in the Maxixe and for directions for other modern dances, address MENTEL BROS. PUBLISHING CO., Cincinnati, Ohio.

50

MENTEL · BROS · PUB · CO ·
CINCINNATI · OHIO

"But the dance, which is the main thing, is beautiful, and like most beautiful dances requires a considerable amount of grace. The steps themselves are not difficult; on the contrary, they are childishly simple; it is the easiest dance of all to do, and I think the hardest of all to do well. My advice to the beginner is to start by being very conservative about it. Get the steps and figures so that you do not have to think about them, and acquaint yourself with the music and rhythm of the dance; after this you may sway the body and try to be graceful. If you feel easy and graceful, you probably are; but if you feel stiff or awkward, go back to the way you first learned and do the dance simply and plainly. For, let me assure you, this dance, with all its bends and swaying, will make a woman appear very attractive or very ridiculous."[26]

The Maxixe had two characteristics setting it apart from its peers: heel digs and notable swaying. The author of *Secrets of the Tango* reports: "I am told by Señor Barrasa that corsets are impossible in the Brazilian Maxixe."[27]

The heel digs can be seen in figures two and four of the sheet music on the preceding page. The side-to-side swaying of Maxixe turns is clear in the image above and in the filmstrip sequences at left, all from *Modern Dancing*.

The Maxixe was an up and coming dance when the Great War began but lost its momentum during the somber war years. Yet its signature moves found new life in another Brazilian export.

Above and far left: The Castles demonstrate the Maxixe's back two step.

Near left: A regular Maxixe two step.

Opposite top: The Maxixe two step lives on in modern Samba rolls.

When Samba emerged from Brazil into the fashionable ballrooms of Europe and North America, it was far too sensual to be accepted without major changes. Dance masters took the name and the music and pieced together a new genre using, in part, steps from the waning Maxixe. The Brazilian Tango's heel digs survive as a Samba move titled, appropriately, the Maxixe, while the swaying turn once called a Maxixe Two-Step is now a Samba Roll.

From its early twentieth-century transformation, International-Style Samba evolved along a totally separate path from Brazilian Samba; today the two are no longer recognizable as the same dance.

The Maxixe may have been the latest dance when 1914 began, but by the end of that year the last of the major Ragtime dances had, quite literally, hit the stage.

Trotting dances had been around for awhile—the much-maligned Turkey Trot, for one—but none with both wide popularity and staying power. Legend has it that one Harry Fox and partner brought a particularly enticing trot to New York's Vaudeville stage in the spring of 1914. Suddenly "Fox's Trot" was *the* dance to learn. The Castles said it was the dance to use when the music was too fast for a One-Step and too slow for a Two-Step.

Below: Vaudevillian Harry Fox managed to permanently attach his name to the immortal Fox Trot.

Right: A 1914 advertisement for dance lessons in Lowell.

Following pages: From Ladies Home Journal, *Dec. 1914 (shown 2/3 size).*

"Before teaching you the steps I should like you to listen to the music. You will find absolutely no difficulty in dancing to it, but the natural inclination is either to dance very fast steps double time to the music or very slow steps with it. The latter is what most people do, and what is more they seem to enjoy it. But it seems to me that, as to keep up the dance one way is too fast and the other too slow, the only real solution is to combine the two. By doing this you not only make the dance more comfortable, but you also make it possible to do a great variety of easy and amusing steps."[28]

Thus, the Fox Trot became the mix of quick and slow steps that still defines it. By September of 1914, dance teachers in Lowell were advertising Fox Trot lessons for their fall terms. By October, stores in Lowell were pushing their phonographs by appealing to Fox Trot lovers in their advertisements:

"FOR DANCING. The Victrola furnishes the best music. The Vernon Castles supervise the making of ALL Victor dance records—of which we carry very large stocks so you can get at once music for any of the newest dances:—THE FOX TROT, THE CASTLE POLKA, or other modern society dances."
—The M. Steinhart & Sons Company, 130 Merrimack Street.[29]

Modern Dance Instruction

MR. and MRS. HUGH PAYNE
Of N. Y. City and Boston

Hesitation Waltz, One-Step, Maxixe, Fox Trot

MIDDLESEX HALL EVERY FRIDAY, 8 to 10.30

Opening night, Friday, Oct. 2nd. You are invited to attend and see exhibitions of all the new dances. Classes will be formed on opening night.

151

MR. AND MRS. VERNON CASTLE'S
III: THE CASTLE FOX TROT
DESCRIBED BY MR. CASTLE

NUMBER ONE

In Taking the Slow Steps the Stride Should be as Long as Possible

NUMBER TWO

This is the Second Slow Step at the Beginning of the Dance

NUMBER THREE

I Walk a Little to the Side Instead of Directly Facing You

NUMBER FOUR

By Stopping Suddenly You Will Find You Unconsciously Fall Into Half a "Grapevine" Step

IN PRESENTING the last of our three modern dances I am obliged to revert to the very old and true saying that "There is no new thing under the sun." However in the present dance you will find a pleasant change, and as it is very like the one-step I think it should become popular. On and off for the last three months we have been introducing this dance at various parties, and it has always been received with a great deal of enthusiasm. So far as the music for this dance is concerned, if you will play an ordinary "rag" half as fast as you would play it for the one-step you will have a pretty good idea of the music and tempo.

And now for the dance itself. Before teaching you the steps I should like you to listen to the music. You will find absolutely no difficulty in dancing to it, but the natural inclination is either to dance very fast steps double time to the music or very slow steps with it. The latter is what most people do, and what is more they seem to enjoy it. But it seems to me that, as to keep up the dance one way is too fast and the other too slow, the only real solution is to combine the two. By doing this you not only make the dance comfortable, but you also make it possible to do a great variety of easy and amusing steps.

The position for this dance is the ordinary one, and I start on my left foot going forward, and you on your right foot going back. We take two slow steps with the music and then four fast steps double time to the music. This completes the step and one bar. We repeat the thing—two slow and four fast steps, and so on around the room. This is very easy, and as it is the main step it should be done in between other more difficult steps. In this way it makes the changing from one step to another more simple. In taking the slow steps in this dance the stride should be as long as possible, as it adds a great deal of grace. (See the first and second photographs.)

The next step is not quite so easy to explain as it is to do. The first two slow steps are the same, except that I walk forward a little to one side, instead of directly facing you (see the third photograph). After the second slow step we spin round for three fast steps, reserving the fourth and last fast step to stop with, because when one begins spinning very fast it is difficult to stop right on the beat, and so we save our last step upon which we stop, and I prepare to go forward again. By stopping suddenly like this you will find you unconsciously fall into half a "grapevine" step (see the fourth photograph), which gives the finish a very pretty effect.

I feel sure it is unnecessary for me to explain what a grapevine step is, as it is far too well known. In the beginning of the dance furore, when all the new steps of the turkey

NEW DANCES FOR THIS WINTER

WITH PHOTOGRAPHS OF EACH STEP
ESPECIALLY POSED BY MR. AND MRS. CASTLE
PHOTOGRAPHS COPYRIGHT BY IRA L. HILL'S STUDIO

trot first came out, the "grapevine" was the standby of all the beginners, and it was about as far as most of them got, for which they should now be thankful.

The counting for the second step is "O–n–e, t–w–o, one, two, three, stop," the first two steps slow and the last three spinning fast.

The third step is much like the first, with the addition of a very pretty little back kick (see the fifth photograph). The first two steps are the same (slow ones, you going back on your right and I forward on my left). We then give a tiny hop and both kick up at the back, you with your right foot and I with my left (see the fifth photograph). This takes up two fast beats, and for the other two remaining beats we take two fast steps in the same direction we started. This completes that step, which takes the same number of beats as the others. The counting is "O–n–e, t–w–o, hop, kick, three, four."

For the next step, instead of taking two slow steps forward we take two drags to the side. This drag is a very old negro step, often called "Get over, Sal." It is done this way: You first take a small hop on your left foot, then quickly throw the weight of the body on the right, dragging the left up to the right. This should take up one long beat. I realize how difficult it is to understand this, but I can think of no simpler way of explaining it, and the sixth photograph should help considerably. In it my wife is just about to drag the left foot up to the right.

After this you do exactly the same step on the other side (see the seventh photograph). This takes up the other long beat; then you finish with four fast steps as in the beginning of the dance. For you the counting is: "Drag to left, drag to right, one, two, three, four." As I am opposite you I have naturally to drag to the right while you drag to the left.

Now here is a step which is, I think, by far the prettiest of all. In order to get into it easily it is necessary to begin in exactly the same way as the first and main step—except that I am at the side instead of directly facing you. We commence "O–n–e, t–w–o, one, two, three, four." Now we take one more slow step, as though we were commencing again, and, instead of taking the second step, we face quickly around in the other direction without changing the position of our feet. This takes up the second long beat (the eighth photograph shows us just after we have made this turn).

The rest is fairly simple. We take four fast steps back in the direction from which we came, and repeat the step, "O–n–e, turn, one, two, three, four," and so on. There is one difficulty in this step, and that is to keep the feet in the same position while you turn around, and, after you have made the turn, to avoid starting off again with the four fast steps ahead of the music.

NUMBER SEVEN

This is Exactly the Same Step on the Other Side

NUMBER SIX

In This Picture My Wife is Just About to Draw the Left Foot Up to the Right Foot

NUMBER FIVE

This Step is Very Much Like the First, With the Addition of a Very Pretty Little Back Kick

NUMBER EIGHT

This Picture Was Taken Just After We Had Made the Turn

By November, Cherry & Webb on John Street was selling "the new Fox Trot coat" (apparently a cloth coat with a particularly full skirt) for $8.98. And early in 1915, the Bon Marche on Merrimack was giving away free copies of a "Fox Trot booklet" as incentive for customers to stop by and peruse the "New Dance Records Just Issued."

Two years earlier, an extraordinary new dance pavilion had opened on Thorndike Street, just a stone's throw from downtown; it would eventually become the famous Commodore Ballroom. The Transit Center garage stands there now.

"Kasino Opens Tonight: Promptly at 8 o'clock tonight, a big orchestra will sound the opening of the Kasino, Lowell's only open air dance hall. By midnight, it is expected that more than 2000 men and women will have tried the floor, which is said to be the very best in New England."

Above: This 1914 Lowell Sun *advertisement touted something called a "Fox Trot Coat" for $8.98.*

Left: The Bon Marche offered free Fox Trot instruction booklets early in 1915 in hope of increasing record sales.

Upper right: A couple demonstrates the Lulu Fado (a.k.a. Lulufado, Lule Fado), one of several Ragtime dances that swept through briefly before disappearing.

Lower right: The house at 58 Highland Street, built in the late 1850s, was once home to a Lowell dancer who landed a spot on the Keith Vaudeville circuit.

"The Kasino is situated opposite the northwest corner of the South common, occupying an elevation overlooking the common, just to the south of the George mansion on Thorndike street. It is said to be the coolest, breeziest spot in the city on a hot day, and as it is at everybody's door, so to speak, there can be no question as to patronage."

"From the Highlands, nearby, will come hundreds of dancers, young and old, while other sections of the city are expected to be correspondingly well represented. The management aims to conduct the best amusement resort of its kind to be found anywhere in the east. Only refined dancing will be countenanced, and the closest attention will be given to the comfort of every patron."

"Between dances, the promenade will be occupied, and here chairs and settees will be placed for the use of Kasino patrons. The capacity of the promenade, like that of the dance hall, will be ample for the crowds that resort to the casino." —*Lowell Sun*, May 28, 1912.

When the Fox Trot craze hit Lowell, the Kasino was right in the middle of it.

"**THE KASINO**. There are three new dances which Lowell people have not seen. They are the fox trot, castle polka and the lulufado. The writer hasn't had the pleasure of seeing either dance, but if advance information is a criterion, the steps are altogether wholesome and pleasing. Tomorrow night, Clayton Robinson and Miss Dornach, well known exponents of the modern dance, will appear at the Kasino and will give exhibitions which will surely interest Lowell people who desire instruction in the three movements. Tonight, as usual, the Kasino will be open, with Miner's orchestra as an incentive to good dancing." —*Lowell Sun*, September 28, 1914.

It wasn't long before the Kasino was holding dance contests—and those dance contests were stepping stones to performance gigs for the winners.

"Canobie Lake. As a special attraction at the Canobie Lake park dance hall on Wednesday evening, the management has secured Harold Maquire of Lawrence and his partner, Miss June Warner of Lowell to give an exhibition of modern dancing including the one step, hesitation and fox trot. This couple were the prize winners at the recent contest in the Kasino at Lowell and also in the Arcadia at Manchester, N. H." —*Lowell Sun*, August 31, 1915.

Some local dancers even gained themselves spots on the Vaudeville circuit.

"Miss Anna G. Leary of 58 Highland street will appear at Keith's theatre next week with her dancing partner, Adelard Victor Gaudreau of Portland, Me. They took their final rehearsal one week ago last Friday and have since received word from New York that their engagement on the Keith circuit had been officially decided upon and that they were booked to begin in Lowell on the week of Feb. 22. Miss Leary is pardonably elated over the assignment as she had worked hard to obtain it. She and her partner will appear in new dances, creations of their own, and Miss Leary will also introduce an original song, entitled 'Perhaps.' Their dances will include the 'Brazilian Polka,' 'Lulu Fado,' 'Balancello,' 'Fox Trot,' and others, some new and some revamped. They will also dance the 'Hesitation' in the music of Miss Leary's original song, 'Perhaps.'" —*Lowell Sun*, Feb. 16, 1915.

One has to wonder what Miss Leary's family thought of this achievement. The house at 58 Highland is a lovely home; it is highly unlikely that any of the Leary girls worked in the mills. Was a job in Vaudeville a step up or a step down? Chances are Miss Leary's parents rued the day the Kasino ever sprouted across the street from their residence!

155

There were still plenty of people who disdained dancing—and even more who disapproved of it as it was done on the Vaudeville stage. Dance teachers in particular railed against Vaudeville's soiling of their proper dances.

"It is not difficult to find the explanation of some of the undesirable dancing. A working man and girl go to a musical comedy. From their stuffy seats high up under the roof they look down upon the dancers on the stage. These are—so the program tells them—doing modern ball-room dancing. The man on the stage flings his partner about with Apache wildness; she clutches him around the neck and is swung off her feet. They spin swiftly or undulate slowly across the stage, and the program calls it a 'Tango.' The man and girl go away and talk of those 'ball-room dances.' They try the steps; they are novel and often difficult; they have aroused their interest. The result is that we find scores of young people dancing under the name of 'One Step' or 'Tango' the eccentric dances thus exaggerated and elaborated to excite the jaded audiences of a roof-garden or music-hall."

> The smooth moves of modern Foxtrot—whether competitive or social style—bear little resemblance to the cheerful trot of earlier days. But the mood of the dance remains the same.
>
> A Foxtrot is, above all, playful. And the best Foxtrots have a mischievous confidence to them, as if the dancers are sure enough of their dance skills (and perhaps some other skills as well) to relax and have fun flaunting them. —Author

FOXTROT

*A plague upon your
modern dance,
Let sulphur flames consume
and burn it!
At forty I'm too old to prance,
I tell you that I cannot learn it.*

*Think you that I will hop about
To strain of sprightly drum and fiddle
Resembling, as an awkward lout,
A chicken on a red-hot griddle?*

*Or that I'll make the thinking grieve
And set your faces broadly grinning
Because I dance the grape-vine weave
With my rheumatic underpinning?*

*And shall I with my collar down
And wet my brow with perspiration,
To ape a Ringling Brothers' clown
When such is not my occupation?*

*What though myself I cannot see
In such fantastic modern reeling,
I'm very sure, take it from me,
Of just how foolish I am feeling.*

*I need no beveled mirror fine
My foolish picture in be spotting;
I know myself that I'm a shine,
I know that I'm too old for trotting.*

*What though I lose the world applause,
Where otherwise I'd stand to win it,
I'm off the fox trot thing because,
I'm naturally "sot agin it!"*

—Edgar A. Guest

"There is no one to tell those young people that they are mistaken in their choice of the steps, that 'society' does not do those dances. They hear hundreds of men and women denouncing the scandalous modern dances, and in their ignorance think that these are the only dances."[30]

Other teachers remarked that: "Objections to dancing have been made on the ground that it is wrong, immoral, and vulgar. This it certainly is not—when the dancers regard propriety. It is possible to make anything immoral and vulgar; all depends on how it is done."[31]

And: "If it leads to perdition, or if it leads to Paradise, fifty other things would do as much."[32]

There were those who considered dancing to be healthy exercise, and who felt that it would be of particular value to the workers of large cities:

"The child of the tenement would be delighted if put into a beautiful, clean, and airy play-room; so will be the men and women of all ages when we show them how to dance the modern dances gracefully and modestly."[33]

Left: This poem by an older gentleman poking fun at the latest dance fad originally appeared in the Detroit Free Press. It was reprinted in the Lowell Sun *late in 1914.*

Opposite page: Dancing and Vaudeville were two hugely popular forms of entertainment in early twentieth-century Lowell, as is clear from this page of advertisements.

"Give them clean fun to offset the hard work of the day. Give them exercise for tired muscles; give them instructors to teach them, without charge, the correct positions and the correct steps for the popular dance, and every girl and boy you teach in this fashion will teach their friends, until by constructive elimination we have done away with what is vulgar by giving our young people something better."[34]

"The lure of the rhythm, the sense of flinging aside the weariness of the working-day, is as strong in the heart of the girl behind the counter as in that of the girl in the private ball-room."

"And what is more, I do not and will not believe that all those young persons, the fathers and mothers of to-morrow, who are working and striving to earn honest livings and to rise in the world connect their moments of recreation with suggestive ideas and unworthy ideals."[35]

One eastern Massachusetts city took the radical step of actually teaching dancing in school!

"To Teach Tango. Lynn School Men Surrender in Fight Against Modern Dances."

"BOSTON, Dec. 3 [1914]—The school authorities of Lynn have surrendered in the fight against modern dances, and, switching their policy completely, are now having lessons given public school pupils in the tango, hesitation, etc., with their approval and under their supervision."

"'The boys and girls are going to learn the dances anyway; why not have them do it right, and under proper guidance?' said the teachers, and the scheme was put in practice. As a result, being kept after school, instead of being a punishment, is now the greatest treat the English high seniors have."[36]

Lowell was not quite so accommodating. Overindulgence in dancing was still seen as frivolous and unhealthy by many, and there were both churches and individuals who, if they couldn't ban it outright, at least sought to discourage it during the holier times of year.

"A Lenten Rest. Even those who are not swayed by the religious significance of Lent will readily admit the need for it and the advantages to be derived from its observance in a physical sense. The religious fasts of simpler days have been for the most part abandoned, but still there is a great deal of voluntary abstention which strengthens the will and benefits the stomach and the nerves. Who will deny that the giving up of smoking, for instance or of excessive candy consumption will benefit the principals? In these lesser things the Lenten season helps to restore balance and makes for permanent physical improvement."

"It is in the tempering down of social observances, however, that Lent does the greatest bodily good. Year after year thousands of young men and women—and a few old ones—enter into the functions of social life with increasing impetuosity. Our social sets have recently set out to tango, fox trot and otherwise cavort their vitality away by an attempt at perpetual

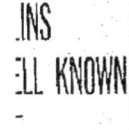
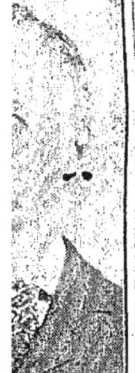

motion. For these, Lent is a safety valve, reminding them gently that while dances, parties, concerts and such things are very good in season—and in moderation—they are the secondary things of life. Those who are disposed to get back into the swirl of all things after the penitential season may pile up a surplus store of energy through the next few weeks so as to be ready for all demands on the feet and on the nervous system when the sober season of Lent is over and festivities break out anew."[37]

Holy season or not, the city government regularly assigned police to be on the lookout for "improper" dancing at Lowell's many venues. It was, frankly, a thankless task. The designated dance inspector was routinely hissed at and ridiculed; and he failed to make any discernible headway against the latest crazes. On top of that, when one couple was actually taken to court for questionable behavior on the dance floor, the press and the public had a field day.

"**POLICE COURT CROWDED AT THE TANGO TRIAL.** Two Officers Demonstrated Movements and Postures of the Defendant Dancers While the Crowd Giggled—Case Resumed This Afternoon."

"The spectacle of two police officers, in uniform, dancing the tango in police court tickled a good many funny bones in Judge Enright's court this forenoon. The court tangoing was resorted to in the case of Frank Hennessy and Angelina Marcotte, whom the official dance inspector, Officer John H. Clark, arrested for exaggerated tangoing at Lincoln hall on the night of February 19. The court room was crowded when Officers Clark and Swanwick took the floor and negotiated all the motions and postures which Officer Clark said the defendants engaged in at Lincoln hall. Other officers in the court room tried in vain to suppress the tittering and the giggling that went the rounds when the sturdy officers chased about the witness stand and 'dipped' near the judge's chair."[38]

"Officer John H. Clark, the official dance inspector, and arresting officer testified.
'I saw the defendants there that night,' he said, 'and spoke to them. I told them to stop such actions on the floor—'
'What actions?' queried the superintendent.
'Indecent actions—'
'Oh, no,' said the court, 'describe them'—and the officer went through the motions on the witness stand—presumably exaggerated tango motions.
'Did they dip?' asked the superintendent.
'They did, and—'
'I object,' said [Defense Atty.] O'Connor. 'You must describe what they did.'"

"The witness then took and attempted to describe 'leg positions' as he observed them."
He said he warned them three times, that they observed the first warning, but not the other two warnings.
The court asked again as to body motions and the officer went through another series of sways, exercising, quite vigorously, his shoulders and hips. 'Will you describe the motions they went through with Officer Swanwick?' asked the superintendent.
'I object,' said Mr. O'Connor.
The court allowed the demonstration and there was great giggling."

"Never before was such a sight witnessed in the local police court and it was impossible to suppress the laughter as the two officers, clasped in each other's arms, à la tango, glided and dipped about the witness stand. It was a sight for the gods and nary a motion of theirs was missed by the courts. He had asked for a demonstration and the officers were doing their 'level best' to describe the naughty dance. Men and women, too, who profess to know all about the tango, declared that Officer Swanwick was the better dancer of the two. He is stouter than Officer Clark, but there is a certain gracefulness about him that seemed to take the curse off the terrible dip that rankles, that makes the tango an outlaw. Men and women in back seats stood up to get a good look at the tangoers and even the defendants seemed to enjoy it. If there are any hip, shoulder, or any other movements that were not described by the officers, they must belong to some other dance than the tango."[39]

"The excitement in and about the Market street building this morning was the most intense of any witnessed there for many moons. Not since the Blondin murder, or perhaps the days when the great textile strike was at its height, and rioters were being carted to the police station as fast as the black Maria could take them in, have so many sought admittance to the police court, where officers were on guard above and below stairs."[40]

And the following morning, when the trial was to conclude, the public was just as eager to be there:

"Trial of the tango case, so-called, was resumed in the police court this forenoon and that interest in the tango-dip-schottische-waltz episode is still in bloom was manifested by the reappearance of yesterday's roaring, surging, billowy crowds, that jammed the doors almost to the point of obliging the officers to use their clubs."

"It was given out as 'honest and true' that the defendants in the case, Angelina Marcotte and Frank Hennessy, would give a tango demonstration just to show to the court that it was physically impossible for them to assume the postures and negotiate the movements described by the 'tangoing' police officers yesterday."[41]

"Reporters, photographers and cartoonists were everywhere, and one unacquainted with the facts might well imagine that something of international importance was taking place or that Harry Thaw [accused of a 1906 murder in the prematurely titled "Trial of the Century"] had struck town."[42]

The onlookers were treated to several exchanges between the defense and Officer Clark regarding why Miss Marcotte and Mr Hennessy had been singled out. What made them "lewd" and "wanton" while others were innocent?

"You have observed sweet, clean, wholesome boys and girls waltzing, and in close contact, haven't you?"
"Yes sir, but as a rule they do not come in very close contact."
"You couldn't put many sofa pillows between them, could you?"
"No."
"Not much more than a sheet of paper?"
"Oh yes, more than that."
"Yes, two or three sheets, I suppose," said Mr. O'Connor.

Opposite page: Tango images from postcards of the era.

Left: The trial was held in the Police Court on the second floor, west end, of Market Street's old Market Building, shown here. Lincoln Hall, where the incident took place, would have been around the corner and several blocks down at the intersection of Gorham and Appleton Streets.

In the end, the judge was reluctantly forced to declare the pair "not guilty."

"He cited cases coming under the same statute as the one under which the complaint against the defendants had been made and could find nothing that would warrant him in holding them. He hoped that the bill now before the legislature providing for elimination of the tango and other dances of a like nature would become law as under the present state of affairs it is impossible for the police to regulate dancing."[43]

It was not simply Lowell, or Massachusetts with its Puritan roots, or even the United States that had issues with the tango; countries in Europe also took steps to keep this "naughty" fad in check. A French journal reported that one enterprising German police chief had even arranged for a tango demonstration for his troops:

"The officers were ordered to observe every move and every step of the couple, to learn it, not to dance, but to be able to recognize improper dancing." ("*Les agents avaient reçu l'ordre de surveiller chaque mouvement et chaque pas du couple, afin d'apprendre, non pas à danser, mais à savoir distinguer les danses excentriques.*")[44]

Why was tango so offensive? Why was a dance defined as elegant by some, considered obscene by others? Why was it singled out? Several factors came into play.

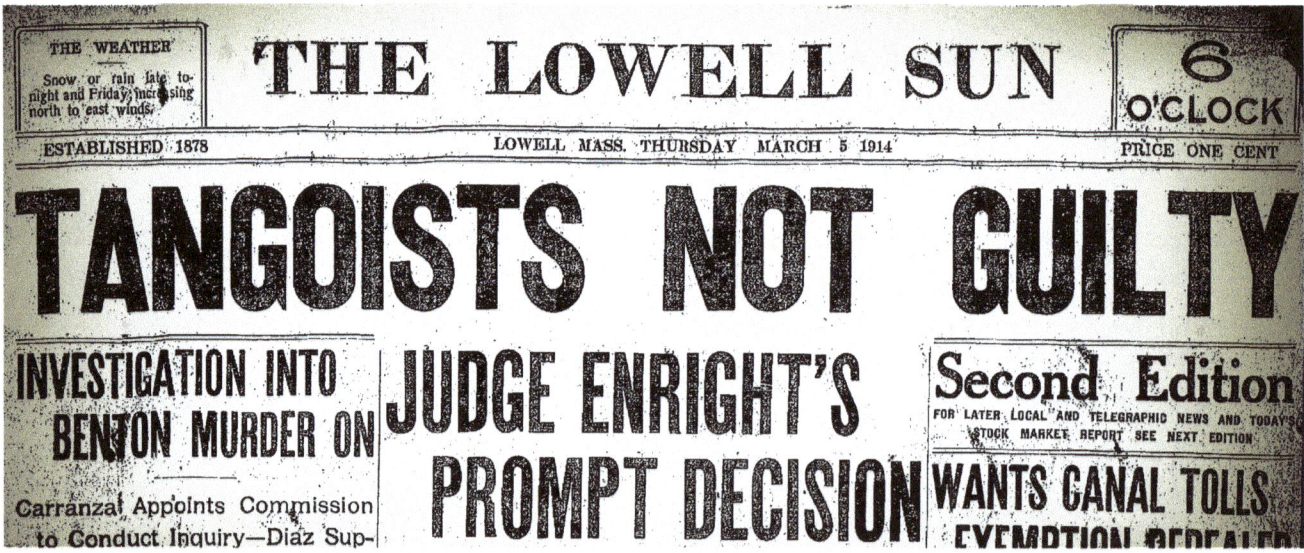

To begin with, Señor Barrasa may have claimed that the cowboys of Argentina brought the tango into existence, but he didn't specify where. It was often done where there were willing women: in brothels. Tango was designed for tight spaces and tight holds. Even after it was cleaned up, the dance had more swiveling moves than traveling ones.

Other dances not only lacked the tango's sordid past, but the power dynamics inherent its story, as well. Less colorful couple dances might expose a girl to a man's embrace, or might prove an avenue to seduction, but the woman was always properly submissive; she was a follower in the most literal sense. In the moody, brooding tango, a woman's attitude could suggest both power and passion—how absolutely shocking! And how very early twentieth century, when the struggle for women's suffrage was reaching its height.

To make matters worse, tango and maxixe—with its swaying, corset-less moves—were often lumped together under the single heading of tango in the minds of the non-tangoing public. The German police demonstration mentioned above included moves from the "craquette," a dance similar, if not identical, to the maxixe.

And Vaudeville didn't help when it eagerly latched onto the drama of the tango and made the most of it. One particular stage act, the "Vampyr Dance," was most likely a tango where the idea of a sensual, powerful woman was carried to its utmost extreme. For some, these sensationalized stage "tangos" were all they knew of the dance.

One writer spelled it out thusly: "The danger in this dance was that, danced by couples, one male and one female, it was easily vulgarised, easily robbed of all its fine innuendo, its voluptuousness left bare and vulgar. When the dance was brought to Broadway, we were to see, clearly enough, how completely it could be stripped of all save its vulgarity."[45]

Back in Massachusetts, Mrs. James Storrow—who went on to found Pinewoods Dance Camp near Cape Cod, and whose husband's name graces Boston's Storrow Drive—directed dance classes for impoverished girls. As a dancer herself, she understood that there were multiple sides to the tango.

"The Tango dance is not only perfectly proper and all right in every way, but is one of the finest dances that has ever been introduced. But please remember that the conditions and associations, after all, are what really count. By being danced correctly, I mean when it is danced as the members of Boston society dance it, and not the way that it is danced in some of the public dance halls, which is shocking."[46]

Opposite page: Possibly because of genuine concern as to the morals of dancers, but more likely because of public fascination with both dance and scandal, the verdict of the "Tango Trial" rated a full-width, banner headline in the Sun.

Above: This 1914 French illustration shows a tango class for police in the German city of Halle. Apparently, couples accused at public balls of improper tango moves would sometimes respond: "But we're dancing the polka!" and police, painfully aware of their own dance ignorance, would hesitate to interfere. The lesson was organized by Halle's chief of police and was designed to enable police to distinguish prohibited dances from acceptable ones.

Left: An image from a vintage postcard, c. 1914, of what one assumes is the final pose in the sensationalistic Vampyr Dance.

161

In the end, for better or for worse, there was no stopping tango. Banning any of the new dances was like trying to sweep back the tide. And the rising tide didn't just affect dancers, it affected fashion. This gave women—dancers and non-dancers alike—freedom from the restrictive dress of the past. Irene Castle explained in *Modern Dancing*:

"In the world of fashion, where there is no appeal from the decree of the great designers, the modern dance has come boldly to the front and demanded, and won, sensible styles. On looking back a few seasons to the clothing worn by women and girls, you will recall long, cruel corsets and garters that trussed them like fowls for the roasting. You will remember, too, the tight snakiness of the hobble-skirt and the hats that were shaped like peach-baskets."

"All women will recall them because all wore them, and all wore tight shoes and heavy petticoats and high, stiff-boned collars. Then Paris began to dance, and of course once Paris began to dance all the world began to tap its feet and try to learn how to pronounce '*thé dansant*' [tea dance]. Then our dancers turkey-trotted. They trotted because that was the best they could do in the fashions old Dame Style had decreed; but it was not comfortable, and they succeeded in doing away with the high collars, and introduced a little slit into the skirts. That was the beginning, the opening gun in the war of the Dance upon the Designer. The Dance has won."

"To-day the average woman is wearing a girdle-like corset with elastic instead of bones, and at most two pairs of garters. All the long, stiff tube corsets are left on the bargain-counters. Nor has this reform stopped with the abolition of the corset, for it is to be noted that the modern shoes are big enough to dance in and are held in place with ribbons. The modern frocks are collarless, and the skirts are subtly cut so that they fall freely and give the perfect ease one must have to dance the modern dances." [Note the shoes in photo at right.]

"Simple coiffures have become the fashion because they do not become untidy when dancing; and for lingerie the dancer now wears a smart pair of silken bloomers and a plaited chiffon or crepe de Chine petticoat that fluffs out gracefully and hides her ankles when she does the little dip that comes in the Hesitation Waltz and other measures."

"The long, awkward, and often soiled train that used to drag behind women in the afternoons and evening is seen no more. The fashions of 1914 have done away with it, because—you could not dance in a train!"[47]

At right: Irene Castle takes some of her own advice in this 1914 photograph.

"While fashion decrees the narrow skirt, the really enthusiastic dancer will adopt the plaited one. A clever woman may, however, combine the two by the use of a split skirt, carefully draped to hide the split, and a plaited petticoat underneath. Thus when she dances the skirt will give and not form awkward, strained lines, and the soft petticoat, fluffing out, will lend a charming grace to the dancer's postures."[48]

Across the country and all about Lowell, dancing was an integral part of social life.

There were *thé dansants* taking place at the Whistler House:

"The third in the series of thé dansants given this winter by Miss Talbot and Mr. Stowell was held yesterday afternoon at the Whistler House. In the general dancing the new fox-trot was most popular."[49]

And the latest dances were demonstrated by increasingly skilled locals at venues such as Associate Hall:

"The decided feature of the evening's festivities came at about 9 o'clock, when Mr. Thomas Garvey and partner, Miss Elsia Grant, gave a very clever interpretation of the maxixe, fox-trot and hesitation canter [a loping version of the hesitation waltz]. The execution of the various steps would have done credit to the celebrated Castles of New York, and the dancers received generous applause at the conclusion of their exhibition."[50]

By the early twenties, regular dancing at regular locations was so much the norm that there was no need to give specifics when a festive holiday came along. The newspaper need only say: "Dancing at all local halls," and everyone headed to the hall of their choice at the appropriate time![51]

Above and at right: Images from an advertisement for Columbia Records. The original text has the headline "Dance!" It goes on to say "Tangos and Maxixes. If you can keep your feet still when you hear them you are music-proof."

163

If dancing was all about having a good time, good times were being had all across Lowell in February of 1898. The *Sun* stated as much:

"In Washington Parties The Social Season Was Joyously Brought to a Close. All the Leading Halls of the City Occupied."

"Washington's birthday was very generally observed last night and particularly so because it wound up the social season before the opening of Lent. In every hall in the city, there was a gathering of merry dancers, making the most of the last hours of mirth and revelry before entering upon the penitential season. In Associate hall, Spindle City Circle, Companions of the Forest danced. In Odd Fellows' hall, the Washington Charity party was held; in Prescott hall, the Washington Associates; in Hibernian hall, the Merrimack corporation employees had a surprise party; in Mechanics' hall, a cotillion under the direction of Miss Cumnock was enjoyed; in Highland hall, the M. S. P. held forth; at Elvin's hall, on Dutton street, a masquerade party was held, while a large number of private parties were enjoyed."[1]

Germans, Grizzlies, and More: Novelties and Fads

Some of those were the same-old, same-old:

"Spindle City Circle had a fine gathering in Associate hall last evening, in observance of the national holiday. There were present about 250 couples, including officers of the local circles and courts."

"The only decoration was on the stage where Florist McManmon had tastefully arranged some tall palms and potted plants in a screen work in front of the orchestra. Hibbard's orchestra played a delightful concert program, which was enjoyed by those who occupied the seats in the gallery and took no part in the dancing that followed. Refreshments were served"[2]

The masquerade mentioned at Elvin's hall would have offered something a bit different for partyers. And then there was this at Burkes' Hall:

"A cake walk was a feature of the Washington's Birthday party at the Burkes' hall last night. It was conducted by the Burke Temperance Institute. The hall was crowded with the merry dancers and when the cake-walkers marched to the floor they were received with applause. Four couples did the walking, which was as good as any ever seen here. The participants were Miss Morris and Mr. Hennesy, Charles Whalen and Miss McKenna, Wm. Kelleher and Frank O'Neil, the latter made up as a girl. Miss Etta Sharkey and William Gleason also participated. The judges had a hard time picking a winner and finally awarded the cake to Miss. Sharkey and Mr. Gleason."[3]

Opposite: The Baby-Polka was a novelty dance that mixed polka and clapping games. An 1890 Maine dance manual included a description, and, at Mrs. Darracott's 1893 recital and dance at Huntington Hall, a group of "tots" performed this novelty dance.

Above right: Postcard image, c. 1914.

Right: "Fascinating, unique and inexpensive costumes may be made for the fancy-dress party or masquerade by the girl who has time and thought to give to their development. A princesse slip of lawn or similar material is used as a foundation on which the crêpe paper is sewed.
—Ladies' Home Journal, 1914.

165

A cakewalk might best be explained as a competitive strut. The following descriptions were set down in the mid-1900s as related by people who had heard them directly from former slaves.

"The cakewalk was originally a plantation dance, just a happy movement they did to the banjo music because they couldn't stand still. It was generally on Sundays, when there was little work, that the slaves both young and old would dress up in hand-me-down finery to do a high-kicking, prancing walk-around. They did a take-off on the high manners of the white folks in the 'big-house,' but their masters, who gathered around to watch the fun, missed the point. It's supposed to be that the custom of a prize started with the master giving a cake to the couple that did the proudest movement."[4]

"Us slaves watched white folks' parties where the guests danced a minuet and then paraded in a grand march, with the ladies and gentlemen going different ways and then meeting again, arm in arm, and marching down the center together. Then we'd do it, too, *but we used to mock em*, every step. Sometimes the white folks noticed it, but they seemed to like it; I guess they thought we couldn't dance any better."[5]

The cakewalk came to be at the heart of any number of racist caricatures of African-Americans, but it seeped into white ballrooms where it was a satire of a satire, whether the society people doing it realized it or not. Most of all, it was fun. And in that spirit of fun, it wasn't unusual for it to be done by two dancers of the same gender (note that William Kelleher and Frank O'Neil competed as a couple at Burke's Hall). Of course, anything that was novel in the dance world was also co-opted by Vaudeville, and cakewalking lent itself readily to both comedy and contortion.

Looking again at Lowell's full slate of dancing on that long-ago holiday, there was another event that mixed playful competition into the evening's entertainment—and with prizes far more varied than a single cake.

"MISS CUMNOCK'S COTILLON. At Mechanics Hall last evening, Miss Grace Cumnock gave another in a series of subscription cotillions. The hall had been beautifully decorated with the national colors and an abundance of flags were used in the decorations. About 50 couples were present, several being from out of town."

"The first part of the cotillion, which was a George Washington party, was in the charge of Mr. J. Tyler Stevens. The favors were silk flags, cherries, hatchets, fancy sashes, gilt wands with bunches of flowers. The first part was continued until 11 o'clock; the American orchestra furnished the music, at which time the D. I. Page Co. served lunch in the upper hall."

"After refreshments the second part of the cotillion began. This was called a Mardi Gras party and was in charge of Mr. Victor I. Cumnock of New York. The favors were from Sherry's in New York and consisted of confetti, papal rockets and tissue flowers."[6] ["Papal rockets" are a bit of a mystery. Best guess is that they were fireworks—perhaps similar to those shot off at the election of a pope—and given the "papal" prefix here to fit in with the Mardi Gras/Lent theme.]

This page: Two postcard images of Vaudeville players performing the Cakewalk.

Opposite top: Illustration from a 1910 magazine article about how to hold a cotillion.

Opposite bottom: Illustration from the Lowell Sun, January 1899.

166

The girls strike the colored golf balls for the men to catch

"Cotillon" was originally the French word for petticoat and came to mean certain types of dances, particularly quadrilles, where the turns and promenades might flash a bit of the women's underskirts. The word could be spelled with or without a second "i," "cotill*i*on" being an English approximation of the French pronunciation. In the mid-nineteenth century a new version of cotillion was introduced, one often referred to as a "German."

"This dance was introduced in New York about the year 1844. At the time the quadrille was the fashionable dance, but was known as the cotillion. To make a distinction between that and this dance, which was known in Europe by the same name, this was called the 'German Cotillion;' gradually the word cotillion was dropped, the dance becoming simply 'The German.'"[7]—from Dodworth's *Dancing and Its Relation to Education and Social Life*

The German—or cotillion—was not a single dance, but rather an entire, carefully planned evening of intertwined games and dances, complete with favors, designed to provide an enjoyable experience for every guest. The majority of games determined who would dance the next dance with whom, as seen in the illustrations above and below.

"Attention to the following five suggestions will give to the cotillion its true character and position, as the representative dance of modern civilization, combining fine music, fine motions, and fine manners," declared Dodworth.

"1st. *Alertness,* each dancer being at all times awake to the duties required of him or her.
2nd. *Promptness* in taking places for the execution of a figure.
3rd. *Silence* and attention during the explanation of any novelty.
4th. *Obedience* at all times to the conductor during the management of the dance.
5th. *Willingness* to sacrifice momentary personal pleasure, so that others may gain."[8]

Favors were provided to the guests in abundance. Sometimes these trinkets were props for the game being played; other times they were prizes or rewards. They were often collected and worn pinned to the shoulder as trophies (see image on following pages). One manual, *The German. How to give it. How to lead it. How to dance it.* offered advice:

"CHOOSING FAVORS. First of all, have a sufficiency of them. Nothing seems to put people in such good humor as receiving a quantity of these pretty and worthless bits of tinsel and toys. Having favors for every figure is not too many; having them for less than half the figures is too few."

"THE LASSO." A FAVORITE COTILLION FIGURE IN THE JANUARY DANCES.

THIS PRETTY FIGURE IS DANCED IN DOUBLE ROWS DOWN EACH SIDE OF THE ROOM. THE GENTLEMEN LASSO THEIR FAIR PARTNERS WITH RIBBON OR WITH LONG STRIPS OF LASSO PAPER WHICH COMES FOR THE PURPOSE

"Pick them out with reference to the following points, in this order: novelty, oddity or absurdity, prettiness, brilliancy and largeness. As to the last quality, we mean that it is well to make as great a display as convenient. Besides the conventional 'German' favors, there are hundreds of toys and trinkets that add very much to the fun of the party. Almost anything of such a size that a pin will support it will answer the purpose, and the odder the better."

"Flowers (of course), drums and whistles, bells, rattles, jumping jacks, colored silk cut to fit coat lapels, bead ornaments, gilt charms, dolls, fans, and pewter and indeed all other kinds of small toys."[9]

THE FAVOR

The subject of Cotillon favors was mentioned regularly in the *Lowell Sun*.

"Some Dainty Bags. There is always a demand for novelties in the way of pretty trifles for the church fair or cotillion favors, and the silk and lace bon-bon bags are among the many dainty gifts. These can be made of all sorts of fine and delicately colored materials, and three novel designs are here reproduced." —*Lowell Sun*, February 15, 1898.

"…There was a cotillion led by Mr. F. W. Stickney, after 12:30 o'clock, and many odd favors were all issued." —*Lowell Sun*, March 2, 1900.

"A Parrot Cotillion. A New Dance Which Will Find Favor With the Smart Set. A cotillion is the most popular form of evening amusement and for this nothing can be prettier than the parrot dance. Veri-colored, life-sized parrots on long gilded sticks are given as favors and are carried through the figure and, sometimes, through the whole dance." —*Lowell Sun*, March 10, 1900.

Despite being designed for private gatherings, and despite having faded from popularity by the mid-teens, some sort of "cotillion" was held at a very large 1920 event at Associate Hall where it was a distinctly separate activity from the general dancing. Based on the newspaper description, it was a type of grand march that somehow included favors.

"Dancing continued until 10:30. Now couples were continually coming in until finally the resources of the checkrooms and even the dance orders were taxed to capacity. The size of the crowd out-distanced the very generous preparations made by the conductors, but eventually everybody was taken care of. The formal cotillion began at 10:30 with those taking part going through the traditional evolutions with grace and precision. More than 150 couples took part and after the preliminary movements, the lines of 16 came down the hall and presented a pretty

SCHEDULE.

(1) No.	(2) Name.	(3) Properties.	(4) No. up. P.	(5) Favors.	(6) Remarks.
1	Basket		P.6	Flowers	
2	Lines		P.6	Noisy Toys	Ladies ½ chain, right and left, countermarch.
3	Cards	Cards	5		Ladies choose 3 gentlemen. Fix chairs.
4	Scarf	12 Scarfs	P.6	Conventional Favors.	Distribute scarfs.
5	Kings and Queens	4 Kings, 4 Queens	4		Gather cards.
6	Causeway		P.6	Bonbon Hats	Have gentlemen all face south.
7	Darts	Target and Darts	4	Cigars to gen.	Fix target. Gentlemen choose gentlemen.
8	Star		P.6	China Dolls	See quadrille form.
9	Boxing G.	4 Boxing Gloves	4		Gentlemen choose 2 gentlemen.
10	Jerusalem	14 Chairs	P.8		7 chairs each end of room.
11	Rain	8 Parasols	P.4	Gilt Charms.	
12	Wind-up		All	Ribbon Bows	
Ex.	Race	8 Whips	P.4		Collect whips and reins.

This will make a very pretty "German" for say twenty-five couples.

(Left margin: 45 / TO THE LEADER.)

Above: A woman pins a favor to her partner's jacket.

Left: Chart for planning a cotillion including the names of the games (col. 2), the props needed to play each one (col. 3), the number of couples for each, plus whether players find their own partners or partners are provided (col. 4), the favors for each game (col. 5), and any other notes (col. 6).

Opposite top: Advertising card showing a cotillion game.

Opposite middle: Y.M.C.I. hall, 1907.

Opposite bottom: 1910 French fashion images of the era's narrow skirts.

sight. Soft lights added much to the beauty of the affair. Many pretty favors were distributed."[10]

Whatever a "cotillion" had become by the twenties, it had clearly ceased to be a private evening of fancy games and dancing—Ragtime informality and wartime austerity had put an end to those. Regardless, the Young Men's Christian Institute continued holding annual cotillions of some type, complete with favors, at their building on Stackpole Street into the 1930s. Today, a "cotillion" is usually a debutante ball.

Considerably more controversial than cotillions were the "animal dances" that gained popularity early in the twentieth century. Some of these dances managed to have a certain degree of grace in spite of their names; others, not so much. With holds and steps that were well outside the norm of "proper" dancing, they were firmly denounced by an assortment of officials. Which, of course, only added to their appeal.

Among the first of these dances was the Turkey Trot, whose awkward gait Irene Castle blamed on the narrow —or "hobble"—skirts of the period.

The narrowest skirts lasted less than a year and were routinely ridiculed in the press. One Lowell Sun article titled "Hobbles, Bobbles, and Wobbles on Fifth Avenue" reported that while Americans blamed Paris for the style, Paris blamed the Americans. It was joked that politicians could easily escape any approaching Suffragettes and their bothersome demands now that these would-be voters were slowed by their skirts.

The Sun noted several falls caused by hobble skirts, including one where a fashionably dressed bride, playfully pursued by members of the wedding party, was tripped up by her skirt and fell out a window. The bride broke her wrist; the honeymoon was delayed.

171

Above and below: Lighthearted postcard illustrations of the Turkey Trot and Bunny Hug.

Opposite page: Dancers doing what appears to be the Grizzly Bear, as seen in a Victrola Advertisement.

Appearing on the west coast around 1909 and generally done to rags, the Turkey Trot devolved into two forms: society's and the "tough" version.

"URGES NEWSBOYS TO BAR TURKEY TROT. MRS STORROW SPEAKS BEFORE YOUNGSTERS ON DANCING. Mrs. James J. Storrow, the wife of the president of the Chamber of Commerce, gave the newsboys of the Happy Twenty Club, of which she is an honorary member, an illustrated talk on the 'turkey trot' at their clubroom last night."

"She expressly asked the boys who had charge of the ball to taboo the 'turkey trot.' Then she explained that the real 'turkey trot' danced in a rhythmical walk, with the right arm extended and with the two partners at least a foot distant, was not only graceful and beneficial in its training and exercise, but entirely unobjectionable from any point of view."

"It was then that Mrs. Storrow tripped back and forth across the end of the room to show just how the 'turkey trot' should be danced."

"But for the 'turkey trot' as it is known in the dance halls, Mrs. Storrow could find no expression severe enough to convey her disapproval."

"That 'tough' dance, misnamed the 'turkey trot,' and allied with the 'bunny-hug' and the 'grizzly-bear,' Mrs. Storrow begged the boys to forbid at their dance. She said that such a dance is extremely harmful not only morally, but physically."[11]

The tough version, of which Mrs. Storrow spoke, would remind a modern onlooker of the Charleston more than anything else, with its energetic bounce and little kicks. But with multiple hops on first one foot and then the other, this dance had its own, quite different, side-to-side sway.[12]

The Bunny Hug was another newcomer with lots of energy but very little movement across the floor. It shared the turkey trot's side-to-side lilt but the hops were replaced by a triple step—L-R-L, R-L-R done on 1-&-2, 3-&-4. It had its own set of embellishments and a radical hold that gave it its name. Partners leaned in, placed their hands on the back of their partner's shoulders and danced away in an ungainly, cheek-to-cheek hug.[13]

Then there was the Lame Duck. In the book, *Modern Dancing*, the Castles describe a waltz step they call the Lame Duck. This step had a two-count dipping action that repeated on the same leg multiple times, giving it a bit of a "limp." They cautioned that it should be done gracefully and on the beat.

"If you do it smoothly it is pleasing to the onlookers and to yourself; if you exaggerate it you lose all the Duck and it is simply Lame."[14]

When the Lame Duck began to be seen as a vulgar dance, it was probably due, in part, to this advice being ignored. The uneven gait of the Lame Duck also gave rise to various types of "canters," the Hesitation Canter, for one.

The Kangaroo Hop, the Chicken Flip, the Grizzly Bear, the Camel Walk and an assortment of other animal-named dances joined the menagerie. The Grizzly Bear was certainly among the silliest, having little resemblance to a dance at all and full of moves designed solely to mimic a bear.

Everybody had something to say about these dances. To the young people, they were harmless fun. Learned from their friends or from watching Vaudeville, dances of this type didn't require hours of practice or expensive lessons that working class fans couldn't afford. But to the cultured, they were vulgar, immoral, and downright dangerous.

"TURKEY TROT PROVED FATAL TO A YOUNG WOMAN. Atlantic City, N. J. —Mrs Agnes Day, 21 years, of 10 Mt. Vernon avenue, with her husband, enjoyed an exhibition of turkey trot on one of the piers last night. When they returned home, in a spirit of fun, she endeavored to show the rest of the family how the dance was accomplished. A sharp pain in her side caused the young wife to stop. Ten minutes later she dropped unconscious to the floor. Before a physician could arrive the girl was dead. She had burst a blood vessel during the dance."[15] —*Lowell Sun*, June 1912.

The classic ballerina, Anna Pavlova, declared the ragtime dances "abominations." She inserted some of them into her 1913 London performances "to show the contrast between the stately grace of one kind of dance and the 'unwholesomeness' of the other." The result was a sensation, although whether it changed anyone's mind is debatable.[16]

A great many people—such as Mrs. Storrow—differentiated between the "proper" version of a dance and the dance hall version. One of these was Miss Helen Keller, a woman deaf and blind from childhood who grew to be a cultured and celebrated individual. When the topic came up in an interview, her response caught the questioner off guard.

173

Interviewer: "What do you think of some of the latest dances such as the turkey trot and the bunny hug?"

"'As I dance them they are all right' —the fact that Miss Keller is a dancer being rather startling to the newspaperman—'but I understand they can be done in a very objectionable manner.'" —*Boston Post*, February 23, 1913.

It was this "objectionable manner" that the Lowell Police Department had in mind when it reassigned Officer Clark.

"Officer John H. Clark, who has been on the Middlesex depot beat during the past few years, will be assigned to 'special duty' at the station during the early night. He will serve as a call man in case of emergency and will probably be associated with the squad of inspectors. His particular job, it is alleged, will be to keep an eye on dance halls with a view to stopping all of the 'animal dances,' so called. It is presumed he is an authority on the intricacies of the tango, the bunny hug, the castlewalk, the Boston, the kangaroo and turkey trot." —*Lowell Sun*, January 6, 1914.

The Massachusetts legislature sought to ban the whole lot of "objectionable" dances early in 1914. A *Lowell Sun* article on the subject included some light-hearted ribbing of the aforementioned dance inspector, the same inspector who had been at the center of the tango trial described in the preceding chapter.

"LEGISLATURE ASKED TO PUT BAN ON DANCES THAT ARE OFF COLOR. One of the freak bills before the legislature this year has to do with dances, including the tango, lame duck, Argentine, chicken flip, bunny hug, grizzly glide, or any dance that indicates a bold departure from the dances indulged in by our illustrious ancestors."

"The bill was not introduced by Police Officer Clark, the man who cries the halt—sometimes—on tangoists in Lowell. There is a bare possibility that Mr. Clark had a hand in the framing of the bill but his name does not appear in connection with it. The passage of the bill, however, would eliminate all the dances enumerated and it would be hardly reasonable to suppose that Mr. Clark would assist in legislating himself out of a job that is not in the least laborious. Perish the thought! The act reads as follows:"

"Section 1. Dancing at public dances, entertainments or gatherings of the so-called tango, lame duck, Argentine, chicken flip, bunny hug, grizzly glide, or any dance participation in which is not conducive to propriety, shall be prohibited."

"Section 2. Violation of this act shall be punished by a fine of not exceeding fifty dollars for the first conviction, and by imprisonment in the county jail for a period not exceeding six months for second and subsequent convictions."

"Section 3. The chiefs of police of cities and towns shall be empowered to enforce the provisions of this act, and shall be the sole judge concerning whether section one is violated."[17]

A month later, the bill died in the House by a vote of 65 to 149. Even without the ban, eventually, "the Zoo was rounded up, and the camels and grizzly bears and snakes and kangaroos were caged again."[18] More new dances were to come along and shock the older folks: the Charleston and its kin, followed by Lindy Hop, Swing, and then by Rock and Roll. But the menagerie of the early 1900s faded away while the century was still young.

There were other, less widely embraced dance novelties that cropped up now and again during Lowell's first hundred years. Back in 1860, an article about dancing on roller skates appeared in the *Lowell Courier*.

"Ladies' 'parlor skates' are noticed for sale in Boston. They are made to all appearances like ordinary skates, but have in the runners little brass wheels, neatly covered with leather, so that the wearer can skate over an ordinary floor with ease and safety. It is said that ball room skating is to be the rage at the watering places this summer."[19]

The concept doesn't seem to have caught on widely, but it reappeared periodically, and on both sides of the Atlantic.

London, 1913: "Tango dancing on roller skates is one of the chief attractions at the newly opened Queen's Rink at Earl's Court. Already some wonderful displays of Tango skating have been held, and at the special 'skating tea' given there the other day, Mr. Percy A. Brown, the skating expert and gold medallist, and his marvelous lady pupil, Mrs. Bramley-Moore, provided a display which was quite a revelation."

"Starting off with a waltz, at a sudden change in the music to [a] two-four, rag-time air, they began the most wonderful series of gyrations ever seen on roller skates. They 'Promenaded,' they 'Cort-éd,' they performed the Tango 'Dip,' the Huite Croisé, 'Scissors,' and even the 'Media Luna,' dancing sometimes facing one another and sometimes side by side, with the gentleman rather behind the lady."[20]

Not surprisingly, Vaudeville embraced this odd combination. The El Rey Sisters skated tango and turkey trot and more on the Vaudeville circuit, including at the Keith Theatre on Bridge Street. From a 1915 *Lowell Sun* review:

"Last but by no means least are the El Rey Sisters, Zoe and Klara, who do wonders on roller skates. They are good to look upon and their act is tip top. They are more at home on rollers than most theatrical critics are on terra firma without rollers. They waltz, maxixe, fox trot, clog dance and wind up with a whirling dervish that stops the breath."[21]

Innumerable other novelties enlivened one event or the other, never to be seen again. One such instance was an 1895 fundraiser at Associate Hall. Men wishing a partner for any of the first four dances were required to "borrow" one from the "Circulating Library." Forty-five rare "volumes," in "silken and gold bindings," were available for loan.

"1. A 'book' can be secured from the library for one dance, by the payment of ten cents."

"2. Any person retaining a 'book' after the dance will be liable to a fine."

"3. No 'book' can be loaned or removed from the hall upon any pretext, and any person transgressing this rule may be fined at the discretion of the Librarian."[22]

This particular novelty was apparently quite the success. Next day's paper reported: "It is needless to state that there were no books allowed to remain long on the shelves, and it was with reluctance that they were returned."[23]

Left: Vaudeville, with its fondness for novelty and sensation, was often blamed for corrupting respectable dances into the vulgar versions that came to dominate public dance halls.

Right: Cover of the "Circulating Library's" fancy, eight page dance card. —Lowell Historical Society.

In the long run, the doubters were right. Lowell's population peaked in 1920 just shy of 113,000 and then began a slow, painful decline. One by one, the city's textile mills fell on hard times, many of them relocating to the southern states in search of lower transportation costs and cheaper labor. In 1926 and 1927 alone, Lawrence Manufacturing, Hamilton Manufacturing, Appleton Manufacturing, Massachusetts Mills, Suffolk Mills and Tremont Mills either shut down, moved south, or changed hands.[1]

The Last Waltz:
From Flappers to Folk Festivals

Other industries picked up some of the slack, for a while. By 1931 the shoe industry was Lowell's largest employer. A decade later, it, too, was in decline. In 1938, 40 percent of the city's residents received government assistance.[2]

World War II brought a spate of new jobs. Parachute manufacturing came to the old Lawrence Manufacturing buildings, and other war-related industries brought employment to many of Lowell's residents. But when the war ended, Lowell's unemployment rate again soared.[3]

Many of the old mill buildings fell into disrepair; some stood empty and decaying for decades, subject to fire, vandalism, and the ravages of New England winters. In 1960 the Merrimack Mills complex was razed. Meanwhile, periodic attempts at urban renewal destroyed swathes of residential neighborhoods deemed unworthy of preservation. Lowell's reputation suffered; to many outsiders, it was a dirty city and a place to be avoided.

Opposite: The Boott Cotton Mill clock tower, c. 1968, before its restoration.

Above right: Empty storehouse at the Boott, c. 1968.

Right: Inside the shell of the Lowell Manufacturing Company's 1899 coal storehouse (2015). It was the shift from water power to coal-produced steam that helped to doom Lowell's textile industry.

Through the city's financial ups and downs, social dancing remained popular. Ballrooms and dance halls still drew crowds, and dozens of venues were available about Lowell, as well as a trolley ride away in the surrounding area.

The open-air dance and roller skating pavilion, the Kasino—once perched where the Gallagher Transit Terminal garage stands today—became the famous, year-round, Commodore Ballroom. In the 1930s, the Commodore promoted itself as a full-fledged "winter resort," complete with an 18 hole Tom Thumb golf course in the basement.[4]

The Commodore thrived for decades, offering a steady stream of top-notch big bands and singers through the thirties and forties, from Frank Sinatra to the Clooney Sisters. In the fifties the music was jazz, and in the sixties, Rock and Roll. The ballroom was popular with the soldiers from nearby Fort Devens and was considered a healthy diversion for teens.[5]

Opposite top: The Massachusetts Mills structures in this 2015 photo were abandoned during Lowell's hard times. They are some of the few mill buildings not yet rehabilitated.

Opposite bottom: The Commodore Ballroom seen from the intersection of Thorndike and Summer Streets in 1931 (Lowell Historical Society). The Sun *advertisement is from 1924.*

Right: The Laurier Hotel boasted the largest rising dance floor in the world as shown on this 1943 postcard.

Below: The Hi Hat Roll-A-Way on Princeton Blvd. offered both roller skating and dancing in the 1950s.

A while back, I exchanged e-mails with a former Lowell resident who laid out the mid-twentieth century dance scene of his youth quite colorfully; he invited me to feel free to quote him.

This gentleman mentioned the High Hat, an establishment whose large wooden floor served both dancers and roller skaters: "In my time, roller skating at the Hi-Hat as a pre-teen was the first initiation to holding a gal to 'The Skater's Waltz' [or] 'Blue Tango.'" *As he grew older and entered high school, he found dancing aplenty in Lowell.*

"Every Friday or Saturday night there were record hops in stinky gyms, like that of (and behind) the Immaculate Conception Church [or at] Keith Academy. The least stinky was at the youth center of the Polish Holy Trinity church, given its being the newest. DJs, mostly from WCAP, stood on stage spinning 45s on actual record players."

"Gals congregated on the sides of the gyms in their crinolined dresses or girdled-tight, straight skirts while wearing fuzzy-wuzzy angora sweaters after having spent hours sitting under plastic, portable hair dryers with mega hair rollers. Most wore 'flats' due to developmental gender differences. Guys always wore at least a sport jacket, often white, with cuff-linked light pink or blue shirts with ties and navy-blue, pegged pants. Hairdos were just as important to guys and typically of the DA (Duck's 'behind') styling per a little dab of Brylcreme or Vaseline hair tonic; whiffles were optional. They usually hid in the darker back trying to get up the nerve to cruise by the gals to risk the Walk of Shame...getting turned down. No matter what, we all did sweat, especially in A/C-less summer!!!"

"If we looked old enough, we could also go dancing to the waning sounds of The Big Bands in more 'sophisticated' Ballrooms like The Commodore on Thorndike St. and The Totem Pole—albeit 'Tote' was down in Norumbega Park... the glorious Totem Pole with their cuddly two seater couches!"

"Just west of the Hat was a Supper Club where you dined to also enjoy a 'mini' dance floor. 'Twas called The Blue Moon."

"THE Dance of the Year [was] The [Lowell High School] Girl Officers Ball at The Auditorium!!!"

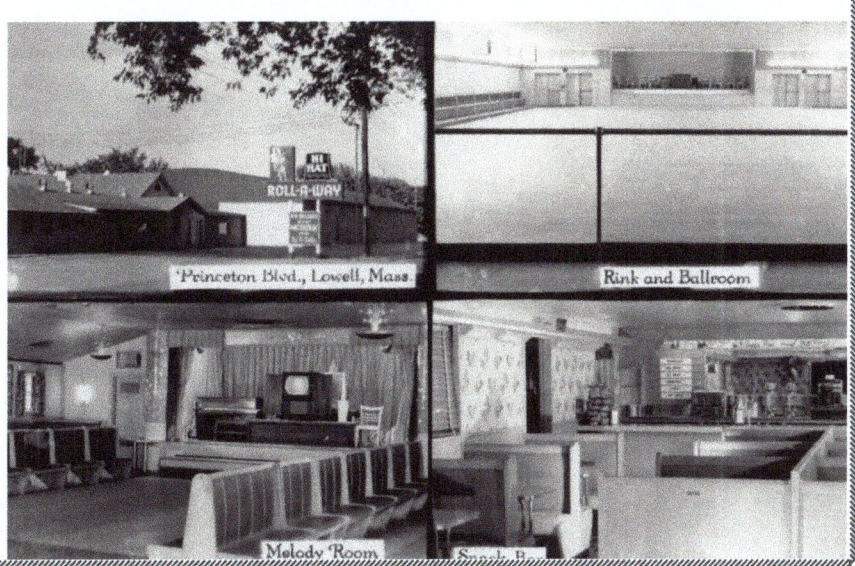

Right: The Totem Pole's "cuddly two seater couches." Norumbega Park can be located on the 1900 trolley map on page 126; the Totem Pole ballroom didn't open until 1930.

Opposite upper: A sign in the middle of the former Lowell Manufacturing complex points the way to the Lowell Folk Festival's dance pavilion (2013).

Opposite lower: The 2013 Lowell Folk Festival dance tent filled with couples swing dancing.

Through the mid-twentieth century, the Commodore and similar venues prospered. But times were changing; eventually even the Commodore fell to the wrecking ball.

So what happened to all that dancing? Why did most people—in Lowell and elsewhere—stop going out for an evening of music and dance when so many earlier generations had enjoyed it?

An obvious culprit was television, with its ready diet of at-home entertainment, but there were other reasons, too.

A wartime "cabaret tax" was enacted in 1944. This 30 percent tax (later reduced to 20) on food or merchandise sold at eateries swank enough to provide entertainment was imagined as a luxury tax. But "cabaret" was defined broadly.[6]

"A roof garden or cabaret shall include any room in any hotel, restaurant, hall or other public place where music or dancing privileges or any other entertainment, except instrumental or mechanical music alone, is afforded the patrons in connection with the serving or selling of food, refreshments or merchandise."[7]

While it was first thought that such a tax "will not hamper the boys and girls out seeking a good time,"[8] nightclubs soon found themselves struggling. Club owners had three choices: bill the 30 percent tax to the customer, absorb the 30 percent hike themselves, or sever the connection between dining and dancing. As a result, restaurant dance floors disappeared and the big bands went with them.

Ballrooms became a separate entity, most of them limited to selling overpriced drinks. But a good-sized dance floor is a lot of real estate to maintain without food sales to help support it. And, unlike nightclubs, ballrooms don't draw in non-dancers for an evening of dining and spectating. Not only that, but a dance floor full of hardcore ballroom fans will often intimidate beginners and choke off the supply of new patrons. A self-perpetuating spiral had begun.

By the time the tax was eliminated in the mid-sixties, only small pockets remained of any type of structured partner dancing. Foxtrot and waltz were old-fashioned; quadrilles (square dances) were hokey; contra dancing was the Virginia Reel in gym class; and tango was something from a Valentino movie. To most folks, Rock and Roll ruled the scene and "touch dancing" meant swaying side to side in a *very* close hold (perhaps even in time to the music!).

Today things have rebounded some. The few surviving New England ballrooms may host mostly concerts and private functions, and restaurant dance floors tend to be the size of postage stamps, but more people are taking a second look at touch dancing. Swing and Salsa—both lead/follow partner dances—have legions of followers. Salsa in particular is popular in ethnically diverse cities such as Lowell. Ballroom dancing is again a much-watched spectator sport, one routinely featured in news reports and gossip. And New England contra dancers can be heard to comment on the rash of enthusiastic—if occasionally etiquette-challenged—young people attending their events.

Lowell, too, has experienced a rebirth. In the mid 1970s a local educator, Patrick J. Morgan, campaigned to make downtown Lowell into the nation's first urban national park. Community organizations and politicians banded together to form plans for the restoration and redevelopment of the city. In 1978, President Carter signed legislation committing forty million dollars to the creation of Lowell National Historical Park. In addition, Congress established the Lowell Historic Preservation Commission to help manage the project.[9]

Since that time, the majority of empty mill buildings have been restored and repurposed. Apartments, theaters, art galleries, museums, condominiums, and a wide range of businesses inhabit these historic structures. The University of Massachusetts Lowell calls the city home, as do the Lowell Spinners, a Red Sox farm team. The city has become a unique and fascinating place to live with a range of concerts and festivals taking place over the course of a year. The population has rebounded—Lowell is a desirable address once again. Downtown boasts a flourishing night life and on a warm, summer evening, music can be heard emanating from a number of clubs, bars, and restaurants.

Alas, Lowell's old downtown dance halls have all been demolished, repurposed, or abandoned. There are ballroom studios elsewhere in the city, and some lovely dance floors a short drive away—a one-time barn hosts twice-weekly contra dances in Concord, and a converted mill has weekly ballroom dancing in North Chelmsford—but the classic dances that filled hall after hall in the city center for a hundred years have vanished.

Except, that is, for a single weekend each summer. On the last full weekend of July, the city hosts the Lowell Folk Festival—the largest free folk festival in the country. For those few days, residents and visitors alike can stroll between multiple stages offering both ethnic and home-grown traditional music. There's also a dance pavilion. Its floor may not have the size or quality of the old ballrooms, but it's enough for a decent polka—or perhaps, just once in awhile, one of those scandalous, whirling waltzes!

Illustrations

Preface
Ill. 1: Ella Carlson, *Ruth and Charles Kitchen Sink Dip* (2011) photograph.
Ill. 2: *Dance Card* (1923), dance card, author's collection.
Ill. 3: *Some Night, Some Waltz, Some Girl #2* (c. 1905), postcard, author's collection.
Ill. 4: *Some Night, Some Waltz, Some Girl #3* (c. 1905), postcard, author's collection.
Ill. 5: B. W. Kilburn, *Spinning Room, Lawrence Mill, Lowell, Mass, USA*, (1891), stereoscope card, author's collection.
Ill. 6: *Hood's Sarsaparilla Calendar for 1891* (1890), printed advertisement, back cover of *Hood's Lovely Woman, A Collection of Fun, Fancy and Fact*, pamphlet.

Introduction

Pages 1 facing and 1
Ill. 1: *Bird's Eye View of Lowell, from Fort Hill Park* (1910), postcard, author's collection.
Ill. 2: (Background image) Ella Carlson, foot detail from *Ruth and Charles Waltz* (2011) photograph.
Ill. 3: Ruth C. Evans, *Page from the 1866 Diary of Clark B. Evans* (2013), diary entry, author's collection.

Page 2
Ill. 1: "Husking the Corn in New England" and "The Dance After the Husking", *Harper's Weekly, A Journal of Civilization*, November 13, 1858, 728-729.

Chapter 1—*At the Bend in the River: Dancing before Lowell*

Pages 4 and 5
Ill 1: *A Plan of Sundry Farms &c. at Patucket in the Town of Chelmsford* (1821), reproduced from the original plan for the Proprietors of Locks and Canals on Merrimack River (1871), map, Norman B Leventhal Map Center at Boston Public Library.
Ill. 2: *Sleighing in Mount Royal Park, MONTREAL* (c. 1900), postcard, author's collection.
Ill. 3: Gen. Joseph Bradley Varnum, *The Lowell Book*, 26-27.
Ill. 4: The Varnum House, Ibid.

Pages 6 and 7
Ill. 1: "The Dancing School", *The Dancing Master; or, Directions for dancing country dances, with the tunes to each dance, for the treble-violin.* (10th ed. corrected, London, Printed by J. Heptinstall, for H. Playford, 1698), frontispiece, Library of Congress, http://memory.loc.gov/ammem/dihtml/dicatlg.html.
Ill. 2: Ruth C. Evans, Mockups created from descriptions in Water's *History of Chelmsford*, 457-458.
Ill. 3: *Danse au Chateau* (1920), postcard, author's collection.

Pages 8 and 9
Ill. 1: *Thanksgiving Ball at Middlesex Tavern*, photograph of an invitation written on a playing card, Lowell Historical Society.
Ill. 2: *Old Middlesex Tavern; Lowell, Mass. At Old Middlesex Village*, postcard, author's collection.
Ill. 3: *La Quadrille Français sous la Restauration*, (c. 1900), postcard, author's collection.

Page 10
Ill. 1: *Increase Mather*, artist's rendering, Library of Congress, http://www.loc.gov/pictures/item/2005692001/.
Ill. 2: *An Arrow Against Profane and Promiscuous Dancing*, 6.
Ill. 3: Elias Howe, "Waltz of Three Steps", *Howe's Complete Ball-Room Hand Book: Containing Upwards of Three Hundred Dances*, illustration, 71.

Chapter 2—*The Early Days: Lowell's Beginnings*

Pages 12 and 13
Ill. 1: "Junction of Concord & Merrimack Rivers," *Ballou's Pictorial Drawing Room Companion*, Vol. X, No. 17, 264.
Ill. 2: B. L. Singley, *Their First Dancing Lesson* (1900), stereoscope card, author's collection.

Pages 14 and 15
Ill. 1: *Interior of Lancashire Cotton Mills* (c. 1913), postcard, author's collection.
Ill. 2: Leo H. Grindon, "In a Cotton Factory," *Lancashire, Brief Historical and Descriptive Notes*, 95.
Ill. 3: Podmore, "A View of New Lanark," *Robert Owen: A Biography*, 48.

Ill. 4: George Hunt, *Mr Owen's Institution, New Lanark* (1825), color graphic printed by Pyall & Hunt. Digital image provided by Jerome Robbins Dance Division, The New York Public Library for the Performing Arts, Astor, Lenox and Tilden Foundations.

Pages 16 and 17

Ill. 1: James Queen, *Detail from the Power of Music* (c. 1872), chromolithograph created by Duval & Hunter and published by A. & C. Kaufmann, Library of Congress, http://www.loc.gov/pictures/item/98516820/.

Ill. 2: "The Effect of Bad and Good Circumstances," woodcuts in *Robert Owen: A Biography*, 112. Originally published in the 1834 reprint of *Owen's Essays on the Formation of the Human Character*.

Ill. 3: "Central View of Waltham, Mass.," *Ballou's Pictorial Drawing Room Companion*, Vol. X, No. 11, 161.

Ill. 4: *Boston Manufacturing Company Cotton Mill* (1906), postcard, author's collection.

Ill. 5: "Wash Room of Waltham Bleachery (c.1852);" *Gleason's Pictorial Drawing-Room Companion*, 1853, 400.

Ill. 6: Ibid, "Boiling Room of Waltham Bleachery."

Ill. 7: *Pawtucket Falls, Lowell, Mass* (c. 1910) postcard, author's collection.

Pages 18 and 19

Ill. 1: *Lowell, Mass. Ayer Home for Young Women and Children* (c. 1907), postcard, author's collection.

Ill. 2: "Old Marshall Tavern on Parker Street," *The Lowell Book*, 6.

Ill. 3: *Old Washington Tavern, First Stage Coach House in Lowell, Mass* (c. 1910), postcard, author's collection.

Ill. 4: Ellen Straw Thompson," Upper Hall of Spaulding House," *New England Magazine* (1907), 186. From the article "Rediscovering an Old House."

Ill. 5: John Lewis Krimmel, *Barroom Dancing* (c. 1820), watercolor, Library of Congress, http://www.loc.gov/pictures/item/2004661961/.

Pages 20 and 21

Ill. 1: *Interior of a Lowell Cotton Mill—Weave Room* (1913), image from postcard, author's collection.

Ill. 2: *Thanksgiving Ball at the Exeter House in Exeter, ME* (1857), dance announcement, author's collection.

Ill. 3: "New Shoe Store Advertisement" *Lowell Courier* (October 10, 1837), printed advertisement.

Ill. 4: Ibid, "Dancing & Waltzing Academy."

Pages 22 and 23

Ill. 1: *Dancing Couple* (1907), postcard, author's collection.

Ill. 2: *St. Anne's Church, Lowell, Mass.* (1911), postcard, author's collection.

Chapter 3—*Mixt Dance: Kissing, Courtship, and Damnation*

Pages 24 and 25

Ill. 1: *Joy and Happiness Untold* (1908), postcard, author's collection.

Ill. 2: *The Waltz* (1913), postcard, author's collection.

Ill. 3: *Risqué* (c. 1910), postcard, author's collection.

Ill. 4: Thomas A. Faulkner, *From the Ball-Room to Hell*, cover art. Black and white image colorized by author.

Ill. 5: Charles Durang, "Valse à Deux Temps", *The Fashionable Dancer's Casket*, 83.

Pages 26 and 27

Ill. 1: *A Solemn Warning to Dancers*, 1.

Ill. 2: *Ye Three Gay Young Gentlemen* (c. 1880), dance card, author's collection.

Ill. 3: *Old Line Ball Invitation*, photograph of vintage invitation, Lowell Historical Society.

Pages 28 and 29

Ill. 1: *Highland Club, Lowell Mass* (1913), postcard, author's collection.

Ill. 2: *Some Night, Some Waltz, Some Girl #1* (c. 1910), postcard, author's collection.

Ill. 3: Frédérique Vallet-Bisson, *After the Ball*, postcard, author's collection.

Pages 30 and 31

Ill. 1: *A Summer Girls Diary* (1910), postcard, author's collection.

Ill. 2a: (Frame) *Lady's Friend Magazine* (1865), cover art.

Ill. 2b: (Background image—also on p. 203) L.A. Tessier, *Tourbillon* (1917), from postcard, author's collection.

Pages 32 and 33

Ill. 1: *Hood's Sarsaparilla Parlor Games* (Lowell, MA: c. 1885), front and back cover art.

Ill. 2: Ibid, 5.

Pages 34 and 35
Ill. 1: *Crescent Moon at the Dance* (1915), postcard, author's collection.
Ill. 2: *E. W. Hoyt & Company Advertisement* (Lowell, MA: 1892), advertising card, author's collection.
Ill. 3: *Dr. J. C. Ayer & Company Advertisement* (Lowell, MA: 1886), advertising card, author's collection.

Chapter 4—*Country Dance: Contras and Quadrilles, Past and Present*
Pages 36 and 37
Ill. 1: Charles Pears, *Sir Roger De Coverly* (A.W. Penrose & Company, 1907), print, author's collection.
Ill. 2: Lucien O. Carpenter, "The Five Positions" *J. W. Pepper's Universal Dancing Master*, 5–6.
Ill. 3: J. Berryman, "The Five Positions of Dancing", *An Analysis of Country Dancing, wherein all the figures used in that polite amusement are rendered familiar by engraved lines* (London: J.S. Dickson, 1811), engraving.

Pages 38 and 39
Ill. 1: Thomas Hillgrove, *Complete Practical Guide to the Art of Dancing*, frontispiece.
Ill. 2: Douglas Plummer, *Dance Line* (2013), photograph. Taken at May Madness Dance Weekend, Clarkdale, AZ.
Ill. 3: Hillgrove, *Complete Practical Guide to the Art of Dancing*, 52, 54.

Pages 40 and 41
Ill. 1: Ibid, "The Moulinet", illustration, 95.
Ill. 2: Douglas Plummer, *Star* (2012), photograph. Taken at the Chehalis Dance Camp in Agassiz, BC.
Ill. 3: Ruth C. Evans, *Star Wrist Hold* (2014), illustration.
Ill. 4: Thomas Wilson, "Right and Left" *The Quadrille and Cotillion Panorama*, illustration, 34.
Ill. 5: Ibid, "Ladies Chain, 2nd Part", 40.
Ill. 6: Ruth C. Evans, *Courtesy Turn*, illustration.
Ill. 7: "Balance", *The Ball-Room Instructor*, illustration, 15.
Ill. 8: Burchenal, "Balance Step", *American Country-Dances*, introduction, xiv. Excerpt from the "Steps " section.

Pages 42 and 43
Ill. 1: Douglas Plummer, *Taking Hands* (2011), photograph. Taken at the New England Folk Festival.
Ill. 2: Ibid, *NEFFA Swing* (2011), photograph. Taken at the New England Folk Festival.
Ill. 3: Burchenal, "Buzz Step", *American Country-Dances*, introduction, xiv. Excerpt from the "Steps " section.
Ill. 4: Wilson, "Swing Corners", *The Complete System of English Country Dancing*, illustration.

Pages 44 and 45
Ill. 1: Hillgrove, "Contra Dance Formation", *Complete Practical Guide to the Art of Dancing*, diagram, 86.
Ill. 2: Wilson, "Ground Plan of a Quadrille", *The Quadrille and Cotillion Panorama*, illustration, 32.
Ill. 3: Howe, "Circular Form", *Howe's Complete Ball-Room Hand Book*, illustration, 21.
Ill. 4: "Money Musk", *The Gentleman & Lady's Companion; Containing*, 17.
Ill. 5: Howe, Elias et. al., "Money Musk", *American Dancing Master and Ball-Room Prompter: containing about five hundred dances*, 80.

Pages 46 and 47
Ill. 1: *"Old Line" Order of Dances* (1850), photograph of a vintage dance card, Lowell Historical Society.
Ill. 2: Ville, Paul, comp., "Lady Walpole's Reel", *Reels, Hornpipes, Jigs, Etc.*, 9.
Ill. 3: Howe et al, "Balance Four in a Line", *American Dancing Master and Ball-Room Prompter*, illustration, 16.
Ill. 4: *First Grand Concert and Ball of Chevalier Lodge, No. 2, K. of P.* (1899), photograph of a vintage dance card, Lowell Historical Society.

Pages 48, 49, 50 and 51
Ill. 1: "Sleighing in New England", *The Graphic*, Dec. 26, 1874, 620–21, illustration.

Pages 62 and 63
Ill. 1: Hillgrove, "The Lancers' Quadrilles", *Complete Practical Guide to the Art of Dancing*, illustration, 97.
Ill. 2: Ibid, "Lancers' Third Figure", 102 - 104.
Ill. 3: Douglas Plummer, *Dance Hall Doorway* (2013), photograph. Taken at the May Madness Dance Weekend in Clarkdale, AZ.

Chapter 5—*'Round the Room: Galop and Polka and Waltz, Oh My!*
Pages 54 and 55
Ill. 1: *The Daily Graphic, An Illustrated Evening Newspaper*, February 23, 1878, Vol. XV, No. 1538, front page.
Ill. 2: Lionel Peraux, *Opening of a French Waltz* (c. 1900), postcard, author's collection.

Pages 56 and 57
Ill. 1: Ferdinand von Řezníček, untitled illustration (c. 1900), postcard, author's collection.
Ill. 2: Hubert Köhler, "Deutsche Volkslieder: Rosenstock, Holderblüt'—danzlied" (c.1905), vintage postcard from author's collection. The title translates to: "German Folksong: Rosetreee, Elder-blossom—dance tune." The title refers to a waltz-time tune/dance, which is quite possibly a Ländler.
Ill. 3: J.R.A. Randall, frontispiece engraving from Wilson's *The Correct Method of Waltzing*. Color photo of frontispiece (1816 edition) provided by John Drury Rare Books, Essex, UK. Image enhanced by author.
Ill. 4: Ibid, title page. Original image recreated by author for legibility.

Pages 58 and 59
Ill. 1: *Valseuses* (1901), postcard, author's collection.
Ill. 2: *Byron Illustrated—The Waltz* (c. 1895), illustration based on painting by F. Stephanoff, postcard, author's collection.
Ill. 3: "The Polka Fashions", *Godey's Ladies' Book*, vol. XXXI, 1845.

Pages 60 and 61
Ill. 1: "Polka Gaiters Advertisement", *The Daily Courier*, May 19, 1848, printed advertisement.
Ill. 2: "Fancy Polka Step," *Howe's Complete Ballroom Handbook*, illustration, 93.
Ill. 3: Jan Moniuszko, *Mazur*, (c. 1908), postcard, author's collection.
Ill. 4: *Varsovienne* (1903), postcard, author's collection.

Pages 62 and 63
Ill. 1: *The Butcher's Dress Ball* (1873), photograph of inside of dance card, Lowell Historical Society.
Ill. 2: *Masquerade Ball* (1873), photograph of dance card, Lowell Historical Society.
Ill. 3: *Gilbert's Round Dancing*, index, 3–8. Original image recreated by author.
Ill. 4: Ibid, "The Five Positions with Modifications", illustration, 25–30.

Chapter 6—*The Middle Years: Dancing 'Round Every Corner*
Pages 64 and 65
Ill. 1: "View of the Boott Cotton Mills, at Lowell, Mass.", *Gleason's Pictorial Drawing Room Companion*, vol. II, no. 22, May 29, 1852.
Ill. 2: *Bird's Eye View of Lowell* (c. 1880), stereoscope card, author's collection.
Ill. 3: "Lowell Court House", *Ballou's Pictorial Drawing Room Companion*, vol. X, no. 17, 265.

Pages 66 and 67
Ill. 1: *The Bloomer Waltz* (1851), sheet music cover, Library of Congress, digital library. http://hdl.loc.gov/loc.pnp/cph.3g03591.
Ill. 2: "Lawrence, Boott and Merrimack Mills", *Lowell Illustrated*.
Ill. 3: *Irish Life: A Jig on the Green* (1909), postcard, author's collection.

Pages 68 and 69
Ill. 1: *Le Bal a la Veillee* (1939), postcard, author's collection.
Ill. 2: "Photograph 32: Tenements of Irish and Greeks, Rear View from Canal Bridge, Broadway", *The Record of a City*, 52—53.
Ill. 3: Ibid, "Photograph 24: Block of Thirty-Two Tenements, Corner of Elm and Linden Streets."
Ill. 4: Ibid, "Map 1: Foreign Districts."

Pages 70 and 71
Ill. 1: "E. Bigelow," *Appleton's Cyclopaedia of American Biography, Vol. 1*, (New York, D. Appleton and Company, 1888) illustration, 260.
Ill. 2: James E. Taylor, *Guiseppina Morlacchi*, portrait, SPC BAE 4605 01602619, National Anthropological Archives, Smithsonian Institution, http://collections.si.edu/search/results.htm?q=record_ID:siris_arc_40622.
Ill. 3: "Civil War Header", *Harper's Weekly, A Journal of Civilization*, vol. VIII, no. 371, February 6, 1864, 81.
Ill. 4: Ibid, "Stag Dance", 93.
Ill. 5: *Patrick S. Gilmore*, photographic print, Library of Congress, http://www.loc.gov/pictures/item/99471795.

Pages 72 and 73
Ill. 1: *Excursion to Lowell* (c. 1882), printed advertisement, author's collection.
Ill. 2: *Lasting Machine Shaping Shoes in a Massachusetts Shoe Factory* (c. 1910), stereoscope card, author's collection.

Ill. 3: Ruth C. Evans, *Pillings Shoe Factory Building* (2014), photograph.
Ill. 4: *A Mule-Spinner and His Assistant (Leopold Daigneau), Chace Cotton Mill, Burlington, VT. May 7, 1909* (1909), photograph, Library of Congress, http://www.loc.gov/pictures/item/ncl2004001517/pp/.
Ill. 5: *Letter Carriers' Ball* (1893), postcard-style handbill, author's collection.
Ill. 6: *Postmaster and Letter Carriers at Post Office*, Bridgeport, Conn. (c. 1909), postcard detail, author's collection.

Pages 74 and 75
Ill. 1: *State Armory at Lowell, Mass.* (c. 1905), postcard, author's collection.
Ill. 2: "Main Floor of Nelson's Colonial Department Store", *Lowell Illustrated*.
Ill.3: *Boston and Lowell Clothing Company Advertisement* (c. 1883), advertising card, author's collection.

Pages 76 and 77
Ill. 1: *Base Ball Polka* (c. 1865), sheet music cover, Library of Congress, http://hdl.loc.gov/loc.pnp/ppmsca.09564.
Ill. 2: *Canal Walk, Lowell, Mass.* (1906), postcard, author's collection.
Ill. 3: *Skating Scene at Shedd Park, Lowell, Mass.* (1912), postcard, author's collection.
Ill. 4: *View in South Common, Lowell, Mass.* (1910), postcard, author's collection.
Ill. 5: *Willow Dale Park, Bower Bros. Props. Lowell, Mass.* (c.1905), postcard, author's collection.

Pages 78 and 79
Ill. 1: "A Partial View of Bowling Alleys and Pool Room, Y.M.C.I. Building", *YMCI Five Year Book*, 312.
Ill. 2: *Merrimack Valley Auto Race Course* (c. 1910), postcard, author's collection.
Ill. 3: *Lowell Skating Rink, Corner of Gorham and Union Streets* (c. 1880), advertising card, author's collection.
Ill. 4: *I'm Making Headway* (1916), postcard, author's collection.
Ill. 5: Ruth C. Evans, *Arm Chair*, clip art.

Chapter 7—*The Ballroom: Its Decorum, Dimensions, and Delights*

Pages 80 and 81
Ill. 1: *The Ballroom—The Waltz* (North Bennington, VT: H.C. White Co., 1902), from stereoscope card, author's collection.
Ill. 2: *To See Another's Arms Around You Dear, Makes My Heart Ache* (1907), postcard, author's collection.

Pages 82 and 83
Ill. 1: "Lynch Advertisement" (1874), *Lowell Directory*, printed ad, 500.
Ill. 2: *Hamilton Hall*, photograph of stereoscope card, Lowell Historical Society.
Ill. 3: *Dance Hall. White City, Worcester, Mass.* (1914), detail from postcard, author's collection.

Pages 84 and 85
Ill. 1: *Ball Given by the City of New York to the Japanese Embassy at the Metropolitan Hotel,* June 25, 1860 (1860), enhanced image, Library of Congress, http://www.loc.gov/pictures/resource/cph.3f06401/.
Ill. 2: *Fig. 10--Verre Du Bec D'Argand* (c. 1869), Library of Congress, http://www.loc.gov/pictures/item/2006691769/.
Ill. 3: "Lowell Gas Light Co. Advertisement," *YMCI Five Year Book*, 124.
Ill. 4: "Main Hall, Y.M.C.I Building", detail from photograph, *YMCI Five Year Book*, facing, 128.
Ill. 5: The Miriam and Ira D. Wallach Division of Art, Prints and Photographs: Photography Collection, The New York Public Library. "Archer and Pancoast Manufacturing Co. [Gas chandeliers exhibit]" New York Public Library Digital Collections. http://digitalcollections.nypl.org/items/510d47e0-b506-a3d9-e040-e00a18064a99.

Pages 86 and 87
Ill. 1: *Hoyt's German Cologne 1892 Calendar* (1892), advertising card, author's collection.
Ill. 2: Hedwig Rosenkranz, *Couple Dancing* (Heidenau, Germany, 1887), photograph, author's collection.
Ill. 3: *Ayer's Hair Vigor* (c. 1890), advertising card, author's collection.
Ill. 4: "Les Mode Parisiennes, July 1865." *Peterson's Magazine, Vol. XLVIII, No. 1*, Philadelphia: July, 1865, 9.

Pages 88 and 89
Ill. 1: Ruth C. Evans, *Ayer Ball*, image derived from "Photograph 48. Ayer Home, Pawtucket Street," *The Record of A City*, facing, 178.
Ill. 2: *Cordial Thanksgiving Greetings*, detail from postcard, author's collection.
Ill. 3: Lewis Wickes Hine, *Doffer Girls in Brookside Worsted Mills. Westford, Mass.* (1909), photograph, Library of Congress, http://www.loc.gov/pictures/item/ncl2004001495/pp/.

Pages 90 and 91

Ill. 1: Charles Jay Taylor, *Rainsford is Right—The Rich Must be Regulated* (1897), detail from lithograph, Library of Congress, http://www.loc.gov/pictures/item/2012647649/.

Ill. 2: *Howe's Complete Ball-Room Hand Book: Containing Upwards of Three Hundred Dances*, title page.

Ill. 3: *Won't You Waltz Home Sweet Home with Me for Old Times Sake?* (1907), postcard, author's collection.

Pages 92 and 93

Ill. 1: "Grand Ball Advertisement," *Lowell Sun*, February 2, 1901.

Ill. 2: *The Ball Room Companion*, cover and frontispiece.

Ill. 3: "Lowell Cadet Orchestra Advertisement". *YMCI Five Year Book*, printed advertisement, 54.

Ill. 4: W.N. Jennings, *Salem Cadet Band—Willow Grove Park, Philadelphia, PA* (1905) photograph of a postcard from CardCow.com.

Ill. 5: *Concert by Salem Cadet Band, Salem Willows, Mass.* (1911), detail from postcard, author's collection.

Pages 94 and 95

Ill. 1: "The Honorable Joseph H. Hibbard," *A Souvenir of Massachusetts Legislators*, 81.

Ill. 2: *Hopkinton Masquerade Card Detail* (1882), dance card, author's collection.

Ill. 3: *Palms in Ballroom* (c. 1914), photograph from the author's collection, deaccessioned by Culver Pictures.

Ill. 4: "Interior of Women's Club", *The Lowell Book*, 45.

Ill. 5: *Columbia Records Graphophone Advertisement* (1914), detail of printed advertisement, author's collection.

Chapter 8—*A Short Tour: The Victorian Dance Halls of Downtown Lowell*

Pages 96 and 97

Ill. 1: G.M. Hopkins, *City Atlas of Lowell Massachusetts*, map. 15, 22, 23, plates B & D.

Ill. 2: "Second Universalist Church on Shattuck Street," *Bay State Monthly*, Vol. I, No. 3, etching.

Ill. 3: Ruth C. Evans, *Athenean Corner* (2013), photograph.

Ill. 4: "Casto Theatre," *Views of Lowell and Vicinity*, photograph.

Pages 98 and 99

Ill. 1: Ruth C. Evans, *Condos and Leo Roy garage* (2011), photograph.

Ill. 2: Cowley, "Lowell Co. Mills," *Illustrated History of Lowell*, illustration, 52.

Ill. 3: "Lowell Manufacturing Co. Advertisement," *Lowell Directory* (1866), printed advertisement, 317.

Ill. 4: "Hamilton Manufacturing Co. Advertisement," *Lowell Directory* (1866), printed advertisement, 318.

Pages 100 and 101

Ill. 1: Ruth C. Evans, *Father John's Building* (2013), photograph.

Ill. 2: *Mechanics Phalanx on Market Street* (c. 1870), photograph of stereoscope card, Lowell Historical Society.

Ill. 3: Ruth C. Evans, *Market House* (2014), photograph.

Ill. 4: "Cotillion Parties Announcement" *Lowell Daily Journal & Courier*, January 26, 1854.

Ill. 5: Ruth C. Evans, *New Mansur Building* (2015), altered photograph (traffic light in foreground edited out).

Pages 102 and 103

Ill. 1: Ruth C. Evans, *Appleton Block* (2011), photograph.

Ill. 2: *Central Street, Lowell, Mass.* (c. 1900), postcard, author's collection.

Ill. 3: "French's Advertisement," *Lowell Directory* (1866), printed advertisement, 337.

Ill. 4: *Union Ball at French's Hall* (1855), photograph of vintage dance card, Lowell Historical Society.

Ill. 5: *Central Street* (c. 1870), photograph of vintage stereoscope card, Lowell Historical Society.

Ill. 6: *Butcher's Dress Ball at Goddard's Hall* (1873), photograph of vintage dance card, Lowell Historical Society.

Ill. 7: "Goddard's Advertisement," *Lowell Directory* (1874), printed advertisement, frontispiece.

Pages 104 and 105

Ill. 1: *The Junction of Prescott and Central St., Lowell, Mass.* (c. 1900), postcard, author's collection.

Ill. 2: "Hibbard Advertisement," *YMCI Five Year Book*, printed advertisement, 44.

Ill. 3: "Burbank Building Advertisement," *Lowell of Today* (Lowell Daily Citizen, 1893) 83.

Ill. 4: George H. Russel, *Central Street Parade* (c. 1914), photograph, author's collection.

Ill. 5: Ruth C. Evans, *Howe building* (2015), photograph.

Pages 106 and 107

Ill. 1: *Merrimack Square, Lowell, Mass.* (c. 1900), photograph of a postcard from CardCow.com.

Ill. 2: Ruth C. Evans, *Fairburn Building and Page's Clock* (2013), photograph.

Ill. 3: "Merrimack Street," *Lowell Illustrated*, photograph.

Ill. 4: *Bridge Street and Keith's Theatre toward Sun Building, Lowell, Mass.* (c. 1912), photograph of a postcard, Lowell Historical Society.

Pages 108 and 109

Ill. 1: *Street Car Waiting Room, Merrimack Square, Lowell, Mass* (c. 1900), postcard, author's collection.

Ill. 2: Ruth C. Evans, *Page's Clock* (2013), photograph.

Ill. 3: *Hildreth Building, Lowell, Mass.* (c. 1900), postcard, author's collection.

Ill. 4: *Ticket to Lowell Mechanic Phalanx Ball* (1875), printed ticket, author's collection.

Ill. 5: *Merrimack Street* (c. 1880), stereoscope card, author's collection.

Pages 110 and 111

Ill. 1: "Freewill Baptist Church," *Lowell Offering*, series 1, no.7 (September 1841), photograph, 263. Image courtesy of Lawrence Public Library.

Ill. 2: Ruth C. Evans, *Pollard Building* (2013), photograph.

Ill. 3: *Central Fire Station, Lowell, Mass.* (c. 1900), postcard, author's collection

Ill. 4: "Burke Temperance Institute Building: Ford and Phillips, Architects," *Lowell Sun*, July 11, 1891.

Ill. 5: Ruth C. Evans, *Institute Building* (2014), photograph.

Page 112 and 113

Ill. 1: Ruth C. Evans, *Bon Marché* (2013), photograph.

Ill. 2: "Nichols and Hutchins Advertisement," *Lowell Directory* (1874), printed advertisement, 482.

Ill. 3: *Merrimack St., Lowell, Mass.* (1916), postcard, author's collection.

Ill. 4: Ruth C. Evans, *Welles Building* (2013), photograph.

Ill. 5: Ibid, *St. Joseph's* (2013), photograph.

Ill. 6: *St. Joseph's Church, Lowell, Mass.* (c. 1900), postcard, author's collection.

Pages 114 and 115

Ill. 1: *Citizens' Union Ball Invitation* (1833), photograph of vintage dance card, Lowell Historical Society.

Ill. 2: Ruth C. Evans, *Old City Hall* (2013), photograph.

Ill. 3: *Old City Hall* (c. 1870), stereoscope card, author's collection.

Ill. 4: *Merrimack Street, Lowell, Mass.* (c. 1900), postcard, author's collection.

Ill. 5: "Urban Hall Advertisement," *Lowell Daily Courier* (September 6, 1873), printed advertisement.

Ill. 6: "Brooks and Davis' Quadrille Band Notice," *Lowell Daily Courier* (March 26, 1866), printed advertisement.

Ill. 7: Ruth C. Evans, *Wentworth Block* (2013), photograph.

Pages 116 and 117

Ill. 1: "Huntington Hall," *Views of Lowell and Vicinity*, photograph.

Ill. 2: "Mechanic's Hall," *Contributions to the Old Residents Historical Association*, photograph, 282.

Ill. 3: Ruth C. Evans, *Mechanic's Hall and Dutton Street* (2013), photograph.

Ill. 4: *Merrimack House* (c. 1870), stereoscope card, author's collection.

Ill. 5: *Associate Hall and Monument Square, Lowell, Mass.* (1909), postcard, author's collection.

Ill. 6: Ruth C. Evans, *Merrimack and Dutton* (2013), photograph.

Page 118 and 119

Ill. 1: Ruth C. Evans, *Representative Arches* (2013), photograph.

Ill. 2: *Fireman's Fund Ball Dance Card* (1890), vintage dance card, author's collection.

Ill. 3: "Shattuck Street side of Huntington Hall," *Ballou's Pictorial Drawing Room Companion*, Vol. X., No. 17, (April 26, 1856), etching, 264.

Ill. 4: "Mechanic's Hall Interior," *Contributions to the Old Residents Historical Association*. Vol. VI, No. 1., 299.

Ill. 5: George Kenngott, "Photograph 8, Mechanics' Hall, now First Trinitarian Congregational Church," *The Record of a City, A Social Survey of Lowell Massachusetts*, facing, 10.

Pages 120 and 121

Ill. 1: *Thanksgiving Ball Invitation* (1839), photograph of vintage dance invitation, Lowell Historical Society.

Ill. 2: *New Merrimac House, Lowell, Mass.* (1907), postcard, author's collection.

Ill. 3: "Merrimack House Advertisement," *YMCI Five Year Book*, printed advertisement, 12.

Ill. 4: *Lowell Elk's Concert and Ball Program*, cover and front page from the author's collection.

Ill. 5: "Associate Hall Advertisement," *Lowell Daily Sun* (January 27, 1894), printed advertisement.

Ill. 6: Trades and Labor Council of Lowell, "Associate Hall," *Lowell: A City of Spindles*, 123.

Pages 122 and 123
Ill. 1: Ruth C. Evans, *Lowell National Park Trolley and Brick Arch* (2013), photograph.

Ill. 2: "Lowell Museum Advertisement," *Lowell Daily Journal and Courier* (January 4, 1850), printed ad.

Ill. 3: "Merrimack Street," *Ballou's Pictorial Drawing Room Companion*, detail of etching, Vol. X, No. 17, 265.

Pages 124 and 125
Il. 1: Trades and Labor Council of Lowell. "View From City Hall," *Lowell: A City of Spindles*, 175.

Ill. 2: Corey Sciuto, "View from City Hall," *History, Urbanism, Photography, and Technobabble from the capital of the Merrimack Valley* (blog), April 1, 2012, http://www.coreysciuto.blogspot.com/2012/04/photo-tour-lowell-city-hall.html. Image used with permission.

Chapter 9—*Out of the City: The Trolley Parks*

Pages 126 and 127
Ill. 1: Robert H. Derrah, *Derrah's Official Street Railway Guide for Eastern New England*, fold-out map.

Ill. 2: Ibid, book cover.

Pages 128 and 129
Ill. 1: *Lakeview Park, Boardwalk in Pavillion, Lowell, Mass.* (1908), postcard, author's collection.

Ill. 2: *Lakeview Park Flyer* (1892), printed advertisement, author's collection.

Ill. 3: Derrah, "Pole Catcher Advertisement," *Derrah's Official Street Railway Guide for Eastern New England*, printed ad on inside of back cover.

Ill. 4: "Lakeview Park Advertisement," *Lowell Sun*, June 14, 1902.

Pages 130 and 131
Ill. 1: *Thomson's Patent Glove-Fitting Corsets Promotional Card*, detail of promotional card, author's collection.

Ill. 2: Derrah, *Derrah's Official Street Railway Guide for Eastern New England*, 56.

Ill. 3: Meyer Billmers, *Cecil Sharp (C#) Pavilion at Dusk* (c. 2008), photograph.

Ill. 4: *A Couple in the Woods* (c. 1900), postcard, author's collection.

Pages 132 and 133
Ill. 1: Derrah, "Trolley Time Table," *Derrah's Official Street Railway Guide for Eastern New England*, 48.

Ill. 2: *Dance Hall, Canobie Lake Park* (1900), postcard, author's collection.

Ill. 3: *Dance Hall, Whalom Park, Mass.* (c. 1900), postcard, author's collection.

Ill. 4: *The Grounds and Skating Pavilion, at the Pines, Groveland, Mass.* (c. 1900), postcard, author's collection.

Ill. 5: *Suntaug Lake Inn, Lynnfield, Mass.* (1922), postcard, author's collection.

Page 134 and 135
Ill. 1: *Interior of Dance Hall, Lake Pearl* (1912), postcard, author's collection.

Ill. 2: *Dance Hall, Lake Pearl, Wrentham, Mass* (1909), postcard, author's collection.

Ill. 3: *Concert by Salem Cadet Band, Salem Willows, Mass.* (1911), postcard, author's collection.

Ill. 4: *Salem Willows, Mass. Dancing Casino, View from the Park* (1911), postcard, author's collection.

Ill. 5: Derrah, "The Cove, Salem Willows," *Derrah's Official Street Railway Guide for Eastern New England*, 30.

Ill. 6: Derrah, "Salem Willows," *Derrah's Official Street Railway Guide for Eastern New England*, 30.

Ill. 7: *Hampton Beach Casino, Hampton Beach, N.H.* (1907), postcard, author's collection.

Ill. 8: *Palm Garden, Paragon Park, Nantasket Beach, Mass* (1924), postcard, author's collection.

Ill. 9: *Entrance to Paragon Park showing New Dance Hall and Roller Coaster, Nantasket Beach, Mass.* (c. 1917), postcard, author's collection.

Pages 136 and 137
Ill. 1: *Round Dance Hall, Salisbury Beach, Mass.* (1909), postcard, author's collection.

Ill. 2: *Square Dance Hall, Salisbury Beach, Mass.* (c.1911), postcard, author's collection.

Ill. 3: *Children's Free Dancing School, Ocean Echo, Salisbury Beach, Mass.* (c. 1920), postcard, author's collection.

Ill. 4: *Glouchester, Mass. The Pavilion, Long Beach, Cape Ann.* (c. 1900), postcard, author's collection.

Ill. 5: *Ocean Pier Dancing Pavilion, Revere Beach, Mass.* (c. 1915), postcard, author's collection.

Ill. 6: *Condit's Dance Hall, Revere Beach, Mass.* (1911), postcard, author's collection.

Chapter 10—*The 1900s Arrive: Ragtime Dances Come to Town*

Pages 138 and 139
Ill. 1: United Press Photo, *Vernon and Irene Castle* (1914), photograph.

Ill. 2: Ruth C. Evans, *1910 Power House* (2015), photograph.

Pages 140 and 141
Ill. 1: Ibid, *1909 Spinning Mill* (2015), photograph.
Ill. 2: Ibid, *Lowell Silk Mills* (2015), photograph.
Ill. 3: "Victrola Advertisement", *The Etude* (c. 1915), printed advertisement, author's collection.

Pages 142 and 143
Ill. 1: *Lowell Elk's Ball Order of Dances* (1909), dance program, author's collection.
Ill. 2: *Joplin's Maple Leaf Rag* (1899), highlighted text added by author, sheet music from the Mutopia Project, http://www.mutopiaproject.org/.

Pages 144 and 145
Ill. 1: Vernon and Irene Castle, "Starting the Castlewalk," *Modern Dancing* (New York: Published by the World Syndicate Co. under an arrangement with Harper & Brothers, 1914), 42.
Ill. 2: Ibid, "Taking a Corner", 42.
Ill. 3: Ibid, "The Spin", 53.
Ill. 4: Louis H. Mentel, "More Mustard Preview," *Mentel's Maxixe* (1914), printed advertisement on back cover, author's collection.

Page 146 and 147
Ill. 1: Vernon and Irene Castle, "Hesitation Waltz Sequence", *Modern Dancing*, 75.
Ill. 2: *Tango/Waltz Dip* (c. 1914), postcard, author's collection.
Ill. 3: *Tango's Corte con Cruzado* (1914), postcard, author's collection.
Ill. 4: United Press International Photo, *Castles Dance the Innovation* (1914), photograph.

Pages 148 and 149
Ill. 1: Vernon and Irene Castle, "The Cortez", *Modern Dancing*, 82.
Ill. 2: *Tango's Corte con Cruzado w/Open Hold* (c. 1914), postcard from the author's collection.
Ill. 3: Adam Taylor, "Paso Doble", *Dancing With the Stars* (2011), photograph, © Taylor/ABC.
Ill. 4: Mentel, *Mentel's Maxixe* (1914), cover of sheet music from the author's collection.

Page 150 and 151
Ill. 1: Vernon and Irene Castle, "Maxixe Two Step Sequence", *Modern Dancing*, 123.
Ill. 2: Ibid, "Maxixe Back Two Step", 118.
Ill. 3: Ailura, *Samba* (2012), performed by Marian Sivak and Kristina Raczova at the 2012 Austrian Open Championships, photograph, distributed under a CC BY-SA 3.0 license.
Ill. 4: Harry Fox, *Pretty Soon* (1914), cover image from sheet music, author's collection.
Ill. 5: "Modern Dance Instruction Advertisement", *Lowell Sun*, September 28, 1914, printed advertisement.

Pages 152 and 153
Ill. 1: "Mr. and Mrs. Vernon Castle's New Dances for this Winter", *Ladies Home Journal*, December 1914, 24–25.

Pages 154 and 155
Ill. 1: "Bon Marche Advertisement", *Lowell Sun,* January 27, 1915, printed advertisement.
Ill. 2: Ibid, "Cherry & Web Advertisement", November 27, 1914.
Ill. 3: "The Lulu Fado Separation Step", *Boston Sunday Post*, November 22, 1914.
Ill. 4: Ruth Evans, *Home at 58 Highland Street* (2015), photograph.

Pages 156 and 157
Ill. 1a: Edgar A. Guest, "Foxtrot Poem", *Lowell Sun*, December 4, 1914.
Ill. 1b: (Background image) *Stumbling: A Fox Trot Oddity* (1921), from sheet music cover, author's collection.
Ill. 2: "Entertainment Advertisements", *Lowell Sun*, July 30, 1912, printed advertisements.

Pages 158 and 159
Ill. 1: *Dances of Today* (c. 1914), postcard, author's collection.
Ill. 1: *The Tango* (c. 1914), postcard, author's collection.
Ill. 2: Ruth C. Evans, *Market Building/Police Court* (2015), photograph.

Page 160 and 161
Ill. 1: "Tangoists Not Guilty" *Lowell Sun*, March 5, 1914, printed banner headline.
Ill. 2: "Le Tango et le Police", *Le Petit Journal* (illustrated supplement), December 21, 1913.
Ill. 3: *Vampyr Dance* (c. 1914), postcard, author's collection.

Page 162 and 163
Ill. 1: United Press International Photo, *Vernon and Irene Castle* (1914), photograph.

Ill. 2: *Columbia Records Advertisement* (1914), modified photograph of item in the author's collection. Image altered to remove text.

Chapter 11—*Germans, Grizzlies, and More: Novelties and Fads*

Pages 164 and 165
Ill. 1: "Baby-Polka," *Gilbert's Round Dancing*, 68.

Ill. 2: *I Will Show You How* (c. 1914), postcard, author's collection.

Ill. 3: "Barnyard Masquerade Costume," *Ladies Home Journal*, November 1914, Curtis Publishing Company, Philadelphia, 29.

Pages 166 and 167
Ill. 1: *Le Cake-Walk, Dansé au Nouveau Cirque, Les Négres* (1905), postcard, author's collection.

Ill. 2: *Cake Walk, Dansé au Nouveau Cirque, Les Elks* (c. 1905), postcard, author's collection.

Ill. 3: C.B. Dillon, "Winter Dances and Cotillions: Golf," *Woman's Home Companion*, November 1910.

Ill. 4: "The Lasso: A Favorite cotillion Figure in the January Dances," *Lowell Sun*, January 21, 1899.

Pages 168 and 169
Ill. 1: Henry Tenré,"Kotillon," 1893 wood engraving from *Moderne Kunst, Illustrierte Zeitscrift* [Modern Art Illustrated Journal], VII, Berlin, 9.

Pages 170 and 171
Ill. 1: "The Favor", from *Dancing* by Marguerite Wilson, 130.

Ill. 2: "Schedule for Leaders" from *The German*, 45.

Ill. 3: *France,—Le Cotillon* (c. 1903), advertising card, author's collection.

Ill. 4: "Main Hall, Y.M.C.I Building", *YMCI Five Year Book*, facing, 128.

Ill. 5: "Hobble Skirt Fashion Illustrations," *La Mode*, April 17, 1910, year 15, no. 16, 8–9.

Pages 172 and 173
Ill. 1: *Le 'Turkey Trot'* (1913), postcard with illustration by Xavier Sager, author's collection.

Ill. 2: *Everybody's Doing It Now* (c. 1913), postcard, author's collection.

Ill. 3: "Victrola Music Gives Dancing New Delight," *Metropolitan Magazine* (c. 1915), advertisement.

Pages 174 and 175
Ill. 1: *Vaudeville Women Dip* (c. 1905), postcard, author's collection.

Ill. 2: *Vaudeville Women Spanish Dance* (c. 1908), postcard, author's collection.

Ill. 3: *Vampyr Dance!* (c. 1914), postcard, author's collection.

Ill. 4: *Circulating Library* (1895), photograph of dance card, Lowell Historical Society.

Chapter 12—*The Last Waltz: From Flappers to Folk Festivals*

Pages 176 and 177
Ill. 1: *Boott Cotton Mill Clock Tower* (c. 1968), photograph, Library of Congress. http://www.loc.gov/pictures/resource/hhh.ma1289.photos.080691p/.

Ill. 2: *Empty Storehouse at the Boott* (c. 1968), photograph, Library of Congress. http://www.loc.gov/pictures/resource/hhh.ma1289.photos.080723p/.

Ill. 3: Ruth C. Evans, *Coal House Ruins* (2015), photograph.

Pages 178 and 179
Ill. 1: Ruth C. Evans, *Abandoned Mills* (2015), photograph.

Ill. 2: "Commodore Advertisement", *Lowell Sun*, May 5, 1924, printed advertisement.

Ill. 3: *Commodore Ballroom* (1931), photograph, Lowell Historical Society.

Ill. 4: *The Laurier Hotel*, 507 Merrimack St., Lowell, Mass. (1943), postcard, author's collection.

Ill. 5: *High Hat Roll-A-Way, Princeton Blvd., Lowell Mass.* (c. 1955), postcard, author's collection.

Pages 180 and 181
Ill. 1: *Totem Pole Ballroom at Norumbega Park—Auburndale, in Newton, Massachusetts* (c. 1940), photograph of a postcard from CardCow.com.

Ill. 2: Ruth C. Evans, *Lowell Festival Courtyard* (2013), photograph.

Ill. 3: Ruth C. Evans, *Lowell Festival Dance Tent* (2013), photograph.

Appendix I:

Trying to analyze all the hidden meanings in this poem is beyond the skills of the author or the purview of this book, but here it is for anyone interested. It is a fascinating look at "respectable" partying in a Massachusetts mill town in the 1860s.

The Donation

J. J. F., Housatonic, MA, January 1861
quoted in *Berkshire County Eagle,* March 27, 1862.

How did the Parson's Donation go o'er?
There was "Great Expectations;"
Much frying and baking,
Some "stewing", and quaking,
      For fear that the "frosting,"
Should spoil in the making.
There were doughnuts, enticing—
Some cakes worth the slicing:
      And *one* with ten dimes
Stuck around in the icing!
There was tea (black and green)
But no coffee was seen;
      And the moon-shine and sleighing,
The best that have been.
Pleasant words were essayed;
      A Poem was read;
And some very nice music,
      Was very well did,
There were Ships filled with "notions"
      (Private *earing*, some said)
That tried, might and *main*,
      To run the blockade.
And a game where you go out,
      A candle to find,
And, ("going it *blind*")
Try hard for a blow out!
There was "crinoline"—plenty—
      And jockies—so jaunty!
(The Dollars collected,
      Were five and twice twenty.)
There was marching (quite solemn!)
'Round the old chimney column;
And plays with the girls,
Where you pull 'em and haul 'em
Now chase 'em, now miss 'em;
Now catch 'em, now kiss 'em,
"Roped in" by that, Drag-on,
They call Copenhagan:'—
Which is just a new name
      For a very old Dagon;
That's worship'd, just now,
      ("Lip-service," I trow!)
As our grandmothers worship'd
      Their *mizzle-toe*-bough!—

With racing and chasing;
And whirling and twirling
And flying and catching;
And snatching and catching;
And shouting and pouting;
And slapping and flapping;
And hurrying and worrying;
And blundering and floundering;
And falling and sprawling;
And giggling and wriggling;
And teasing and squeezing;
And musing and bussing,
And may be, some cussing,
Round the rope—whose bare touch
Has a magic that's such
      It almost beat the devil—
And it quite "beats the Dutch."
There was capering and prancing;
Retreating, advancing!
      (But never a fiddle—
For then there'd be "dancing!")
There's a needle, whose eye,
      No one could pass through,
Without finding "knots,"
      Very hard to undo,
While the thread (a whole skein)
Makes a musical din,
As if 'twere a new sewers' singing machine!
      And this is its song,
      As it gallops along,
While heart, hand and foot,
      Keep time to the tongue.
"This needle's eye, what can surpass
      The thread that trips it through?
It has caught many a smiling lass
      And now it has caught *you!*"
And, so being caught,
You cannot do ought,
But kiss or *be* kissed,
'Till you are nearly distraught:
Then you "all hands around,"
Tripping lightly the ground,
And "forward and back"wards
Most gaily you bound.

('Tis very "fast *walking*"—
    As the dance you were mocking
        But not a "cotillion"—
For that would be shocking!)
And, then, there's a "mill,"
    With very queer "hoppers,"
(We don't call them dancers,
    For "dancing's improper!")
And this is, good lack!
The gist of its clack,
As it goes round and round,
But not "forward and back."
    "Happy is the Miller-Boy,
        He lives alone by stealth;
    As the wheel turns round,
        He gathers up his wealth;
    One hand in the hopper
        The other in the bag,
    As the mill goes 'round,
        He calls out—"*Grab*"

He then "grabs" your partner,
And you "grab" another,
And, if you get "sack'd,"
    Oh, ain't there a bother!
But 'round goes the Mill again;
Music you trill again;
Hands clasp hot hands,
Till they tingle and thrill again;
    Your cheek in a blaze—
Your blood in a bound—
    You romp and you race,
While the Mill goes round.
    Sly glances, half-hidden,
Bold kisses unbidden,
    But not any "*dancing*"
For *that* is forbidden!

Appendix II:

A Joyful Account of a Joyous Occasion.
A Lowell Party as Seen Through Boston Spectacles.
Quoted in the *Lowell Daily Courier*, February 10, 1871

Miss Joy, who is one of the reportorial staff of the *Boston Post*, thus does the party given by Mrs. Ayer on Wednesday evening:

It is very probable that there is no other city of its size in New England, or for that matter, outside of it where there is so much social gaiety as in Lowell. Unlike Boston in many particulars, although so near it, it partakes more of the character of New York, and seems rather to belong to it than to New England. The people are eminently social and hospitable, and dispense their hospitality in the most genial and charming manner. All winter long one entertainment follows another in rapid succession with scarcely a lull in between. There is very little need for the inhabitants of the pleasant little city to turn longing eyes on other cities and pass their lives in vain regretting. They have every facility for enjoyment in their own midst, and very sensibly they make the most of what they have, and life in the city of mills, as so many persons see and experience it there, is not at all an unpleasant phase of existence. Every building is not a factory, nor every block a colony of operatives' boarding-houses. Stretching out over the hills in all directions away from business and manufacture, the town lies along the winding Merrimack over looking its tumultuous waters from an elevated perch on numberless hills.

Substantial houses in the midst of well-kept grounds attract the stranger, and give an idea of the comfort and worldly prosperity of the inhabitants. One of the most substantial of these houses is a large, staunchly built, spacious gray stone mansion, situated on a high eminence overlooking the Merrimack, just where it comes tumbling and foaming over its bed of rocks, that are scarcely covered, except when the water is very high. It is a house everybody notices. It has a tempting look, suggestive of roominess and comfort. Just such a house as one always longs to see the inside of, knowing all there must be of comfort, good cheer and luxury. This is the residence of the well-known Dr. J. C. Ayer, and is one of the pleasantest places in the city. On Wednesday evening the house was opened for a large party given by Mrs. Ayer, which was one of the most recherché and brilliant affairs that Lowell has ever seen. More than a week ago the cards were issued and numberless people have been anticipating and planning all the days since. Not only did the list of invited guests include all the elite of Lowell, but cards were sent to many distinguished persons both in this State and New Hampshire. Gov. Claflin, Speaker Jewell and several members of the Legislature were invited, as was Gov. Stearns, of New Hampshire, and a score of other State dignitaries. The severe storm kept some of these officials away, but nearly all the invitations were accepted.

Although it was snowing steadily and persistently outside, the scene inside was like a peep into fairy-land. Carriage after carriage rolled up to the door, and deposited its precious freight underneath the broad awning, which stretched from the gate to the steps. Dainty feet stepped lightly over the carpet put to shield them from the ground, which was kept clean and dry by busy hands, which brushed away the snow as persistently as it fell. Through the spacious doorways they flitted, mysterious bundles done up in multitudinous wraps, through the brilliantly lighted hall, up the broad staircase into the dressing-rooms, where presently from each dull chrysalis would emerge a brilliant, bewildering butterfly. Up the stairs came floating the sweet, soft strains of music, and mingled with them was the murmur and ripple of soft voices, and gurgling, musical laughter from pretty white throats. The blue and green and brown veils were carefully untied, and fair girl heads, wonderful with their glory of curls and frisées, and braids would emerge. Off from plump, pretty shoulders heavy wraps were removed, trains were adjusted, gloves drawn on, one last parting glance at the long mirror was stolen, and down stairs they swept, wave after wave of bright-hued sylphs in billows of tarletane and lace, into the drawing room where Mrs. Ayer received her guests, assisted by Mrs. Frazer of Boston. Mrs. Ayer was elegantly attired in a pink silk dress, with a court train trimmed with an exquisite point lace flounce. The overdress was of point, looped up with bunches of pink rosebuds. The body was low and pointed with puffed sleeves, and a berth of point. The bouquet de corsage was of exquisite French roses and buds, while bunches of the same ornamented each shoulder. Around her neck was a heavy gold chain, to which was suspended a magnificent diamond cross, while large solitaire diamonds glistened in her ears. In her dark hair, which was arranged in long, loose curls at the back, with puffs on the top, was a bunch of pink rosebuds. Mrs. Frazer wore a French gray silk with point lace and exquisite stone cameo ornaments. The drawing-room was one mass of flowers. Numberless bouquets of white and scarlet carnations hung from the chandeliers, and long sprays of smilax drooped from them. On the walls hung several rare paintings, and in the corners stood exquisite marble busts.

In the centre of the room was a life-size statue of Nydia, the blind girl of Pompeii. From the top of the long mirror, and from all the doors and windows, drooped long sprays of smilax, that were fastened back and held in place by bunches of carnations. The piazza at the back of the house was made into a cunning little room, being closed in by boards and lined entirely with pink cambric. Here the band was stationed, and thither came charming young couples, who preferred quiet tête-à-tête to dancing.

Supper was served in both the library and dining-room. On the table in one room were found all the solid and substantial things, while the other was devoted to more delicate viands. The tables were exquisitely arranged, and the supper prepared by Mr. J. B. Smith, of this city. Flowers bloomed everywhere in the greatest profusion in the supper room as well as in the drawing-room. Rare bronzes ornamented the mantels and costly pictures hung on the walls. The tables glistened with the display of silver and beautiful china. Rare wines sparkled in crystal glasses, and tempting fruits loaded the dishes. In the centre of one table was a large china punchbowl, filled almost to the brim with some deliciously mysterious and fragrant compound. In and out of these pleasant rooms the company drifted at will until after 10 o'clock, busy with salads, toying with ices and daintily sipping sparkling champagne, and through it all the Germanias kept playing delicious Strauss waltzes and wild galops, while merry feet and chattering tongues kept time to their strains.

The ladies were, without exception, exceedingly pretty, and the display of toilettes very fine. Mrs. Frederick Ayer wore a delicate green silk with black lace over dress and diamond ornaments.

Her niece, Miss Moffatt, wore a rose pink silk, with trimmings of the same, and ornaments of Roman gold.

Mrs. Harvey Jewell, of Boston, wife of the Speaker of the Massachusetts House of Representatives, looked quiet and matronly in heavy black silk and rich lace.

Mrs. Thomas Talbot was stylishly dressed in deep lavender silk, with white muslin over dress, trimmed richly with duchesse lace.

Miss Fanny Talbot wore pale lilac silk with puffed muslin over dress, with bands of velvet running between the puffs. Ornaments of pearls.

Miss Whitney, a pretty blonde, was charmingly dressed in pale blue silk with pearl ornaments.

Miss Boyden, an equally pretty brunette, wore white tarletane, trimmed with plaitings of the same.

Miss Lillie Ayer, daughter of the host, wore a cherry silk, made short, with an overskirt of the same, and a square body.

Miss Swett, of Exeter, wore white tarletane, with black velvet trimmings.

Miss Reed was prettily and becomingly dressed in a lilac and white train over a plain lilac skirt.

Mrs. Stott was unusually pretty, in a white silk with lace overdress, and springs of smilax in her hair.

Mrs. Sweetser wore lavender silk, over which was an elaborately embroidered French muslin overdress.

Between two and three hundred people must have been present from ten until twelve, when they began to retire, the older ones first, leaving more room for the dancing, which was kept up until two o'clock, when the still unwearied dancers gave a sigh as the last notes of a galop died away and the musicians closed their books, and all bade Dr. and Mrs. Ayer a reluctant good night.

To say the ball was a success, is but simple truth. The participants were cordial and profuse in their praise, the enjoyment being uninterrupted from the beginning to the close. The easy grace and affability with which the guests were welcomed, the sumptuous care which had provided for every gratification, and the refined hospitality which was continually manifesting itself, all gave a character to the event which metropolitan life may emulate, but cannot surpass." —*Lowell Daily Courier,* February 10, 1871.

Endnotes

Chapter 1—*At the Bend in the River: Dancing before Lowell*
1. Charles Cowley, *Illustrated History of Lowell*, rev. ed. (Boston: Lee & Shepard, Lowell: B. C. Sargeant and Joshua Merrill, 1868), 17.
2. Wilson Waters, *History of Chelmsford, Massachusetts*, 76.
3. Frederick W. Coburn, *History of Lowell and Its People*, vol. I, 69–71.
4. Thomas Wilson, *Analysis of the London Ball-room*, 67.
5. Waters, *History of Chelmsford*, Massachusetts, 456.
6. Ibid.
7. Ibid, 457.
8. Deduced from multiple sources: Waters, *History of Chelmsford, Massachusetts*, 349 (map), 397, 441; *The Lowell Book*, 6; *A Plan of Sundry Farms & c. at Patucket in the Town of Chelmsford* (1821)
9. *Contributions of the Lowell Historical Society*, Vol. I, No. 2, 196–197.
10. *The Laws of Etiquette; or, Short Rules and Reflections for Conduct in Society*, introduction. http://memory.loc.gov/ammem/dihtml/dicatlg.html.
11. Ibid, chap. XI.
12. *An Arrow Against Profane and Promiscuous Dancing Drawn Out of the Quiver of Scriptures/By the Ministers of Christ at Boston*, 14. The writing contained in this work is believed to be that of Increase Mather. The passage used is attributed to Perrin's History of The Doctrine and Discipline of the Waldenses as a quote from St. Augustine.
13. Ibid, 2.
14. Ibid, 3.
15. *Contributions of the Lowell Historical Society*, 183.
16. Waters, *History of Chelmsford, Massachusetts*, 405–406.
17. Larkin, Jack, "Early Taverns and the Law", *Old Sturbridge Village Visitor*, Fall 2005, http://www.teachushistory.org/detocqueville-visit-united-states/articles/early-taverns-law.
18. Waters, *History of Chelmsford, Massachusetts*, 685. Also: http://www.chelmsfordgov.com/CHCwebsite/Meeting_Halls.htm and http://www.uuchelmsford.org/about-us/our-history.html, both accessed February 28, 2016.
19. Waters, *History of Chelmsford, Massachusetts*, 685.

Chapter 2—*The Early Days: Lowell's Beginnings*
1. Chaim M. Rosenburg, *The Life and Times of Francis Cabot Lowell, 1775-1817*, 176.
2. Ibid, 192.
3. Frank Podmore, *Robert Owen: A Biography*, 48.
4. John Griscom, *A Year in Europe, Comprising a Journal of Observations*, vol. II, 251.
5. Michael Chevalier, *Society, Manners and Politics in the United States*, 129 (footnote).
6. Rosenburg, *The Life and Times of Francis Cabot Lowell*, 1775–1817, 214.
7. Ibid, 232.
8. Cowley, *Illustrated History of Lowell*, 43.
9. Coburn, *History of Lowell and Its People*, 203.
10. Cowley, *Illustrated History of Lowell*, 43.
11. *The Lowell Book*, 8.
12. Ibid, 9.
13. Jack Larkin, "In All Its Crowd and Tumult: Tavern Life and Entertainments in New England," *Old Sturbridge Village*, http://resources.osv.org/explore_learn/document_viewer.php?DocID=953.
14. Coburn, History of Lowell and Its People, 204.
15. Harriet H. Robinson, *Loom & Spindle or Life Among the Early Mill Girls*, 37.
16. Ibid, 2.
17. Ibid, 38.
18. Parker Lindall Converse, *1642–1842 Legends of Woburn*, 48–50.
19. Charles Lucius Anderson, letter, November 24, 1853.
20. Harriet Martineau. *Society in America*, vol. II, 96.
21. Ibid.
22. Carl Gersuny, "A Devil in Petticoats", 138.
23. Robinson, *Loom & Spindle or Life Among the Early Mill Girls*, 30.

24. Theodore Edson, *Reverend Theodore Edson's Diaries*, entry for February 23, 1839.
25. Robinson, *Loom & Spindle or Life Among the Early Mill Girls*, 9.
26. *The Laws of Etiquette; or, Short Rules and Reflections for Conduct in Society*, introduction.

Chapter 3—*Mixt Dance: Kissing, Courtship, and Damnation*
1. Thomas A. Faulkner, *From the Ball-Room to Hell*, 66.
2. Ibid, 25.
3. Ibid.
4. Ibid, 26.
5. Ibid, 26–27.
6. *A Solemn Warning to Dancers*, 1.
7. Faulkner, *From the Ball-room to Hell*, 71.
8. *A Solemn Warning to Dancers*, 2.
9. Faulkner, *From the Ball-room to Hell*, 11–12.
10. "A Manufacturing Population", *Boston Daily Times*, July 17, 1839.
11. Ibid, July 18, 1839.
12. "A Manufacturing Population", *Boston Daily Times*, July 17, 1839.
13. "The Lowell Courier", *Boston Daily Times*, July 19, 1839.
14. "A Manufacturing Population", *Boston Daily Times*, July 18, 1839.
15. *Northern Junket*, January 1973, vol. 11, issue 3, 40–41.
16. "Sampas Scoopies", *The Lowell Sun*, October 10, 1972.
17. Ibid, October 11, 1966.
18. A Manufacturing Population", *Boston Daily Times*, July 17, 1839.
19. A Letter from a Lowell Factory Worker, quoted in Chevalier, *Society, Manners and Politics in the United States,* 139 and H.C. Carey, Essay on Wages, 89.
20. Allen Dodworth, *Dancing and its relations to education and social life*, 4.
21. J. J. F. Housatonic, *Berkshire Courier*, January 1861, quoted in *Berkshire County Eagle,* March 27, 1862.
22. William James McKnight, *A Pioneer History of Jefferson County, Pennsylvania*, 162.
23. *Hood's Sarsaparilla Parlor Games*, 5.
24. Thomas Watson, *The Select Works of the Rev. Thomas Watson*, 46.
25. James Boïelle, *A New French and English Dictionary*, 97.
26. *Dictionary.com Unabridged* (Random House, Inc.) s. v. "willy-nilly", accessed June 27, 2014, http://dictionary.reference.com/browse/willy-nilly.
27. Wikipedia contributors, "Ramiel," *Wikipedia, The Free Encyclopedia*, accessed June, 27, 2014, http://en.wikipedia.org/w/index.php?title=Ramiel&oldid=607149078.
28. *Dictionary.com Unabridged* (Random House, Inc.) s. v. "tweedledum and tweedledee", accessed June 27, 2014, http://dictionary.reference.com/browse/tweedledum and tweedledee.
29. Faulkner, *From the Ball-room to Hell*, 47.
30. T. W. Higginson, "A Day of Scottish Games", *Scribner's Monthly*, January 1872, 334–335.
31. *Hood's Sarsaparilla Parlor Games*, 23.
32. Ibid, 24.
33. Ibid, 25.
34. Ibid.
35. Ibid.
36. Ibid, 23.
37. Ibid, 25.
38. Ibid.
39. McKnight, *A Pioneer History of Jefferson County*, 163.
40. Ibid.
41. John M. Todd, *A Sketch of the Life of John M. Todd*, 332.
42. Chevalier, Society, *Manners and Politics in the United States*, 139.

Chapter 4—*Country Dance: Contras and Quadrilles, Past and Present*
1. *The Ball-Room Instructor; Containing a Complete Description of Cotillions and Other Popular Dances*, 6.
2. L. De G. Brookes, *Brookes on Modern Dancing*, 24–25.
3. Ibid, 25.

4. Edson, *Reverend Theodore Edson's Diaries*, entry for February 23, 1839.
5. Douglas Kennedy, *English Folk Dancing Today and Yesterday*, 83.
6. Elizabeth Burchenal, "The Steps", *American Country-Dances*, introduction, xiv.
7. Brookes, *Brookes on Modern Dancing*, 4.
8. Thomas Wilson, *The Complete System of English Country Dancing*, 56.
9. Ibid, 10.
10. Burchenal, "The Steps", *American Country-Dances*, introduction, xiv.
11. Richard Herndon and Edwin M. Bacon, *Boston of Today*, 265–266.
12. *Contributions of the Lowell Historical Society*, 196–197.
13. Lillie Pierce Coolidge, *The History of Prescott Massachusetts*, 65.
14. Ralph Page. "A History of Square Dancing," *Square Dancing Magazine*, 1972–1974.
15. *Weekly Wisconsin*, Feb 1, 1856.
16. "Country Sleighing in New England", *The Graphic*, Dec. 26, 1874, 619.
17. *The Ball-Room Instructor*, 11.
18. *Webster's Seventh New Collegiate Dictionary*, s. v. "lancer."

Chapter 5—'Round the Room: Galop and Polka and Waltz, Oh My!

1. Thomas Wilson, *The Correct Method of Waltzing*, 63.
2. Sylvanus Urban, *The Gentleman's Magazine: and Historical Chronicle*, January to June, 1817, vol. 87, part 1, 345.
3. *Bangor Daily Whig and Courier*, October 18, 1837.
4. Betty-Bright Low and Jacqueline Hinsley, *Sophie Du Pont, A Young Lady in America*, 63.
5. *Bangor Daily Whig and Courier*, October 18, 1837.
6. *Contributions of the Lowell Historical Society*, 196–197.
7. Thomas Hillgrove, *Complete Practical Guide to the Art of Dancing*, 168.
8. *Lowell Weekly Sun*, October 4, 1884.
9. *Lowell Daily Courier*, January 6, 1848.
10. Hillgrove, *Complete Practical Guide to the Art of Dancing*, 159.
11. Ibid, 181.
12. Ibid, 164.
13. Ibid.
14. Ibid, 160–161.
15. Ibid, 158.

Chapter 6—The Middle Years: Dancing 'Round Every Corner

1. Cowley, *Illustrated History of Lowell*, 44–57.
2. Charles Lucius Anderson, letter, November 24, 1853.
3. Ibid.
4. Cowley, *Illustrated History of Lowell*, 142.
5. Josephson, *The Golden Threads New England's Mill Girls & Magnates*, 214.
6. Ibid, 221.
7. Ibid, 9–10.
8. Dane Yorke, *The Men and Times of Pepperell*, 75.
9. Coburn, *History of Lowell and Its People*, 343.
10. Dane Yorke, *The Men and Times of Pepperell*, 75.
11. "Photograph 24", *The Record of a City*, 52–53.
12. Coburn, *History of Lowell and Its People*, 345.
13. Ibid, 346.
14. *Lowell Daily Courier*, March 30, 1868.
15. Ibid, November 14, 1868.
16. Ibid, June 30, 1871.
17. *Merchants' Magazine and Commercial Review*, from January to June, 1854, inclusive, vol. 30 (New York: Freeman Hunt, 1854), 165.
18. "Old Suffolk Hall", *The Lowell Sun*, March 19, 1915; "Texas Jack and the Peerless Morlacchi", Center for Lowell History—University of Massachusetts Lowell Libraries, http://library.uml.edu/clh/Texas/T1.Html.
19. Irene Castle, *Castles in the Air*, 141.

20. *Lowell Journal and Courier*, January 19, 1860.
21. *Lowell Daily Sun*, March 7, 1896 (article edited for space).
22. Ibid, April 20, 1894 (article edited for space).
23. Ibid, May 29, 1894 (article edited for space).
24. Ibid, February 18, 1896 (article edited for space).
25. Ibid, February 20, 1895 (article edited for space).
26. Ibid, February 20, 1895 (article edited for space).
27. Ibid, February 1, 1893 (article edited for space).
28. Ibid, January 3, 1896 (article edited for space).
29. Ibid, April 20, 1895 (article edited for space).
30. Ibid, February 18, 1896 (article edited for space).
31. Ibid, April 20, 1895 (article edited for space).
32. Ibid, January 4, 1896 (article edited for space).
33. Ibid, February 16, 1895 (article edited for space).
34. Ibid, April 20, 1895 (article edited for space).
35. Coburn, *History of Lowell and Its People*, 316.
36. Charles W. Stein, *American Vaudeville as Seen By Its Contemporaries*, preface, xi.
37. *Lowell Weekly Sun*, December 20, 1884.
38. Ibid.

Chapter 7—*The Ball Room: Its Decorum, Dimensions, and Delights*

1. Howe, *American Dancing Master*, 5.
2. *Lowell Daily Courier*, December 21, 1868.
3. Ibid, November 16, 1871.
4. *Lowell Daily Sun*, February 20, 1895.
5. Ibid, February 1, 1893.
6. Ibid, January 17, 1895.
7. Faulkner, *From the Ball-Room to Hell*, 33–34.
8. *Daily Journal and Courier*, December 5, 1848.
9. E. I. Woodhead, C. Sullivan, and G. Gusset, *Lighting Devices in the National Reference Collection, Parks Canada* (Canada: Parks Canada, 1984), 60, http://www.sha.org.
10. *Lowell Daily Courier*, November 15, 1871.
11. Ibid, November 5, 1868.
12. *The Ball-Room Guide. With Coloured Plates*, 21–23.
13. Howe, *Complete Ball-Room Hand Book*, 10.
14. *The Ball-Room Guide*, 17.
15. Ibid.
16. Ibid, 18.
17. Ibid, 19.
18. Ibid, 18.
19. *Lowell Daily Courier*, February 10, 1871.
20. *Northern Junket*, Vol. 11, No. 5, May 1973, 35–36.
21. *The Complete Ball-Room Handbook*, 14.
22. A Day of Scottish Games, 334.
23. *Northern Junket*, Vol. 5, No. 10, April 1957, 9–10.
24. *The Complete Ball-Room Hand Book*, 3.
25. Ibid, 5.
26. Ibid, 9.
27. Ibid, 6.
28. Ibid, 7.
29. Ibid, 12.
30. Ibid, 11.
31. Ibid.
32. Ibis, 8.
33. Ibid, 16.

34. *The Complete Ball-Room Guide*, 12.
35. *The Complete Ball-Room Hand Book*, 16.
36. *The Lowell Sun*, February 1, 1901.
37. *Lowell Daily Sun*, February 3, 1893.
38. *A Souvenir of Massachusetts Legislators*, 132.
39. *The Lowell Sun*, January 18, 1900.
40. Ibid.
41. Ibid, January 7, 1889.

Chapter 8—*A Short Tour: The Victorian Dance Halls of Downtown Lowell*

1. Shepley Bullfinch Richardson and Abbott, "Lowell Mfg Co. research report," Digital Initiatives @ UMass Lowell, accessed April 20, 2015, http://libhost.uml.edu/items/show/106.
2. *Lowell Daily Courier,* March 21, 1848.
3. Ibid.
4. Ibid.
5. Hannah Josephson, *The Golden Threads New England's Mill Girls & Magnates*, 83.
6. *Burlington Hawkeye,* [Burlington, Iowa], November 23, 1848.
7. *Daily Journal and Courier*, July 5, 1848.
8. Shepley Bullfinch Richardson and Abbott, "Market Street, 73, 79, 91—Father John's Medicine," Digital Initiatives @ UMass Lowell, accessed April 20, 2015, http://libhost.uml.edu/items/show/589.
9. Cowley, *Illustrated History of Lowell*, 117.
10. George Adams, *The Lowell Directory*, 227.
11. Ibid, 255.
12. Shepley Bullfinch Richardson and Abbott, "Prescott Street, 36—The *Lowell Sun* Building," Digital Initiatives @ UMass Lowell, accessed April 20, 2015, http://libhost.uml.edu/files/show/790.
13. *Lowell Daily Sun*, April 3, 1893.
14. *Lowell Daily Sun*, January 27, 1893.
15. Grace May Burke. Interview by Suzette Jefferson. *Oral History Collection: The Working People of Lowell*. University of Massachusetts Lowell Center for Lowell History and Lowell National Historical Park, http://library.uml.edu/clh/OH/WPOL/Burke.pdf (November 7, 1985).
16. *Lowell Sun*, September 16. 1910.
17. *Lowell Daily Sun*, September 13. 1911.
18. Anita Wilcox Lalacheur. Interview by Sylvia Contover. *Oral History Collection: The Working People of Lowell*. University of Massachusetts Lowell Center for Lowell History and Lowell National Historical Park, http://library.uml.edu/clh/OH/WPOL/Lelacheur.pdf (October 22, 1985).
19. Cowley, *Illustrated History of Lowell*, 92–94.
20. Shepley, Bullfinch, Richardson, and Abbott, "Middle Street, 83—Pollard Building," Digital Initiatives @ UMass Lowell, accessed April 20, 2015, http://libhost.uml.edu/files/show/672.
21. *The Lowell Book*, 46.
22. *Lowell Sun,* April 29, 1911.
23. *Lowell Weekly Sun*, February 17, 1883.
24. *Lowell Sun*, July 11, 1891.
25. Alan F. Kaplan, building owner, in response to online queries by author, September 13, 2014 and July 2, 2015.
26. Shepley, Bullfinch, Richardson, and Abbott, "Merrimack Street, 143—Bon Marché Building/Railroad National Bank Building," Digital Initiatives @ UMass Lowell, accessed April 20, 2015, http://libhost.uml.edu/files/show/639.
27. Ibid, "Merrimack Street, 175—Welles Block," Digital Initiatives @ UMass Lowell, accessed April 20, 2015, http://libhost.uml.edu/items/show/644.
28. *Lowell Daily Sun*, May 19, 1893.
29. *Lowell Sun,* November 8, 1895.
30. Coburn, *History of Lowell and Its People*, 204.
31. *The Lowell Weekly Sun*, January 7, 1881.
32. Shepley Bullfinch Richardson and Abbott, "Merrimack Street, 262-266—Site of Huntington Hall / Boston and Lowell Railroad Depot," Digital Initiatives @ UMass Lowell, accessed April 20, 2015, http://libhost.uml.edu/items/show/651.

33. Cowley, *Illustrated History of Lowell*, 152–153.

34. Shepley Bullfinch Richardson and Abbott, "Dutton Street, 167—Middlesex Mechanics Association Building," Digital Initiatives @ UMass Lowell, accessed April 20, 2015, http://libhost.uml.edu/items/show/371.

35. *Lowell Courier*, March 9, 1837.

36. *Lowell Sun*, February 16, 1898.

37. Shepley Bullfinch Richardson and Abbott, "Dutton Street, 141—Site of Merrimack House ," Digital Initiatives @ UMass Lowell, accessed April 20, 2015, http://libhost.uml.edu/items/show/368.

38. Coburn, *History of Lowell and Its People*, 210.

39. Cowley, *Illustrated History of Lowell*, 80.

40. *Lowell Daily Sun,* March 29, 1893.

41. Ibid, May 7, 1895.

42. Jay Pendergast, *Images of America, Lowell,* vol. 2, 99.

Chapter 9—*Out of the City: The Trolley Parks*

1. Robert H. Derrah, *Derrah's Official Street Railway Guide for Eastern New England*, 8–9.

2. Ibid, 57.

3. Valentine Chartrand, interview by Diane Novelli, *Oral History Collection: The Mill Workers of Lowell.* University of Massachusetts Lowell Center for Lowell History and Lowell National Historical Park, http://library.uml.edu/clh/OH/MWOL/Chartrand.pdf (October 8, 1984).

4. Edward D. Hart, interview by Kathleen Curtin, *Oral History Collection: The Mill Workers of Lowell.* University of Massachusetts Lowell Center for Lowell History and Lowell National Historical Park, http://library.uml.edu/clh/OH/MWOL/Hart.pdf (October 10, 1984).

5. Edward Harley, interview by Paul Page, *Oral History Collection: The Working People of Lowell.* University of Massachusetts Lowell Center for Lowell History and Lowell National Historical Park, http://library.uml.edu/clh/OH/WPOL/Harley.pdf (October 29, 1985).

6. *Lowell Sun,* November 9, 1885.

7. Ibid, March 4, 1886.

8. *Report of the Massachusetts Commission for the Investigation of the White Slave Traffic*, 19–20.

9. "Canobie Lake Park History," *Canobie Lake Park*, accessed Feb. 6, 2014, http://www.canobie.com/history.php.

10. Ibid.

11. Derrah, *Derrah's Official Street Railway Guide for Eastern New England*, 134.

12. Ibid, 75.

13a. *Massachusetts Reconnaissance Survey Town Report: Groveland, 1985*, 15–16.

13b. Wikipedia Contributors, "Groveland, Massachusetts," *Wikipedia, The Free Encyclopedia,* last modified November 14, 2013, http://en.wikipedia.org/wiki/Groveland,_Massachusetts#The_Pines_Recreation_Area.

14. Warren H. Falls, *Images of America: Lynnfield*, 124.

15. *Lowell Sun*, March 27, 1915.

16. "Suntaug Lake Inn," *Restaurant Ware Collectors Network*, last modified August 23, 2011, http://www.restaurantwarecollectors.com/forums/showwiki.php?title=Suntaug+Lake+Inn.

17a. "Elegant Wedding Reception Facility," *Lake Pearl Function Facility*, accessed February 6, 2014, http://www.lakepearl.com.

17b. "The History of Lake Pearl Park," accessed February 6, 2014, http://mysite.verizon.net/vzeqc9sm/lakepearlhistory.html.

18. "Salem Willows Park," *Examiner Online,* Sept. 3, 2010, http://www.examiner.com/article/salem-willows-park-salem-massachusetts.

19. "Casino Ballroom History," *Casino Ballroom*, accessed February 6, 2014, http://www.casinoballroom.com/history.php#6.

20. "Paragon Park," *Boston Globe Online,* June 7, 2013, http://www.bostonglobe.com/arts/theater-art/2013/06/07/from-globe-archives-paragon-park/s2FPLle7TGNO1G0legPgYM/story.html.

21. *Boston Sunday Globe,* June 11, 1905.

22. Ibid.

23. Pamela Mutch Stevens, *Images of America: Salisbury Beach*, 90.

24. Ibid, 4.

25. *Lowell Sun*, July 22, 1931.

26. Derrah, *Derrah's Official Street Railway Guide for Eastern New England*, 39.

27. "The Pavilion, Long Beach, Gloucester, Circa 1910," *Vintage Rockport* (blog), September 16, 2011, http://vintagerockport.com/2011/09/16/the-pavilion-long-beach-gloucester-circa-1910/.

28. "History: City of Revere," *City of Revere, Mayor's Office*, accessed February 6, 2014, http://www.revere.org/mayors-office/history.

29. Ibid.

30. *Report of the Chief of the Massachusetts District Police for the Year Ending Oct. 31, 1917*, 53.

31. "A Brief History of Revere Beach, America's Oldest Public Beach," *NoBo Magazine*, March 15, 2012, http://www.nobomagazine.com/2012/03/15/a-brief-history-of-revere-beach-americas-oldest-public-beach/.

Chapter 10—*The 1900's Arrive: Ragtime Dances Come to Town*

1. Trades and Labor Council of Lowell, Mass., *Lowell: A City of Spindles*, 197–198.
2. Coburn, *History of Lowell and Its People*, Vol. 1, 352–353.
3. Lloyd Shaw, *The Round Dance Book*, 3rd printing, 299.
4. Ibid, 301.
5. Ibid.
6. Vernon and Irene Castle, *Modern Dancing*, 161.
7. Henri Cellarius, *Drawing Room Dances*, 33.
8. Vernon and Irene Castle, *Modern Dancing*, 161.
9. *Lowell Sun*, June 26, 1902.
10. Vernon and Irene Castle, *Modern Dancing*, 43.
11. Ibid, 39.
12. Ibid, 44–47.
13. Ibid, 47.
14. Ibid, 52.
15. Shaw, *The Round Dance Book*, 301.
16. Vernon and Irene Castle, *Modern Dancing*, 72.
17. Ibid, 72–74.
18. S. Beach Chester, *Secrets of the Tango*, 40.
19. Ibid, 57.
20. Vernon and Irene Castle, *Modern Dancing*, 83–84.
21. Kelsey Jost-Creegan, "The Argentines Descended from the Boats: Migration in Argentina" *Argentina Independent*, September 4, 2012, http://www.argentinaindependent.com/top-story/the-argentines-descended-from-the-boats-migration-in-argentina/. Original quote attributed to Juan B. Alberdi.
22. Chester, *Secrets of the Tango*, 19.
23. Vernon and Irene Castle, *Modern Dancing*, 86–89.
24. Chester, *Secrets of the Tango*, 53. Quote attributed to a Miss Chase.
25. Vernon and Irene Castle, *Modern Dancing*, 107.
26. Ibid, 107–108.
27. Chester, *Secrets of the Tango*, 18, footnote.
28. Vernon Castle "New Dances for this Winter", *Ladies Home Journal*, November 1914, 24–25.
29. *Lowell Sun*, October 27, 1914.
30. Elisabeth Marbury, introduction to *Modern Dancing*, by Vernon and Irene Castle, 26–27.
31. Vernon and Irene Castle, *Modern Dancing*, 32.
32. Chester, *Secrets of the Tango*, 21.
33. Marbury, introduction of *Modern Dancing*, 24–25.
34. Ibid, 24.
35. Ibid, 25.
36. *Lowell Sun*, December 3, 1914.
37. Ibid, February 19, 1915.
38. Ibid, March 4, 1914.
39. Ibid.
40. Ibid.
41. Ibid, March 5, 1914.
42. Ibid.
43. Ibid.

44. *Le Petit Journal* (illustrated supplement), December 21, 1913.
45. Pollard, Percival, *Their Day in Court*, (New York, Neale Publishing Company, 1909), 68.
46. *Denver Republican*, May 4, 1913 (copyright by New York Herald Company, 1913)
47. Vernon and Irene Castle, *Modern Dancing*, 144–145.
48. Ibid, 139–140.
49. *Lowell Sun*, February 23, 1915.
50. Ibid, January 21, 1915.
51. Ibid, October 11, 1923.

Chapter 11—*Germans, Grizzlies, and More: Novelties and Fads*

1. *Lowell Sun*, February 23, 1898. Of the halls listed that are not included in "Downtown Halls," Odd Fellow's Hall was at 361 Bridge Street and Elvin's hall on Dutton was an unidentified hall where William Elvin taught dancing in the 1890s. Highland Hall was likely the one in the Urban block, although a second Highland Hall was listed at 131 Branch street by the early 1900s.
2. Ibid.
3. Ibid.
4. Baldwin, Brooke, "The Cakewalk: A Study in Stereotype and Reality," *Journal of Social History*, Vol. 15, No. 2 (Oxford University Press, 1981), 208. www.jstor.org/stable/3787107.
5. Ibid.
6. *Lowell Sun*, February 23, 1898.
7. Dodworth, *Dancing and Its Relation to Education and Social Life*, 145.
8. Ibid, 146–147.
9. *The German. How to give it. How to lead it. How to dance it, by two amateur leaders*, 41 - 42.
10. *Lowell Sun*, February 5, 1920.
11. *Boston Post*, January 10, 1913.
12. Description based on vintage film clips, online sources, and general familiarity with vintage dance. This style of dance was rarely described in standard dance manuals of the period and probably varied from place to place.
13. Ibid.
14. Vernon and Irene Castle, *Modern Dancing*, 80.
15. *Lowell Sun*, June 11, 1912.
16. *Boston Sunday Post*, June 29, 1913. (The newspaper used the correct spelling, "Pavlowa," not today's more common, anglicized "Pavlova.")
17. *Lowell Sun*, February 7, 1914.
18. Shaw, *The Round Dance Book*, 25. Tense changed to better fit narrative.
19. *Lowell Courier*, May 29, 1860.
20. Gladys Beattie Crozier, *The Tango and How to Dance It*, 137–138.
21. *Lowell Sun*, September 8, 1915.
22. *"Circulating Library" Fundraiser Program* (1895), photograph of dance card from the Lowell Historical Society.
23. *Lowell Sun*, January 23, 1895.

Chapter 12—*The Last Waltz: From Flappers to Folk Festivals*

1. "Lowell History Chronology", *Lowell Historical Society Website*, accessed April 13, 2015, http://www.lowellhistoricalsociety.org/lowell_history.htm.
2. Ibid.
3. Ibid.
4. *Lowell Sun*, October 31, 1930.
5. "Memories of the Commodore Ballroom", *UML Center for Lowell History*, accessed April 13, 2015, http://library.uml.edu/clh/Exhibit/mcom03.htm.
6. Eric Felten, "How the Taxman Cleared the Dance Floor", *The Wall Street Journal*, March 17, 2013, http://www.wsj.com/articles/SB10001424127887323628804578348050712410108.
7. Ibid.
8. Ibid. Quote originally published in *Billboard Magazine*, 1944.
9. *Lowell National Historical Park 1978 - 2008, 30 Years of Preservation and Innovation for Future Generations*, June 2008, http://www.nps.gov/lowe/learn/management/upload/NPS_30th%20-%20small.pdf.

Bibliography

Adams, George. *The Lowell Directory, Containing the City Record, Schools, Churches, Banks, Societies, Etc., Names of the Citizens, A Business Directory, An Almanac for 1855, and a Variety of Miscellaneous Matter.* Lowell, MA: Oliver March and Merrill & Straw, 1855, accessed April 20, 2015, https://archive.org/details/lowellmassachuse1855adam.

American Society of Mechanical Engineers Landmark Report: Lowell Water Power System. Lowell, MA: American Society of Civil Engineers and the American Society of Mechanical Engineers, 1985, accessed April 8, 2014, http://files.asme.org/ASMEORG/Communities/History/Landmarks/5589.pdf.

An Arrow Against Profane and Promiscuous Dancing Drawn Out of the Quiver of Scriptures/By the Ministers of Christ at Boston. Boston: Printed by Samuel Green, 1684. Reproduction, New York: New York Public Library, 2013.

Bacon, George B. "A Day of Scottish Games." *Scribner's Monthly, an illustrated magazine for the people*, Vol. III, Issue 3, January, 1872. 345–355. accessed April 20, 2015, http://digital.library.cornell.edu/cgi/t/text/text-idx?c=scmo;cc=scmo;idno=scmo0003-3;view=toc;node=scmo0003-3%3A1.

Bartlett, Elisha. *A Vindication of the Character and Condition of the Females Employed in the Lowell Mills: against the charges contained in The Boston times, and The Boston quarterly review.* Lowell : L. Huntress, printer, 1841, accessed April 20, 2015, https://archive.org/details/101161910.nlm.nih.gov.

Bay State Monthly. Vol. I, No. 3, Boston: John N. McClintock and Co., 1884.

Ballou's Pictorial Drawing Room Companion. April 26, 1856, Vol. X., No. 17.

Ballou's Pictorial Drawing Room Companion. March 15, 1856, Vol. X., No. 11.

The Ball-room Guide. With coloured plates. London, F. Warne and co., 1866, accessed April 20, 2015, http://memory.loc.gov/ammem/dihtml/dicatlg.html.

The Ball-Room Instructor; Containing A Complete Description of Cotillons and Other Popular Dances. New York: Huestis & Craft, 1841, accessed April 20, 2015, http://memory.loc.gov/ammem/dihtml/dicatlg.html.

Bessie; or, Reminiscences of a Daughter of a New England Clergyman of the Eighteenth Century : simple facts, simply told, by a grandmother. New Haven, CT : J. M. Benham, 1861, accessed April 20, 2015, http://babel.hathitrust.org/cgi/pt?id=yale.39002005707816;view=1up;seq=4

Boïelle, James. *A New French and English Dictionary Compiled from the Best Authorities in Both Languages.* New York: Funk & Wagnalls Company, 1903.

Breul, Karl. *A German and English Dictionary Compiled from the Best Authorities in Both Languages.* New York: Funk & Wagnalls Company, 1906.

Brookes, Lawrence De Garmo. *Brookes on Modern Dancing, Containing A Full Description of All Dances as Practised in the Ball Room and at Private Parties, Together with An Essay on Etiquette.* New York: n.p., 1887. accessed April 20, 2015, http://memory.loc.gov/ammem/dihtml/dicatlg.html.

Burchenal, Elizabeth. *American Country-Dances: Twenty-Eight Contra-Dances Largely from the New England States.* New York: G. Schirmer, Inc., 1918.

"Canobie Lake Park History," *Canobie Lake Park*, accessed February 6, 2014, http://www.canobie.com/history.php.

Carpenter, Lucien O. *J. W. Pepper's Universal Dancing Master, Prompter's Call Book and Violinist's Guide.* Philadelphia: J. W. Pepper, 1882. accessed April 20, 2015, http://memory.loc.gov/ammem/dihtml/dicatlg.html.

Castle, Irene. *Castles in the Air.* 1st ed. Garden City, NY: Doubleday, 1958.

Castle, Vernon and Irene. *Modern Dancing.* New York: Published by the World Syndicate Co. under an arrangement with Harper & Brothers, 1914.

Cellarius, Henri. *The Drawing-Room Dances.* Boston: Dinsmore & Co., 1858, accessed April 20, 2015, http://memory.loc.gov/ammem/dihtml/dicatlg.html.

Chester, S. Beach. *Secrets of the Tango*. London: T. Werner Laurie, Ltd., 1914.

Chevalier, Michael. *Society, Manners and Politics in the United States: Being a Series of Letters on North America*, translated from the third Paris Edition. Boston: Weeks Jordan and Company, 1839, accessed April 20, 2015, https://archive.org/details/societymannerspo00chev.

Clendenen, F. Leslie. *Dance Mad or The Dances of the Day*. St. Louis, MO: Arcade Print Co., 1914.

Coburn, Frederick W. *History of Lowell and Its People*. Vol. 1. New York: Lewis Historical Publishing Company, 1920, accessed April 20, 2015, https://archive.org/details/historyoflowelli01cobu.

Contributions of the Lowell Historical Society. Vol. I, No. 2. Lowell, MA: Butterfield Printing Co., 1911, accessed April 20, 2015, https://books.google.com/.

Contributions to the Old Residents Historical Association. Vol. VI, No. 1. Lowell, MA: Published by Old Residents Historical Association and printed by Courier-Citizen Company, 1896, accessed April 20, 2015, https://books.google.com/.

Converse, Parker Lindall. 1642 –1842. *Legends of Woburn. Woburn, Mass*: Printed for Subscribers only, 1892, accessed April 20, 2015, https://archive.org/details/legendsofwoburn02conv.

Coolidge, Lillie Pierce. *The History of Prescott Massachusetts*. N.p.: n.p., n.d., accessed April 20, 2015, https://archive.org/details/historyofprescot00cool. E-book, multiple formats.

Cowley, Charles. *Illustrated History of Lowell*. Rev. ed. Boston: Lee & Shepard, Lowell, MA: B. C. Sargeant and Joshua Merrill, 1868, accessed April 20, 2015, https://archive.org/details/illustratedhist00cowlgoog.

Crozier, Gladys Beattie. *The Tango and How to Dance It*. London: Andrew Melrose, Ltd., 1913.

Derrah, Robert H. *Derrah's Official Street Railway Guide for Eastern New England*. Boston: Derrah Excursion and Publication Co., 1900.

Dodworth, Allen. *Dancing and its relations to education and social life, with a new method of instruction...* New York and London: Harper & brothers, 1900, accessed April 20, 2015, http://memory.loc.gov/ammem/dihtml/dicatlg.html.

Durang, Charles. *The Fashionable Dancer's Casket, or the Ball-Room Instructor*. Philadelphia: Fisher & Brother, 1856, accessed April 20, 2015, http://memory.loc.gov/ammem/dihtml/dicatlg.html.

Edson, Theodore. *Reverend Theodore Edson's Diaries, December 1822 through April 1841*. Transcribed by Walter Hickey with an introduction and history by Martha Mayo. Lowell, MA: Lowell Historical Society, accessed April 20, 2015, http://library.uml.edu/clh/all/ed1.pdf.

Falls, Warren H. *Images of America: Lynnfield*. Charleston, SC: Arcadia Publishing, 1998.

Faulkner, Thomas A. *From the Ball-Room to Hell*. Chicago: Henry Publishing Co., 1892, accessed April 20, 2015, http://memory.loc.gov/ammem/dihtml/dicatlg.html.

The Gentleman & Lady's Companion; Containing, The Newest Cotillions and Country Dances; to which is added, Instance of Ill Manners to be carefully avoided by Youth of both Sexes. Norwich, Ct: Printed by J. Trumbull, 1798, accessed April 20, 2015, http://memory.loc.gov/ammem/dihtml/dicatlg.html.

The German. How to give it. How to lead it. How to dance it. By two amateur leaders. Chicago, Jansen, McClurg and Co., 1879, accessed April 20, 2015, http://memory.loc.gov/ammem/dihtml/dicatlg.html.

Gersuny, Carl. "'A Devil in Petticoats' and Just Cause: Patterns of Punishment in Two New England Textile Factories," *The Business History Review*, Vol. 50, No. 2, 131 - 152, Cambridge, MA: President and Fellows of Harvard College, 1976, accessed April 20, 2015, http://www.jstor.org.

Gilbert, M. B. *Round Dancing*. Portland, ME: M. B. Gilbert, 1890.

Grindon, Leo H. Lancashire, *Brief Historical and Descriptive Notes*. London: Seeley and Co., Ltd, 1892, accessed April 20, 2015, https://archive.org/details/cu31924028040032.

Griscom, John. *A Year in Europe, Comprising a Journal of Observations in England, Scotland, Ireland, France, Switzerland, The North or Italy, and Holland. In 1818 and 1819.* Vol. II. New York: Collins and Hannay, 1824, accessed April 20, 2015, https://books.google.com/.

Herndon, Richard (compiler) and Edwin M. Bacon (editor). *Boston of Today: A Glance at its History and Characteristics with Biographical Sketches and Portraits of Many of its Professional and Business Men.* Boston: Post Publising Company, 1892, accessed February 9, 2016, https://archive.org/details/bostonoftodaygla01herna

Hillgrove, Thomas. *Complete Practical Guide to the Art of Dancing.* New York: Dick & Fitzgerald, 1864. Reprint, N.p.: Da Capo Press, 1981.

Hood's Sarsaparilla Book of Parlor Games, Lowell, MA: C.I. Hood & Co., c. 1885.

Hopkins, G.M. *City Atlas of Lowell Massachusetts.* Philadelphia, 1879, accessed April 20, 2015, http://archives.lib.state.ma.us/handle/2452/127861.

Howe, Elias et. al., *American Dancing Master and Ball-Room Prompter: containing about five hundred dances; including all the latest and most fashionable.* Boston: Elias Howe, c. 1862. Reprint, N.p., n.p., n.d.

Howe, Elias et. al., *Howe's Complete Ball-Room Hand Book: Containing Upwards of Three Hundred Dances, Including All the Latest and Most Fashionable Dances, With Elegant Illustrations.* Boston: Ditson & Co., 1858, accessed April 20, 2015, http://memory.loc.gov/ammem/dihtml/dicatlg.html.

Josephson, Hannah. *The Golden Threads New England's Mill Girls & Magnates.* New York: Duell, Sloan and Pearce, 1949.

Kennedy, Douglas. *English Folk Dancing Today and Yesterday.* London: G. Bell and Sons Ltd., 1964.

Kenngott, George F. *The Record of a City. A Social Survey of Lowell, Massachusetts.* New York: The Macmillan Co., 1912, accessed April 20, 2015, https://archive.org/details/recordofcitysoci00kenn.

The Ladies' Home Journal. November, 1914. Philadelphia: The Curtis Publishing Company, 1914.

The Ladies' Home Journal. Christmas, 1914. Philadelphia: The Curtis Publishing Company, 1914.

The Laws of Etiquette; or, Short Rules and Reflections for Conduct in Society, introduction. Philadelphia : Cary, Lea, and Blanchard, 1836, accessed April 20, 2015, http://memory.loc.gov/ammem/dihtml/dicatlg.html.

Low, Betty-Bright and Jacqueline Hinsley. *Sophie Du Pont, A Young Lady in America. Sketches, diaries, & Letters 1823–1833.* New York: Harry N. Abrams, Incorporated, 1987.

The Lowell Book. Boston: Printed by George H. Ellis, 1899.

The Lowell Directory 1866. Boston: Sampson, Davenport, and Co., 1866, accessed April 20, 2015, https://archive.org/details/lowellmassachuse1866merr.

The Lowell Directory 1874. Boston: Sampson, Davenport, and Co., 1874, accessed April 20, 2015, https://archive.org/details/lowellmassachuse1874merr.

Lowell Illustrated. Lowell, MA: Nelson Colonial Department Store, 1907.

Martineau, Harriet. *Society in America*, Vol. II. Paris: Baudry's European Library, 1837, accessed April 20, 2015, https://books.google.com/.

Massachusetts Reconnaissance Survey Town Report: Groveland, 1985. Boston: Massachusetts Historical Commission, 1985, accessed April 20, 2015, http://www.sec.state.ma.us/mhc/mhcpdf/townreports/Essex/grv.pdf.

McKnight, William James. *A Pioneer History of Jefferson County, Pennsylvania and my first recollections of Brookville, Pennsylvania 1840–1843, when my feet were bare and my cheeks were brown.* Philadelphia: J. B. Lippincott Company, 1898, accessed April 20, 2015, https://archive.org/details/pioneerhistoryof00mckniala.

Page, Ralph. "A History of Square Dancing," *Square Dancing Magazine*, 1972–1974, accessed May 26, 2014, http://library1.du.edu/site/sites/default/files/Page_Contra_Dances_197401.pdf.

Page, Ralph. *Northern Junket Magazine*. Volumes I,IV,V, & VIII-XIV, 1949–1984, accessed May 26, 2014, http://www.izaak.unh.edu/dlp/northernjunket/pages/intro.htm#NJ.

Pendergast, Jay. *Images of America: Lowell*. Vol. II. Charleston, SC: Arcadia Publishing, 1997.

Podmore, Frank. *Robert Owen: A Biography*. Vol. I. New York: D. Appleton and Company, 1907, accessed April 20, 2015, https://books.google.com/.

Powell, R. *Powell's Art of Dancing; or Dancing Made Easy*. Louisville, KY: Printed by Harney, Hughes & Hughes, 1848, accessed April 20, 2015, http://memory.loc.gov/ammem/dihtml/dicatlg.html.

Report of the Chief of the Massachusetts District Police for the Year Ending Oct. 31, 1917. Boston: Wright & Potter Printing Co., State Printers, 1918, accessed April 20, 2015, https://archive.org/details/reportofchiefofm00mass_13.

Report of the Massachusetts Commission for the Investigation of the White Slave Traffic, So Called, February, 1914. Boston: Wright & Potter Printing co., State Printers, 1914, accessed April 20, 2015, https://books.google.com/.

Richardson, Phillip J.S. *The Social Dances of the 19th Century*. London: Herbert Jenkins, Ltd. Printed by Charles Birchall & Sons, Ltd., Liverpool and London, 1960.

Robinson, Harriet H. *Loom & Spindle or Life Among the Early Mill Girls*. Rev. ed. Kaliua, Hi: Press Pacifica, 1976.

Rosenburg, Chaim M. *The Life and Times of Francis Cabot Lowell, 1775–1817,* Lanham, MD: Lexington Books, 2010.

Shaw, Lloyd. *The Round Dance Book*. 3rd printing. Caldwell, Idaho: The Caxton Printers, Ltd., 1950.

Shepley Bulfinch Richardson and Abbott, "Lowell National Historical Park and Preservation District: Cultural Resources Inventory Report," 1980, Digital Initiatives @ UMass Lowell, accessed April 20, 2015, http://libhost.uml.edu/items/show/1784.

A Solemn Warning to Dancers. New York: N. Bangs and J. Emory for the Tract Society of the Methodist Episcopal Church, inter 1824 and 1832, accessed April 20, 2015, http://memory.loc.gov/ammem/dihtml/dicatlg.html.

Souvenir of Grand Concert and Ball of Lowell Lodge #87 Benevolent and Protective Order of Elks (B.P.O.E.) Boston: The Statist Publishing Co., 1908.

A Souvenir of Massachusetts Legislators, 1909. Volume XVIII (Issued Annually). Stoughton, MA: A. M. Bridgman, 1909, accessed April 20, 2015, https://archive.org/stream/souvenirofmassac1909brid#page/n3/mode/2up.

Stein, Charles W. *American Vaudeville as seen by its Contemporaries*. New York: Alfred A. Knopf, 1984.

Stevens, Pamela Mutch. *Images of America: Salisbury Beach*. Charleston, SC: Arcadia Publishing, 2000.

Todd, John M. *A Sketch of the Life of John M. Todd (Sixty-two Years in a Barber Shop) and Reminiscences of His Customers*. Portland: William W. Roberts Co., 1906, accessed April 20, 2015, https://archive.org/details/sketchoflifeofjo00todd.

Théleur, E.A. *Letters on Dancing, Reducing This Elegant and Healthful Exercise to Easy Scientific Principles*. London: Sherwood & Co., 1832, accessed April 20, 2015, http://memory.loc.gov/ammem/dihtml/dicatlg.html.

Trades and Labor Council of Lowell. *Lowell: A City of Spindles*. Lowell, MA: Printed by Lawler & Company, 1900, accessed April 20, 2015, https://archive.org/details/lowellcityofspin00lowe.

Urban, Sylvanus. *The Gentleman's Magazine: and Historical Chronicle*. January to June, 1817. Vol. 87, Part 1. London: Printed by Nichols, Son, and Bentley, 1817, accessed April 20, 2015, https://books.google.com/.

Views of Lowell and Vicinity. Lowell, MA: Published exclusively for S.H. Knox and Company, 1905. Copyright by L.H. Nelson Company, Portland, ME.

Ville, Paul, comp. *Reels, Hornpipes, Jigs, Etc., The Universal Favorite Contra Dance Album*. New York: Carl Fischer, 1905.

Waters, Wilson. *History of Chelmsford, Massachusetts*. Lowell, MA: Printed for the town by the Courier–Citizen Company, 1917, accessed April 20, 2015, https://archive.org/details/historychelmsfo00perhgoog.

Watson, Thomas. *The Select Works of the Rev. Thomas Watson, Comprising his Celebrated Body of Divinity in a series of Lectures on the Shorter Catechism and Various Sermons and Treatises.* New York: Robert Carter & Brothers, 1855, accessed April 20, 2015, https://archive.org/details/selectworksofrev00wats.

Webster's Seventh New Collegiate Dictionary. Springfield, MA: G. & C. Merriam Company, 1976.

Wilson, Marquerite. *Dancing.* rev. ed. N.p.: The Penn Publishing Company, 1913.

Wilson, Thomas. *An Analysis of Country Dancing: wherein are displayed all the figures ever used in country dances, in a way so easy and familiar, that persons of the meanest capacity may in a short time acquire (without the aid of a master) a complete knowledge of that rational and polite amusement.* London: Printed by W. Calvert, 1808, accessed April 20, 2015, http://memory.loc.gov/ammem/dihtml/dicatlg.html.

Wilson, Thomas. *An Analysis of Country Dancing, wherein all the figures used in that polite amusement are rendered familiar by engraved lines.* London: J.S. Dickson, 1811, accessed April 20, 2015, http://memory.loc.gov/ammem/dihtml/dicatlg.html.

Wilson, Thomas. *Analysis of the London Ball-Room: in which is comprised, the history of the polite art, from the earliest period, interspersed with characteristic observations of each of its popular divisions of country dances, which contain a selection of the most fashionable and popular quadrilles and waltzes.* London: Printed for Thomas Tegg, Cheapside, and R. Griffen and Co., 1825. Reprint, N.p., n.p., n.d.

Wilson, Thomas. *The Complete System of English Country Dancing, containing all the figures ever used in English country dancing, with a variety of new figures, and new reels.* London: Sherwood, Neeley and Jones, c. 1815, accessed April 20, 2015, http://memory.loc.gov/ammem/dihtml/dicatlg.html.

Wilson, Thomas. *A Description of the Correct Method of Waltzing: the truly fashionable species of dancing, that from the pleasing Beauty of it Movements has attained an ascendancy over every other Department of that Polite Branch of Education. Part I. Containing a correct explanatory description of the several movements and attitudes in German and French Waltzing.* London: Sherwood, Neely, Jones, and Paternoster Row, 1816.

Wilson, Thomas. *The Quadrille and Cotillion Panorama, or, Treatise on Quadrille Dancing, in Two Parts: with an explanation, in French and English, of all the quadrille & cotillion figures generally adopted, as described by diagrams on the plate.* New York: R. & E. Williamson, 1822, accessed April 20, 2015, http://memory.loc.gov/ammem/dihtml/dicatlg.html.

Y.M.C.I. Five Year Book. Lowell, MAs: Y.M.C.I. Choral Society, 1907.

Yorke, Dane. *The Men and Times of Pepperell.* Boston: Pepperell Manufacturing Company, 1945.

Index

Animal dances, 171–174
Appleton Bank, *96 (map)*, 101, 102, *102*,
Auto racing, 78, *78*
Ayer, Mr. and Mrs. J. C., 18, *18*, *35 (advertising card)*, 87, 88
Ball-Room to Hell, 25, *25*, 26
Ballrooms, 178–181. *See also Halls. See also Parks*
    Chateau. *See Parks, Paragon*
    Commodore, 174, 178, *178*, 179, 180
    decline of, 180
    Hi Hat Roll-A-Way, 179, *179*
    Kasino, 154, 155, 178
    Laurier Hotel, *178*
    Totem Pole, Norumbega Park (Auburndale, MA), 179, *180*
Baseball, 75–76, *76*
Bigelow, Erastus, 70, *70*
"Blow Out" balls, 19, 20, 98–99
Boott Mills, 65, 66, 140, *176*, 177, *177*
Boston Associates, 18
Boston Manufacturing Company, 16–18, *17*
Boston Times, 25–28
Bowling, 78, *78*, 110, 128, 137
Buildings. *See also Halls*
    Armory on Middle, *96 (map)*, 111
    Armory on Westford, 74, *74*, 83
    Bon Marché. *See Halls, Nichols and Hutchins*
    Central Fire Station, *96 (map)*, 111, *111*
    Fairburn. *See Halls, Prescott*
    Hildreth, 108–110, *108*
    Howe. *See Halls, Hibernian*
    Institute. *See Halls, Burke*
    Lowell Museum. *See Halls, Central*
    Mansur. *See Halls, Mathews*
    Market House, *96 (map)*, 100, 101, *101*, *159*
    Old City Hall, *106 (map)*, 114, *114*
    Pollard. *See Halls, Colonial*
    Runels. *See Halls, Prescott*
    Wentworth, 114, *115*, 122
Canal walk, *76*
Canals, Middlesex, 8, 18
Canals, Pawtucket, 17–18
Carleton and Hovey Company, 100
Castle, Vernon and Irene, 71, *138*, 142–153, *144*, *146*, *147*, *148*, *150*, *152–153*, 162, *162*, 163
Charles River, 17
Chelmsford, Massachusetts, *4 (map)*, 7–11, 18, 19, 139
Chevalier, Michael, 16, 35, 67
Churches
    First Trinitarian Congregational, 119, *119*
    Freewill Baptist, 108, *109*, 110, *110*, 123
    Immaculate Conception Church, 179
    Polish Holy Trinity, 179
    Second Universalist, 97, *97*
    St. Anne's, 23, *23*
    St. Joseph's, *96 (map)*, 113, *113*
Circulating library, 175, *175*
Civil War, 52, 68, 71
Coburn, Frederick, 18, 120
Concord River, *12*, 18, 140
Corn husking, *2*, 7
Copenhagen (game or tobacco), 32, 33, 192
Cowley, Charles, 18, 65, 101, 108–110, 118, 120
Dance bands and orchestras, 72–74, 81, 91–95, 99, 101, 102, 115
    American Orchestra, 72, 73, 112
    Hibbard's Orchestra and American Band, 75, 94, *96 (map)*, 104, *104 (advertisement)*, 111, 113, 121, 165
    Lowell Cadet Orchestra, *93*, 94
    Salem Cadet orchestra, 74, 92, *93*
Dance figures
    Balance, 41–43, *41*, *47*
    Buzz Step, 43, *43*, *144*, 145
    Circle, 46, 99
    Contra Corners, 43, *43*
    Cortez, 147, 148, *148*
    Dip, *64*, 146, *146*, 158–159, 162, *162*, 165
    Hands Across. *See Dance figures, star*
    Hey, 6, 40
    Honor your Partner, 39, *39*,
    Ladies Chain, 6, 41, *41*, 46
    Mill. *See Dance figures, star*
    Moulinet. *See Dance figures, star*
    Right and Left, 6, 40, *40*, 41, 46
    Right Hand Turn, 42, 45
    Star, 32, 40, *40*
    Swing Corners. *See Dance figures, contra corners*
    Swing, 42, 43, *43*, 45, 46, 51, 52, 90, 144–145
    Tango figures, 148, 175
    Walking step, 39
Dance
    attire, *57*, *59*, 65, *66*, 73, 74, 83, 86, *86*, 87, *87*, 88, 89, *92*, 110, 115, 142, 162, *162*, 165, 171, *171*
    Ballet, 7, 37–39, *37 (five positions of)*, 42, 56–57, 70
    balls & receptions, 8, 9, 11, 13, 19–20, 22, 27, 47, 52, 65, 72–75, 83, 87–88, 89, 98, 101, 102, 106, 110, 111, 112, 113, 119, 121
    cards. *See Dance, invitations and programs*
    decline of, 180
    etiquette, 9–10, 23, 86, 89, 90, 91
    favors, 166–171, *168–169*
    health benefits, 30, 156–157
    in advertising, *21*, *35*, 60, *60*, 75, 154, *163*, 171, *173*
    in the home, 5–6, 33, 79, 81
    in the mills, 22, 98–99

Dance (continued)
  invitations & programs, *7, 8, 21, 27, 46, 47, 62, 73, 103, 109, 114, 120, 121, 142, 175*
  lead/follow, 62, 142–147, 180
  lessons & schools, 7, *7*, 8, *13*, 19, 21, *21*, 22, 89, 104, 119, 136, *136*, 157
  Modern Ballroom. 55, 146, 148, 151, 156
  morality of, 25, 31, 33, 58, 69, 70, 115, 129, 130, 131, 156–161, 172–174
  music, 5, 9, 46, 47, 67, 76, *76*, 91, 92, 93, 94, 95, 141, 143, *143*
  poetry, 30–31, 50–51, 59, 156, 192
  religious views of, 10, 22, 23, 26, 31, 70, 157
Dances
  Baby Polka, *164*, 165
  Boston, 38, *55*, 146, 174
  Bunny Hug, 172, *172*, 174
  Cake-walk, 165–166, *166*
  Chase the Lady, 47
  Chorus Jig, 9, 21, 45
  circular, 45, *45*
  College Hornpipe, 47
  contra, 6, 9, 21, 37–53, *44*, 58, 67, 90, 119, 142, 180
  cotillon/cotillion, 9, 45, 51, 58, 99, 166–171, *167, 168–169, 171*. See also Dances, quadrille.
  Durang's Hornpipe, 47
  Fisher's Hornpipe, 9, 21, 45
  Foxtrot, 151–156, *152–153*, 162, 175, 180
  Galop/Galopade, 58, 59, 61, 63, 73, 88, 90, 112, 141
  German. See Dances, cotillon
  Grand March, 73, 74, 75, 83, 84, 93, 94, 112, 166, 170
  Grizzly Bear, 172–175, *173*
  Highland Reel, 47
  Hull's Victory, 21, 42, 47
  Ladies Triumph, 47
  Lady Walpole's Reel, 46, *46*, 47
  Lady Washington's Reel, 9, 45, 46
  Lame Duck, 172, 174
  Lancers' Quadrilles, 31, 32, 52, *52*, 53, 90
  Landler, 56
  Lulufado, 155, *155*
  Maid in the Pump Room, 47
  Maxixe, 144, 148, *149*, 150, *150*, 151, 160, 163, 175
  Mazourka/Mazurka, 52, 60–61, *61*, 63, 112
  Milonga, 147
  Minuet, *56*, 63, 166
  Money Musk, 9, 21, 45, 47, 51
  One-step, 143–145, *144, 145*
  Paso Doble, 148, *148*
  Polka, 31–32, 38, 52, 59, *59*, 60–63, *60*, 76, 90, 102, *139*, 141, 151, 155, 161, *164*, 181
  Portland Fancy, 9, 21, 45, 46, 47
  quadrille 9, *9*, 31–32, 37–53, *44*, 67, 73, 89, 90, 112, 115, 119, 142, 145, 167, 180

quadrilles by name, 52. See also Dances, Lancers' Quadrilles
Redowa, 61, 63, 112
round 9, 38, 55, 62, 63, *63*, 90. For alternate meaning, see Dances, circular.
Samba, 151, *151*
Schottisch, 31–33, 52, 61–63, 142, 159
Scotch Reel, 47
Sir Roger De Coverly. See Dances, Virginia Reel
Speed the Plough 9, 45
square. See quadrille
stag, 71, *71*
Tango, 38, 55, 144, *146*, 147–148, *147, 148*, 157, 156–163, *158, 160 (trial headline), 161*, 162, 174, 175, 179, 180. See also Maxixe
Tempest, 47
Turkey trot, 151, 162, 171, 172, *172*, 173, *173*, 174, 175
Twin Sisters, 47
Two Step, 60, 119, 141–143, 145, 150, 151
Valse à Deux Temps, 59, 63, 141, 142
Vampyr dance, 160, *161*
Varsovienne, 61–63, *61*
Virginia Reel, 6, 21, *36*, 47, *48-49*, 51, 180
Waltz, 9, 21, 25, *29*, 31–32, 38, 45, 52, *54, 55*, 55–59, *57, 58*, 61–63, 72, 73, 88, 90, 99, 101, 112, 119, 141–142, 144–146, 159, 175, 179–181
  Hesitation, 145–146, 155, 157, 162, 163, 172
Dodworth, Allen, 30
Edson, Rev. Theodore, 23, 38
Faulkner, T. A., 25, 26
Father John's Medicine, 100
Fox, Harry, 161, *151*
French Revolution, 56
French-Canadians, 68, *68*, 69
From the Ball Room to Hell, 25, *25*, 26
Gilmore, Patrick, 71, *71*
Greeks, 68, 69
Griscom, John, 16
Hadley, Hon. Samuel, 9, 10, 45, 58
Hall decorations, 73, 74, 75, 82, 93, 94, *94*, 95, 165
Halls (in Lowell),
  Associate, 75, 84, *96 (map)*, 113, *117*, 121, *121, 125*, 142, 165, 170, 175
  Burbank. See Halls, Shattuck
  Burke, 72, *96 (map)*, 111, *111*, 165
  Central, *96 (map)*, 102, *103*, 108–110, *109, 123*
  Colonial, *96 (map)*, 95, *95*, 110–111
  Darracott's. See Halls, Prescott
  French's, 81, *96 (map)*, 101, 102, *103*, 105, 112
  galleries, 73, 74, 82–85, *83*, 93, *95*, 121, 165
  Goddard's. See Halls, French's
  heating and ventilation, 82, 85, 86
  Hibernian, 75, *96 (map)*, 100, 104, 105, *105*, 165

210

Halls (continued)
  Highland, 85, *96 (map)*, 113, 114, *115 (advertisement)*, 165
  Huntington, 52, 65, 72, 73, 75, 83, *83*, 86, 92, 93, *96*, *116*, 118, *118*, 120, 122, *124*, 165
  Lester's. *See* Halls, Shattuck
  Lynch's, 82, 100, *100*
  Map of, *96*
  Mathews, 72, 101, *101*
  Mechanics, 21, 23, 58, *96 (map)*, *116*, 119, *119*, *125*, 165, 166
  Merrimack House, 84, *96 (map)*, *117*, 120, *120*, *124*
  Nichols and Hutchins, *96 (map)*, 112, *112*, 115
  Prescott, 82 (as Darracott's), *96 (map)*, 106, *106*, 107, *107*, 165
  Runels. *See* Halls, Prescott
  Russian, 82, 114, *115 (advertisement)*
  Shattuck, 75 (as Lester's), *96 (map)*, 104, *104*
  Suffolk 70
  Urban, 52, 63, 82, 85, *96 (map)*, 114, 115, *115 (advertisement)*
  Welles, *96 (map)*, 106, 113, *113*
  Wells', 75, 106
Hamilton Manufacturing Company, 22, 65, *96 (map)*, 98, 99, *99 (directory listing)*, *124*, 177
Health, 22, 27, 30, 85, 87, 156–157
Hi Hat Roll-A-Way, 179, *179*
Hibbard, Joseph H., 94, *94*, 104, 113. *See also,* Dance bands and orchestras, Hibbard's
Highland Club, 28, *28*
Hillgrove, Thomas, *39 (images of bows as described by)*, 52, 53, 60–62
Hobble skirts, 171, *171*, 162
Howe, Elias, 45, *47 (illustration from)*, 52, 60, 81, 86, 89, 90–92
Hoyt, Eli, *35 (advertising card)*, 86
Immigration, 67, 68, 69
Individual Sovereignty, 3
Inns & Taverns,
  Davis Inn, *19*, 18–19
  laws against dancing, 10–11, 158–160
  Mansion House, 18
  Marshall Tavern, *18*, 19
  Middlesex Tavern 8, *8*, 9
  Old Stone House Inn (later Ayer Home), 18–19, *18*, 29, 87–88, *88*, 194–195
  Washington Tavern, *19*
Irish, 1, 23, 67, *67*, 69, 71, 75, 90
Jackson, President Andrew, 120
Jewish, 68, 69
Keith Academy, 179
Keller, Helen, 173–174
Kissing games, 10, 31–35
Lakeview Park. *See* Parks, Lakeview

Lancashire, England, 13, 14, *14*
Lighting, gas 65, 84, *84*, 85, *85*, 95
Lowell Folk Festival, 181, *181*
Lowell Offering, 97, 110
Lowell, decline of. *See* Textile mills, decline of
Lowell, Francis Cabot, 13–17
Lowell, Hannah, 13
Lowell Manufacturing Company, 65, 70, 98, *98*, *99 (directory listing)*, *124*, *140*, 177, *177*, *181*
Lynch, Patrick, 82, 100
Marriage, 20, 25, 35
Martineau, Harriet, 22
Mather, Rev. Increase, 10, *10*
Mechanics Phalanx, 74, *96 (map)*, *100*, 101, *101*, 111
Merrimack River, *12*, 140
Middlesex Canal. *See* canals
Mill Girls, 20, *32*, 22, 27–30, 38, 47, 52, 67, 76, 87, 89, *89*, 97, 108, 110, 120, 131
Mills. *See* Textile Mills
Morlacchi, Giuseppina, 70, *70*
Native Americans, 5
New Lanark, Scotland, 14, *15*, 16
Nichols and Hutchins, 81, 112, *112 (advertisement)*
Old Line, 27, *27 (invitation)*, 28, 29, *46 (dance program)*, 84
Old Stone House. *See* Inns & Taverns
Owen, Robert, 14, 16
Page, Ralph, 46, 90
Page's Clock, *96 (map)*, 108, *108*
Parks,
  Canobie Lake (Salem, NH), 132, *132*, 155
  Hampton Beach (NH), 135, *135*
  Lake Pearl (Wrentham, MA), 134, *134*
  Lakeview (Dracut, MA) 107, 108, 128–130, *128*
  Long Beach, Cape Ann (MA), 137, *137*
  map of, *126*
  Paragon Park, Nantasket Beach (MA), 135, *135*
  Pines, The (Groveland, MA), 133, *133*
  Revere Beach (MA), 137, *137*
  Salem Willows (MA), 93, 134, *134*
  Salisbury Beach (MA), 136, *136*
  Shedd Park (Lowell), 77
  Suntaug Lake (Lynnfield, MA), 133, *133*
  Whalom Park (Lunenburg, MA), 133, *133*
  Willow Dale (Tyngsboro, MA), 77, *77*
Pastimes, 7, 10, 33–35, 76–79
Pavlowa (spelling is often anglicized as Pavlova), Anna, 173
Pawtucket canal. *See* canals
Pawtucket falls, *17*, 18
Pennacooks, 5
Phonograph, 95, 141, *141*, 151, 163
Pic-Nic(s) 98–99
Pinewoods Dance Camp, *131*, 161
Playford, *The Dancing Master*, 6
Prohibition, 140

Prostitution, 25–29, 130
Ragtime, 42, 143–155, 171–175
Rape, 113, 129, 130
Robinson, Harriet, 20, 22–23
Roller Skating, 78, *78*, 79, *79*, 175, 178, 179
Sexual Harassment, 27, 30, 32
Shaw, Lloyd, 141, 142, 145
Sleighing, 5, *5*, 7, *48–49*, 50–51, 72, *72*, 77, 192
Social classes, 23, 29, 38, 43, 67–69, 88
Sousa, John Philip, 71, 142, 143
South Common, 77, *77*, 155
Spaulding Hall, 8
Spaulding House, 19, *19*
Storrow, Mrs. James, 161, 172, 173
Street Cars—*see Trolleys*
Taverns—*see Inns & Taverns*
Tax, Cabaret 180
Tea dances, 162, 163
Textile mills,
    at Lowell, by name, 65, 177
    conditions in Lowell, 14, 66, 67
    decline of, 139, 176–178, 181
    See also Boott Mills, Hamilton Manufacturing, Lancashire, Lowell Manufacturing, New Lanark, and Waltham
Theaters, Casto (Savoy), 78, 97, *97*, 124
Theaters, Keith's, *96 (map)*, 107, *107*, 155, 175
Thomas, Abel 97
Trials, 113, 129, 158–160
Trolleys, 77, 104, 107, *108 (waiting room)*, *122*, 126–137, *126 (map)*, *129, 136, 137*
Varnum, Squire John 5, 6, 8
Vaudeville, 78, 97, 107, 151, 155, 156, *157 (advertisement)*, 160, *161, 166,* 173, *174,* 175
Waltham, Massachusetts, 16, *16*, 17, 20, 22
Waters, Rev. Wilson 7, 10
Wilson, Thomas, 6, 40, 42, 56–58, *57 (waltz frontispiece)*
Women's suffrage, 140, 160, 171

At the other extreme from the factual research tome, *Twirling Jennies, A History of Social Dance in the City of Spindles 1820–1920*, is Ruth Evans's novel, a fantasy written under the pen name Christina Briley.

The Raven Coronet takes Ms. Evans' knack for storytelling and uses it to create an imaginary world filled with interesting characters and intriquing situations. Sex, swordplay, and magic combine to offer grand adventure and an unconventional romance, one both bawdy and sweet.

The Raven Coronet, by Christina Briley, is available online in e-book and in print (softcover) via the usual suspects. A preview can be found via the Author page of twirlingjennies.com.

Even the youngest child in the United Lands knew the legend of The Raven Coronet—the crown of charisma that had united the world under one ruler —but no one believed that it still existed.

Or almost no one.

Young Thaedra's difficult childhood becomes an even more trying womanhood when her stepfather marries her off as part of a scheme to obtain the storied artifact.